T0333959

New India

New India

Reclaiming the Lost Glory

ARVIND PANAGARIYA

Oxford University Press is a department of the University of Oxford. It furthers the University's objective of excellence in research, scholarship, and education by publishing worldwide. Oxford is a registered trade mark of Oxford University Press in the UK and certain other countries.

Published in the United States of America by Oxford University Press
198 Madison Avenue, New York, NY 10016, United States of America.

Library of Congress Cataloging-in-Publication Data
Names: Panagariya, Arvind, author.
Title: New India : reclaiming the lost glory / Arvind Panagariya.
Description: New York : Oxford University Press, 2020. |
Includes bibliographical references and index.
Identifiers: LCCN 2020011521 (print) | LCCN 2020011522 (ebook) |
ISBN 9780197531556 (hardback) | ISBN 9780197531570 (epub) |
ISBN 9780197531587
Subjects: LCSH: India—Economic policy—21st century. |
Business enterprises—India. | Labor market—India. | Banks and banking—India.
Classification: LCC HC435.4 .P36 2020 (print) |
LCC HC435.4 (ebook) | DDC 330.954—dc23
LC record available at https://lccn.loc.gov/2020011521
LC ebook record available at https://lccn.loc.gov/2020011522

1 3 5 7 9 8 6 4 2

Printed by Sheridan Books, Inc., United States of America

To
Ananth and Ajay

Contents

Preface ix

I. A BRIGHT FUTURE AWAITS

1. Reclaiming the Lost Glory 3
2. From Command and Control to a More Liberal Order: 1950–2018 12

II. UNDERSTANDING THE CHALLENGE OF TRANSFORMATION

3. Underemployment in Agriculture 33
4. Underemployment in Industry and Services 56
5. Walking on Two Legs 72

III. THE ROAD TO REFORMS

6. Reforms for Export-Led and Manufacturing-Fed Growth 83
7. Urbanization: Making Room for Migrant Workers 105
8. Investing Productively: The Securities Market 130
9. Investing Productively: The Banking Sector 145
10. Transforming Higher Education 179
11. Governance 205
12. Nuggets: A Miscellany of Reforms 227
13. In Conclusion: Revisiting the Past, Looking to the Future 242

References 259
Index 265

Preface

I first used the term "New India" in June 2012 in my tribute to Prime Minister Narasimha Rao on the ninety-first anniversary of his birth. I began the tribute thus: "Fifty years from now, when historians take stock of the makers of the new India, two individuals from our times will figure prominently on their lists: Prime Ministers P. V. Narasimha Rao and Atal Bihari Vajpayee. If justice prevails, by then the nation would have also honored them with Bharat Ratna."[1]

It was not a coincidence that I chose the term "New India" and not "modern India" in the tribute. I was acutely aware that historians had already been using the latter term to refer to freedom fighters and to leaders in the immediate post-independence era. I wanted to sharply distinguish the contributions of Rao and Vajpayee from those of these earlier leaders. To the latter group, no doubt, belonged the credit for winning political freedom and laying a sound foundation of democracy in India. But in the economic sphere, they were responsible for placing post-independence India on the road to socialism, with its attendant command-and-control policies. That in turn condemned India to the status of a "miserably poor country" for more than three decades.[2] Rao and Vajpayee launched the movement to free India from the stranglehold of socialism. They placed it on course toward a market economy that has subsequently delivered sustained rapid growth and a sharp reduction in abject poverty.

It is against this background that I was happily surprised when Prime Minister Narendra Modi independently adopted the term "New India" to describe a transformed India, which he seeks to build in the years to come. It is my conviction that a critical component of this New India is economic prosperity for all. Achieving such prosperity requires further movement away from socialist policies that continue to hold the Indian economy back from realizing its true potential. Keeping this in view, the present volume is devoted to outlining a set of mutually reinforcing economic reforms that would help India grow at near double-digit rates during the next two decades. As the experience of every single successful country shows, only sustained rapid growth can bring prosperity on a large scale within a matter of two to three decades.

With its GDP having reached $2.6 trillion, today India is poised to become the world's third-largest economy in less than a decade. Yet only fifteen years ago, most analysts would have summarily dismissed this possibility as pure fantasy. Even a decade ago, commenting on the title of my book *India: The Emerging Giant*, a reviewer recalled with a touch of skepticism the remark by political scientist Stephen Cohen that one is tempted to ask whether "India is always destined to be 'emerging' but never actually arriving."[3]

India's poor economic performance during the first four decades of independence had, justifiably, left even many of its early admirers pessimistic about its future. But we need to remember that for much of the known history of humankind, the country has been home to one of the world's largest and richest economies. During the first one and a half millennia of the Common Era, India accounted for a quarter or more of global income. Indeed, as late as 1820, it accounted for one-sixth of global income and was second in size only to China. True, the Industrial Revolution, which occurred first in Europe and later spread to North America, was responsible for the relative decline of India and China during the nineteenth and twentieth centuries. But it was the self-serving and exploitative policies of the British colonizers that greatly impoverished India even in absolute terms. By the time the British were forced out of the country, India had been reduced to what may be the worst poverty any nation has ever experienced.

India's present pursuit of prosperity is not an excursion into the unknown; instead, it is a quest to reclaim the country's past glory. The difference is that, unlike in the past, India has many competitors in the world today. Rather than lead, it is playing catch-up. Therefore, it needs to foster policies that allow its entrepreneurs to take advantage of available technologies while also innovating new products and processes to deliver double-digit growth.

My book *India: The Emerging Giant* was a comprehensive volume that contained more than five hundred pages and covered nearly all aspects of the economy, including a detailed history of post-independence economic policies. Subsequently, in response to continued skepticism from many scholars and policy analysts about the centrality of growth to poverty alleviation, I offered a comprehensive case for growth as the single most important instrument to combat poverty in my 2012 book *Why Growth Matters*, jointly authored with Jagdish Bhagwati.

In this book I need not be as comprehensive as I was in *India: The Emerging Giant*. Indeed, doing so would only lead to undue repetition. With the importance of growth now gaining wide acceptance, there is no need to comprehensively make the case for it either. Therefore, in this volume I concentrate on the question of how India can achieve sustained rapid growth over the next two to three decades while also creating well-paid jobs for the vast number of workers who lack or have limited skills. I also answer the question of how India can transform its primarily agricultural, rural, and traditional economy into an industrial, urban, and modern one.

Part I of the book serves as an introduction to the Indian economy. It makes the case that within the next one to two decades India can return to being one of the world's major economies, as it was during the entire first millennium and four-fifths of the second. It also takes a brief look at India's development experience in the post-independence era, principally to take stock of what worked and what didn't work as far as growth and poverty alleviation are concerned.

Parts II and III constitute the core of the volume. Part II, containing three chapters, systematically documents the existence of widespread underemployment or low-productivity employment in all sectors of the economy: agriculture, industry, and services. It argues that there is no way to significantly improve the lives of agricultural workers without moving half or more of them into industry and services. It further shows that even within industry and services, the bulk of the workforce is employed in tiny low-productivity enterprises in which they earn at best subsistence-level incomes. This part of the book argues that the only way to create well-paid jobs for the masses is for India to create a business environment in which many more medium and large firms can emerge, especially in employment-intensive sectors such as apparel, footwear, furniture, and other light manufactures. It concludes by arguing that creation of good jobs in large numbers would require capturing a significantly larger share of the world export market and that neither the current wave of protectionism nor rising automation renders the export-led and manufacturing-fed growth model irrelevant.

Part III, consisting of eight chapters, discusses specific policy reforms in the key areas necessary to launch India onto a near double-digit growth trajectory and create well-paid jobs. These include trade liberalization, trade facilitation, labor and land market reforms, urban development, development of the securities market, banking reform, improvements in governance, and a miscellaneous set of reforms such as privatization of public sector enterprises, consolidation of rural subsidies into a single cash transfer, scaling down the Food Corporation of India, and a set of macroeconomic reforms. Each of these subjects is discussed in considerable detail.

Reflecting my comparative advantage, the focus of the volume is on policies rather than programs and projects. Therefore, I do not discuss the important subject of infrastructure, including the creation and expansion of digital platforms. Luckily, the present government is already moving at a fast pace to build infrastructure and increase the role of digitization. Acceleration in growth, which would accelerate revenue collection, will help the government speed up this process yet further.

Additional important areas that I do not cover in the book are school education (although there is a brief section on the reform of the Right to Education Act), health, environment, and energy. These are all very important areas, and progress in them has a direct bearing on growth. A good case can be made for their inclusion in a book like the present one. But I felt that the book had already become overly long and that I should resist the temptation to add yet more chapters to it.

I am indebted to my brilliant former student Rana Hasan, who currently works in a senior position at the Asian Development Bank, for extremely helpful comments on Parts I and II of the book. Comments by two anonymous reviewers on the penultimate draft led to numerous improvements. I also wish to thank B. Venkatesh Kumar for his excellent comments on the chapter on higher education, Rahul Ahluwalia for providing estimates of workforce across broad sectors of the economy and Radhicka Kapoor for estimates of employment by firm size in manufacturing. As with my 2008 book, the excellent online data depositories on the website of the Reserve Bank of India, especially the digital *RBI Handbook of Statistics on Indian Economy*, have been invaluable in writing this one. The RBI has done an excellent job of providing extensive time series data on nearly all aspects of the Indian economy in accessible form. I am grateful to the RBI staff, especially Rajiv Ranjan, who promptly responded to all my data queries in the course of preparing the manuscript.

Finally, as usual, I must thank my wife, Amita, who served as the reader of first resort for many draft chapters. Whenever I was in doubt regarding clarity or feared that a sharp critical tone might offend potential readers, I sought her advice. The book is fondly dedicated to my two children, Ananth and Ajay, who have grown up loving India just as much as the country of their birth and citizenship, the United States. I am sure they too will contribute to building bridges between the two nations in their own ways.

Arvind Panagariya
Columbia University
June 15, 2020

Notes

1. Panagariya 2012. Bharat Ratna is the highest honor India confers on an individual for contributions in any field.
2. The characterization of India as a "miserably poor country" is from Fields 1980, 204.
3. See Kishore 2008; Cohen 2001, 2.

PART I
A BRIGHT FUTURE AWAITS

1
Reclaiming the Lost Glory

According to estimates by economic historian Angus Maddison (2006), India accounted for nearly 30 percent of the world's gross domestic product (GDP) from 1 CE to 1000 CE (Figure 1.1). Though this share declined subsequently, it remained approximately a quarter of the world's GDP until the year 1700. As recently as 1820, India contributed a hefty 16 percent of global GDP.[1] China was the other major economy of the world during this period, with the two nations together accounting for half of global GDP during approximately two millennia ending in 1820.

By the early nineteenth century, the Industrial Revolution was well under way and the center of gravity of the global economy had begun to shift from India and China to Europe. Simultaneously, with the British East India Company having acquired control of much of India, the country was in decline. The situation remained unchanged after control of India passed from the East India Company to the British Crown in 1858. With the policy framework designed entirely to serve the interest of the colonial power, per capita incomes in India saw hardly any improvement during the first half of the twentieth century. Consequently, by the time the British left India, the country's share in world GDP had fallen to 4.2 percent.

Though India managed to accelerate growth in the post-independence era by reorienting its policies to serve the national interest, it failed to achieve its full potential because of the dirigiste policy regime it adopted. Indeed, it continued to grow more slowly than the rest of the world during the early decades of independence, with the result that its share in global GDP dropped yet further to 3.1 percent by 1973. Only after the oil crisis that year led to a substantial slowdown in the global economy and India began to shift to a more liberal policy regime did the declining trend reverse. According to Maddison's original estimates, by 2001 India's share in global GDP had climbed back up to 5.4 percent.

After 1820, China's share in global GDP declined as well. From 33 percent that year, it fell steadily to just 4.6 percent in 1973. Since then, China too has recovered; according to Maddison, its share rose to 12.3 percent in 2001.

The robust picture of India's economy until 1820 is tempered by the fact that despite its large share in global GDP, the country enjoyed only marginal advantage over other countries in terms of per capita GDP, and that only until 1000 CE. A large population was thus the principal driver of the country's large GDP

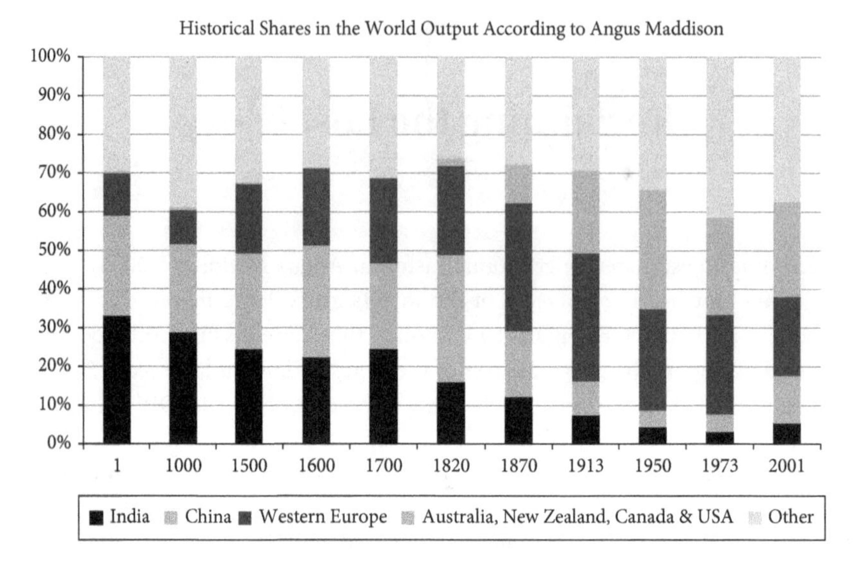

Figure 1.1 GDP Shares of Major Countries and Regions
Source: Author's construction using estimates in Maddison 2006, 639, table 8b.

share. By 1500, the country's per capita GDP had fallen significantly below that of most west European countries. According to Maddison, India's per capita GDP in the year 1000 was $450 (in 1990 Geary-Khamis dollars), compared with $400 in Europe and Latin America and $425 in Japan. But by 1500, per capita GDP in India, at $550, had been surpassed by western Europe at $771. Indeed, by this time even the world per capita GDP, at $566, had come to exceed India's.

The Promise of the Future

In thinking about India's future, we must keep this historical context in mind. Except for the most recent two hundred years, India has been a large contributor to global output. Now that India has opened its economy, introduced numerous pro-growth reforms, and created a large GDP base, it can aspire to return to the prominent position it enjoyed in the global economy for the better part of the last two millennia. Given where India stands currently, a prima facie case for the realization of such an ambition can indeed be made.

During the fifteen years ending with fiscal year 2017/18, India's real GDP at market prices grew at an annual rate of 7.7 percent in real rupees and 9.9 percent in real dollars.[2] This is despite the fact that policy mistakes led to a significant decline in the growth rate from 2011/12 to 2013/14. With GDP at $2.6 trillion in 2017/18, India ranked sixth globally in GDP in 2017.[3]

Against this background, consider the implication of 8 percent average annual grows in real dollars, an outcome well within India's grasp. Such growth would raise India's GDP to $7.2 trillion by 2030/31. This would be sufficient to place the country comfortably in third place in GDP rankings worldwide. The GDP of Japan, currently the third-largest economy, was $4.9 trillion in 2017. Today, no one predicts that Japan will grow faster than 1.5 percent annually in real dollars from 2017 through 2030. At this pace, its economy would rise to only $6 trillion by 2030.

With India's population in 2030 predicted to be 1.5 billion, a GDP of $7.2 trillion would translate into an annual per capita GDP of $4,810 in 2017/18 constant dollars. This figure will still be far from the per capita GDP in the developed countries, but it will be enough to virtually eliminate abject poverty from India and bring prosperity to a large proportion of its population. Seen this way, India's prospects for becoming a prosperous nation at home and a leading economic power globally are excellent.

Yet one thing India's economic history teaches is that nothing can be taken for granted. By 2010/11, India's economy had already seen growth above 8 percent for eight years, and it had come out of the global financial crisis of 2008 unscathed. It seemed then that nothing could slow down this large economy. However, the government's cumulative policy mistakes administered a major blow to the economy, and the growth rate first fell to 6.7 percent in 2011/12 and then plummeted to 5.5 percent in 2012/13.

Growth has two main sources: growth in resources such as labor and capital, which are used to produce goods and services, and growth in productivity, which measures the volume of goods and services that can be produced from a given basket of resources. The amount of capital is constrained by savings, and the amount of labor is constrained by demography. Growth in productivity, which allows more GDP to be produced from the same volume of resources, critically depends on economic policies. When policies retard the efficiency of resource use, policy reform promotes greater efficiency and higher levels of productivity. This is the central reason sustaining and accelerating economic reforms is essential to sustaining and accelerating growth in the forthcoming years.

Accordingly, the central objective of this volume is to outline reforms that India must undertake in the years to come in order to achieve the objective of eliminating abject poverty and bringing prosperity to large segments of its population. As India pursues these objectives, it must also substantially urbanize and modernize its economy over the next two decades. With new technologies emerging at an accelerated pace, the task of modernization assumes special significance.

Before I turn to a detailed discussion of the necessary reforms, however, it is useful to briefly outline the post–Second World War experience of a handful of countries that have successfully transformed their economies. Even though the economic and technological environment today is significantly different from that during the decades immediately following the Second World War, the experience of these economies provides useful lessons for India.

Lessons from the Miracle Economies of East Asia

There are six East Asian entities—Japan, Hong Kong, Singapore, South Korea, Taiwan, and China—that grew at rates ranging from 8 to 10 percent on a sustained basis following the Second World War. These countries successfully achieved the kind of transformation within three decades that took Western economies a century or longer. Table 1.1 provides the growth rates and the associated periods of transformation in these countries.

These countries' growth experiences have several features in common. They all witnessed an exceptionally rapid growth of exports. They also saw a rapid rise in manufacturing's share in GDP, especially the manufacturing of labor-intensive products. Accelerated manufacturing growth, which placed rapidly rising purchasing power in the hands of citizens, expanded the demand for services and thus accelerated services growth as well. Rapid expansion of manufactures and services pulled workers out of agriculture in vast numbers (except in Hong Kong and Singapore, where agriculture had at best a limited presence) and led to rapid urbanization. Productivity grew sufficiently fast in this process to raise wages in manufacturing and services by 8 to 10 percent annually at the same time that

Table 1.1 Growth Rates in Miracle Transformers

Country	Period	Average annual growth rate
Japan	1946–75	8.80%
Hong Kong	1961–80	9.95%
Singapore	1961–80	9.80%
Taiwan	1962–89	9.30%
South Korea	1963–96	8.30%
China	1981–2013	10%

Source: Ito and Weinstein 1996, 209, table 1, for Japan, and author's calculations using online World Development Indicators, World Bank, for other countries.

workers migrated in large numbers into these sectors. Poverty levels saw a rapid decline in relatively short periods of time.[4]

The Experience of South Korea

The experience of South Korea, summarized in Figures 1.2 to 1.5, best illustrates the process of transformation in these economies. In 1963, when the country began growing rapidly, exports' share in its GDP was less than 5 percent (Figure 1.2). During the following decades, that share grew exceptionally rapidly, reaching 38.3 percent in 1987. With GDP itself growing at a rate of 8 percent plus, exports had to grow at an average rate exceeding 20 percent to produce such a large increase in the exports-to-GDP ratio.

This export growth was accompanied by a rapid expansion of manufactures initially. But as incomes rose and the demand for services expanded, services growth accelerated as well (Figure 1.3). The share of agriculture in GDP, which stood at 39 percent in 1965, fell to just 9 percent by 1990. Industry and services came to account for more than 91 percent of GDP in 1990. Within twenty-five years, South Korea went from an agrarian economy to one dominated by industry and services.

A remarkable feature of South Korea's transformation was the large shift in the employment share of agriculture that accompanied the large shift in the output

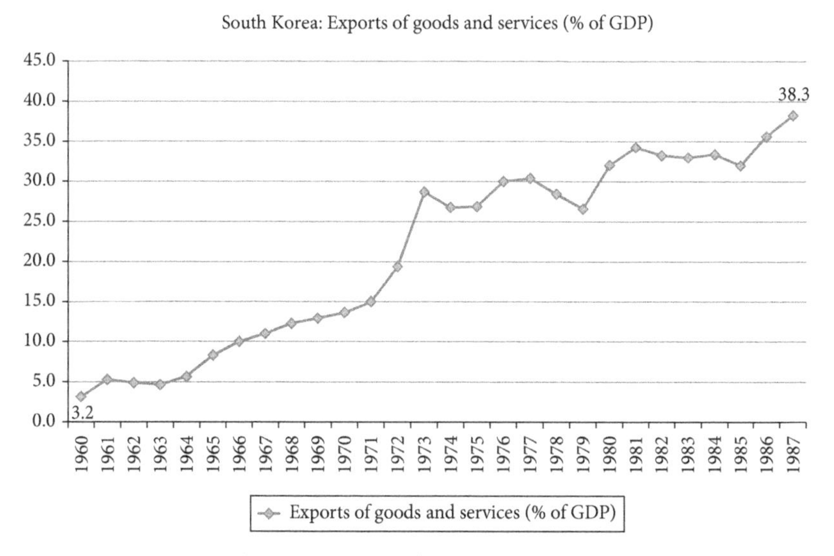

Figure 1.2 Exports-to-GDP Ratio in South Korea: 1960–1987
Source: Based on the author's calculations using online World Development Indicators, World Bank.

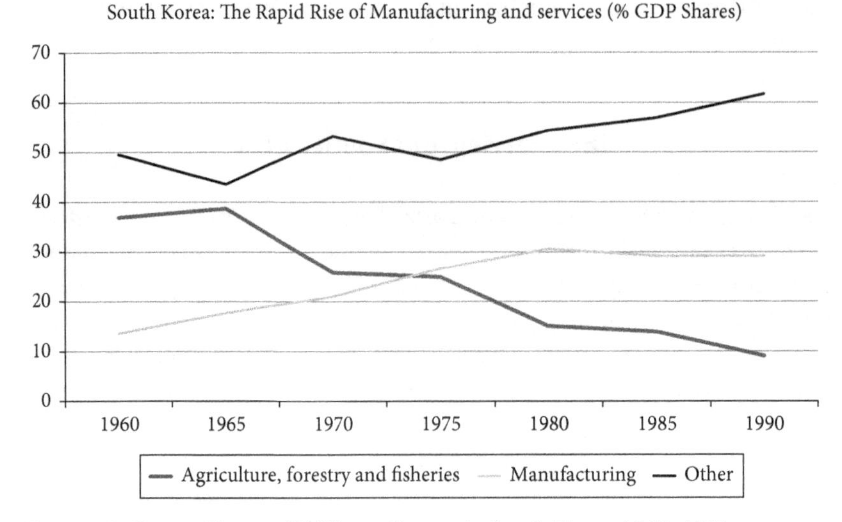

Figure 1.3 Output Shares of Different Sectors in South Korea: 1965–1990
Source: Author's construction using data in Yoo 1997.

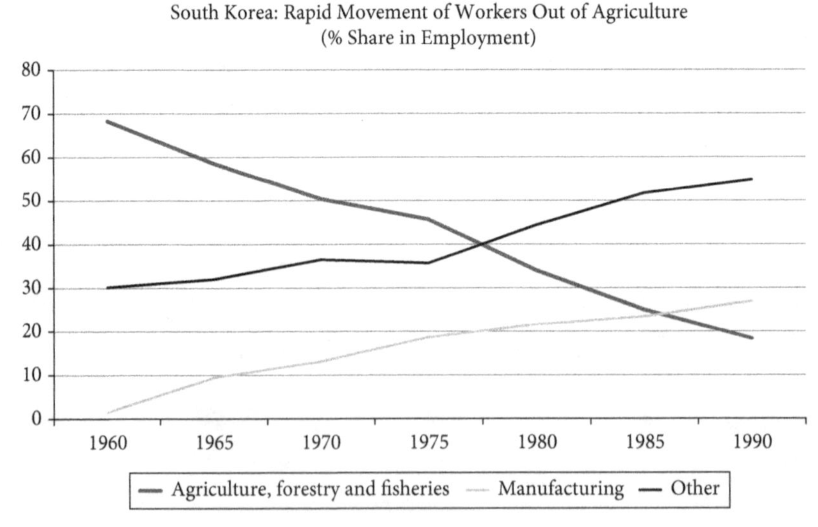

Figure 1.4 Employment Shares of Broad Sectors in South Korea: 1965–1990
Source: Author's construction using data in Yoo 1997.

share of that sector. In 1965, 59 percent of the Korean workforce was employed in agriculture (Figure 1.4). By 1990, this share had dropped to 18 percent. Even as industry and services absorbed large volumes of workers, with productivity rising rapidly, real wages paid in those sectors rose approximately 10 percent annually.

Movement out of agriculture into industry and services was accompanied by urbanization. In the mid-1960s, the urban population in South Korea was 29 percent of the total (Figure 1.5). But once growth accelerated and workers began shifting from agriculture to industry and services, urbanization spread rapidly. By 1990, urbanization in South Korea had crossed the 74 percent mark, and by 1999, it had reached 88.3 percent. This urbanization took place not just because workers moved from rural to urban areas but also because many previously rural regions became urban alongside the shift in the pattern of employment in favor of non-agricultural activities.

This transformation of Korea saw abject poverty virtually eliminated. At the poverty line of 121,000 won per month for a household of five members, the proportion of households below the poverty line fell from 40.9 percent in 1965 to 14.8 percent in 1976 and 7.6 percent in 1991. In rural areas, poverty fell from 54.9 percent in 1965 to 18.1 percent in 1976 and 8.7 percent in 1991. In urban areas, the reduction was from 35.8 percent in 1965 to 11.7 percent in 1976 and 2.8 percent in 1991.[5]

Remarkably, this decline in poverty took place almost entirely through growth, since very few Korean benefited from anti-poverty programs. In 1961, Korea had introduced a public assistance program, which was based on strict means tests. In 1965, the program covered 13.66 percent of the population. But

Figure 1.5 Urbanization in South Korea: 1955–1999
Source: Author's construction using data in Yoo 1997.

this proportion fell to 3.77 percent in 1975 and then rose modestly to 5.26 percent in 1990.[6]

Concluding Remarks

Historically, India and China have been the two largest economies in the world. Until as recently as 1820, together they contributed half of the world's GDP. But as the Industrial Revolution lifted per capita incomes first in Europe and then in the United States, the economic center of gravity of global economy shifted to those regions.

In India, with the British following policies that were entirely designed to serve the interest of their own country's economy, there was prolonged stagnation or decline during the second half of the nineteenth century and the first half of the twentieth. The country's share in global GDP fell from 16 percent in 1820 to just 4.2 percent by the time the British left in 1947. Once a national government committed to promoting the country's interest came to the helm in India, per capita incomes did begin to rise. But the choice of a command-and-control model during the first four decades of independence, driven by the socialistic thinking embraced by the leadership of the day, failed to deliver the high rates of growth that the country needed to rid itself of abject poverty.

A review of East Asia's fastest-growing economies shows that an important key to near double-digit growth remains openness. A detailed look at the development of South Korea from the early 1960s to 1990 shows that once this country opened its economy to world markets, growth in exports of labor-intensive manufacturing initially and in services subsequently allowed it to move the workforce out of agriculture into non-agricultural activities. During this period wages rose at approximately 10 percent per year in industry and services sectors, helping to eliminate poverty in the country.

Stories of the other East Asian miracle economies, including China, Hong, Kong, Singapore, and Taiwan, are different in details but very similar in substance. Those economies also opened up to international trade and built their successes on expansion of exports and imports. Large global markets allowed them to scale up their export industries and reap economies of scale. Competition against the best manufacturers in the global economy and exposure to new products and technologies allowed them to achieve rapid productivity growth. The result was near double-digit growth and a sharp decline in abject poverty.

Until the 1980s, many analysts had argued that exports could serve as the engine of growth only for small economies such as Singapore, Hong Kong, Taiwan, and South Korea. In particular, it was thought, populous countries such as China and India could not achieve high growth rates on the back of the world market.

But after China opened its economy and more or less repeated the performance of the four smaller economies of East Asia, this argument lost its force. When in 1991 India too decided to open to world markets, albeit cautiously and gradually, its experience turned out to be no different from that of China. This is the story I turn to in Chapter 2.

Notes

1. Estimates by Maddison are in 1990 purchasing parity dollars using the Geary-Khamis method. For details on the Geary-Khamis method, see https://stats.oecd.org/glossary/detail.asp?ID=5528 (accessed February 10, 2018).
2. Throughout the book, I use a slash (/) to indicate India's fiscal year, which begins on April 1 and ends on March 31. Therefore, 2017/18 refers to the period beginning April 1, 2017, and ending on March 31, 2018. Growth in real rupees is based on the GDP series at 2004/5 prices for the years 2003/4 to 2011/12 and at 2011/12 prices for the years 2012/13 to 2017/18. Growth in real dollars is derived as follows. Using the nominal GDP data from 2002/3 to 2010/11 at 2004/5 prices and from 2011/12 to 2017/18 at 2011/12 prices and applying the corresponding average annual dollar-rupee exchange rate, the nominal dollar GDP in India grew at an average annual rate of 11.9 percent from 2003/4 to 2017/18. With the growth in the GDP deflator in the United States averaging 2 percent during the same period, annual GDP growth in real dollars in India works out to 9.9 percent.
3. India's nominal GDP in 2017/18 was INR 167.73 trillion. The average exchange rate during 2017/18 being INR 64.4549 per dollar, this figure translates as $2.6 trillion.
4. Detailed experiences of these countries, except Japan, are documented in Panagariya 2019a.
5. Kwon and Yi 2008, table 2.
6. Kwon and Yi 2008, table 1.

2
From Command and Control to a More Liberal Order: 1950–2018

India exhibited a very different growth trajectory than the four East Asian miracle economies during the early decades of development. In spite of a rapidly expanding global economy during these decades, which helped pull up per capita incomes at significantly high rates in many developing countries, India saw only a modest turnaround in its performance. This was progress compared to its abysmal performance during the first half of the twentieth century, when the entire policy and administrative apparatus had been geared to serving the interest of the colonial power.

As was true of other developing countries around the time, India had started extremely poor. But unlike Singapore, South Korea, and Taiwan, which successfully overcame much of their abject poverty during the first few decades following the Second World War, India remained mired in extreme poverty. As late as 1980, economist Garry Fields described India as a "miserably poor country" whose poverty problem was so acute that it was "debatable whether any internal policy change short of a major administrative overhaul and major redirection of efforts might be expected to improve things substantially."[1]

An Overview of Post-Independence Growth Experience

In broad terms, the economic history of India from 1950/51 to 2017/18 can be divided into four distinct phases (Table 2.1).[2] In Phase I, spanning three decades from 1950/51 to 1980/81, India grew 3.7 percent annually, with per capita income growing at just 1.6 percent per annum. In Phase II, the transition phase—and therefore the shortest of the four phases, lasting from 1981/82 to 1987/88—the GDP growth rate accelerated to 4.9 percent. During Phase III, covering the years 1988/89 to 2002/3, there was further acceleration in GDP growth to 5.7 percent. Finally, in Phase IV, encompassing the years 2003/4 to 2017/18, India grew at a yet higher rate, 7.7 percent.[3]

This summary of growth rates illustrates the varied performance of the economy during nearly seven decades beginning in 1950/51. A finer division of the period shows even more variation. In an earlier book, I further subdivided

Table 2.1 Four Phases of Growth in India

Period	Growth in real GDP at market prices	Growth in real per capita GDP at market prices
Phase I (1951–81)	3.7%	1.6%
Phase II (1981–88)	4.9%	2.8%
Phase III (1988–2003)	5.7%	3.7%
Phase IV (2003–18)	7.7%	6.4%

Source: Author's calculations based on CSO GDP data.

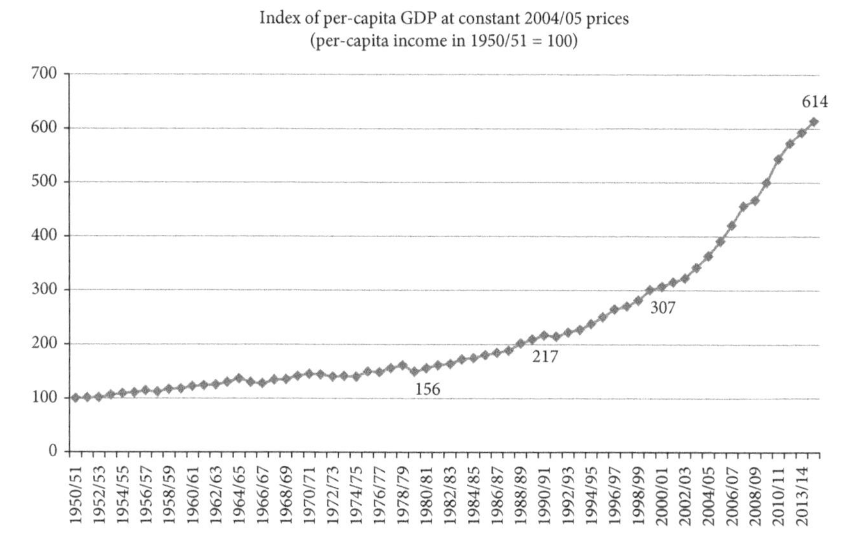

Figure 2.1 Evolution of Per Capita Income in India: 1950/51 to 2011/12
Source: Author's construction using CSO data.

Phase I into two parts: 1951/52 to 1964/65, when the economy grew 4.3 percent annually, and 1965/66 to 1980/81, when it grew only 3.2 percent per year.[4] Indeed, since India's population during the latter period grew faster, the difference in per capita income growth between the two subperiods was event larger: 2.3 percent versus just 0.9 percent per year. From an economic standpoint, the period from 1965/66 to 1980/81 was by far the worst, with a hardly perceptible change in living standard.

To help the reader appreciate better the implications of India's varied performance over these four phases, Figure 2.1 shows the evolution of per capita income at constant 2004/5 prices from 1950/51 to 2013/14, with per capita income in 1950/51 set at 100. I terminate Figure 2.1 in 2013/14 because a continuous GDP series at the same base year, 2004/5, is available only until that year.

The slow growth during Phase I translated in per capita income rising just 56 percentage points over three decades. In 1980/81, the index of per capita income stood at just 156, compared with 100 in 1950/51. In contrast, the modest acceleration and slightly higher base ended up yielding a 61 percentage point rise in per capita GDP during the 1980s over the level prevailing in 1950/51. Acceleration during the 1990s yielded another 90 percentage point rise. Finally, a growth rate over 8 percent for nine years beginning in 2003/4 and the higher base of per capita income allowed the economy to add 307 percentage points during the first thirteen years of the twenty-first century. Put another way, whereas India added just 207 percentage points to per capita income over its 1950/51 level during the entire second half of the twentieth century, it managed to add 307 percentage points in just thirteen years during the twenty-first century.

According to estimates by Maddison, between 1913 and 1950, GDP in India grew a mere 0.23 percent per year. Judged against this performance, a growth rate of 3.7 percent during the first three decades of development may seem satisfactory. Some may even characterize it as a big leap. But such a comparison is what one astute commentator has called "both fatuous and facetious" because the near lack of growth from 1913 to 1950 was the result of a policy designed to serve solely the interest of Great Britain.[5] Any policy that placed the interest of India at its center was likely to produce some acceleration in growth. The real question is whether the policies India adopted in the immediate post-independence era fully exploited the country's growth potential. As the experience of the East Asian economies testifies and India's own superior performance following post-1991 economic reforms demonstrates, India's potential went badly unrealized during those early decades of development.

Policy Mistakes and Corrections

In the early 1950s, South Korea, Taiwan, Singapore, China, and India had comparable per capita incomes. The first three of these countries switched to outward-oriented policies in the early to mid-1960s, resulting in wholesale economic transformation during the following three decades. China and India remained inward-oriented and found themselves at significantly lower per capita income levels in the late 1970s. With its per capita income slightly below that of India, China too made a switch to outward-oriented policies in the late 1970s. Within three decades, it managed to achieve a transformation similar to what South Korea, Taiwan and Singapore had achieved earlier. India persisted in maintaining its inward-looking policy regime much longer and therefore saw its transformation much delayed. In the following, I briefly review the policies India pursued during various periods, their rationale, and the country's eventual shift away from them.[6]

The Lost Decades: 1950/51 to 1980/81

Two key objectives underlying the development model that India's political leadership favored in the 1950s were self-sufficiency and industrialization. In the immediate post-independence era, it was natural for the leadership to seek to reinforce hard-won political independence with economic independence. Industrialization, on the other hand, was seen as synonymous with development and modernization, and it was considered essential for accelerated growth. Growth, in turn, was viewed as the key instrument for ridding India of its abject poverty.

A movement toward self-sufficiency also found broad support among Indian and foreign economists of the day, though for a very different reason. These economists' policy instincts were rooted in what has been called "export pessimism." They held that the comparative advantage of developing countries was in primary products. Therefore, reliance on trade as the engine of growth would mean that these countries would specialize in and export primary products.

But this was a losing proposition for two reasons. First, world demand for primary products was not very responsive to price change. Therefore, to get industrial countries to buy more of these products, prices would have to fall by a large amount. It followed that the benefits of any expansion of exports of these products following trade liberalization or productivity enhancement would pass through to importing industrial countries through substantially lower prices. Second, as incomes rise, demand shifts away from primary products toward manufactured products. This meant that by shifting demand away from primary products, rising incomes in industrial economies would drive down their prices. As a result, specialization in primary products would not pay. The case for import substitution industrialization (ISI), which relied on protection for industry and a movement of the economy away from specialization in primary products, followed.

Nearly all developing countries, including South Korea, Taiwan, Singapore, China, and India, began with ISI in some form in the 1950s. What distinguished the first four of these countries was that, one by one, they decisively opted out of this model. They could escape the curse of export pessimism by specializing in and exporting light manufactures, which did not suffer from the price reductions that threatened primary product exports.

Unfortunately, India persisted much longer with the ISI model. In the early post-independence decades, it pursued two key elements of industrial policy. First, it gave the public sector a dominant role in the development of heavy industry. This was premised, arguably erroneously, on the assumption that efficient operation in heavy industry would require investment on a scale that was beyond the capacity of the private sector. Second, the policy regulated private sector investment flows through strict licensing. This decision was premised on the assumption that, absent licensing, private investment would follow profits and would therefore flow into sectors that did not necessarily serve the nation's interest and priorities.

Combined with the objective of self-sufficiency, this industrial policy gave rise to a highly inefficient economy. Self-sufficiency required that India quickly diversify its production basket to align it with its consumption basket. If bicycles were needed, assembling them domestically was not sufficient; the parts used in the bicycles, the steel used in the parts, and the machines necessary to produce the parts had to be produced domestically as well. Given limited resources, such wide diversification got in the way of exploiting scale economies. Many products were also beyond the country's technological capability at the time, which resulted in abysmal product quality.

Employment being an important objective, the leadership of the day also decided to leave the production of light manufactures to small and household enterprises, called "cottage industry" in those days. It was expected that much of the available capital would be absorbed by formal heavy industry, which was unviable without some minimum scale of operation. Therefore, light manufactures would have to be produced with minimal capital, principally using labor, in a cottage industry setting.

The decision was therefore made that the government would give investment licenses only for products such as chemicals, fertilizers, machinery, and consumer durables that could not be produced by small household enterprises. Later, beginning in 1967, Prime Minister Indira Gandhi formalized this policy via the introduction of the small-scale industries (SSI) reservation. Under the SSI reservation, a list of labor-intensive products was drawn up, with these products reserved for exclusive manufacture by small enterprises. In turn, small enterprises were defined as those with a investment ceiling of just 750,000 rupees or, at the prevailing exchange rate of 7.5 rupees per dollar, $100,000.

On the surface, this was a coherent strategy to stimulate growth and employment while promoting self-sufficiency. But in practice, it undermined both growth and employment creation by undermining efficiency. The strategy greatly underestimated the productivity gains associated with specialization according to comparative advantage and competition in the world markets. Specialization in a handful of products, which can be partially exchanged in the world markets for products not produced at home, allows the firms to achieve high productivity through several channels:

- Insofar as the country specializes in the exports of labor-intensive manufactures in the early stages of development and is consequently able to import machinery and other capital-intensive products, it is better able to utilize its scarce capital.
- Firms that operate in export markets are inevitably exposed to competition with the most efficient producers in the world. This fact forces them to continuously update their technologies, management practices, and product quality to remain competitive.
- Large world markets allow the exporting firms to achieve a scale that makes it attractive for them to employ machinery, which in turn creates skills and raises labor productivity and wages. Use of extra machinery does not undermine the employment objective, since employment per unit of capital is large in labor-intensive products that the country exports, and the vast world market allows exporting firms to operate on a large scale.
- World markets give firms access to high-quality inputs and machinery, which in turn allows them to produce high-quality products demanded by sophisticated global customers.
- Continuous upgrading of technology and management by export-oriented firms gives rise to continuous upgrading of skills and thus better prepares the workforce for the next generation of technologies and innovations in management techniques.

Confined predominantly to the domestic market in the early decades, Indian firms remained stuck in old technologies, low-quality products, and low levels of productivity. The greatest loss of efficiency was in light manufactures, precisely the products in which the country had potential comparative advantage because of its vast labor force. Hamstrung by the investment cap of just $100,000, these products could neither achieve an efficient scale nor take advantage of technological progress or advances in product quality that were taking place elsewhere in the world.

A look at the evolution of exports as a proportion of GDP over time illustrates the detrimental effect that India's policies had on export performance (Figure 2.2). As in South Korea, this ratio was low in India in the 1950s. But in contrast to South Korea, it declined over time in India even though GDP exhibited a mildly rising trend. In 1958/59, for the first time, the ratio fell below 5 percent and remained there during every year until as late as 1974/75. In contrast, in South

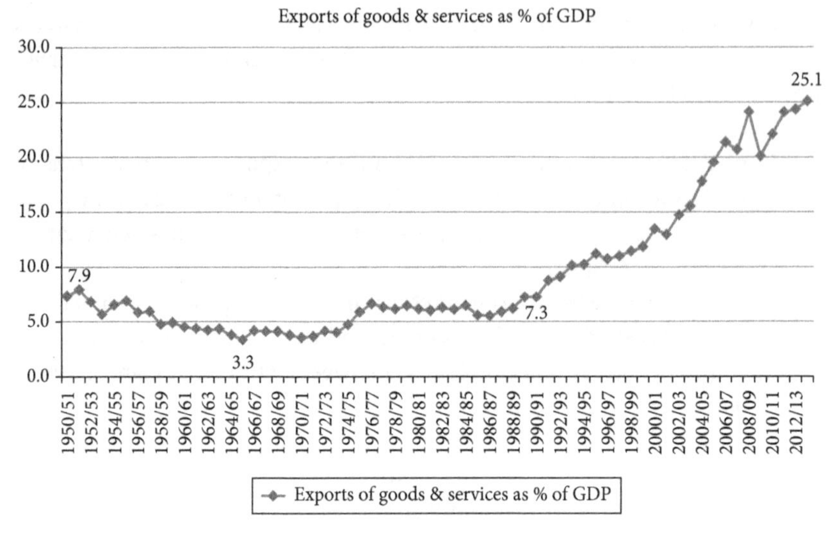

Figure 2.2 Exports as a Proportion of GDP in India: 1950/51 to 2011/12
Source: Author's construction using data from *RBI Handbook of Statistics*, 2014.

Korea, the ratio rose steadily after the mid-1960s and reached above 25 percent in 1973. A declining exports-to-GDP ratio in a growing economy is rare and symptomatic of near-autarkic trade policies and a highly overvalued domestic currency.

With limited access to external sources of financing, imports into India were constrained by revenues generated by exports. Therefore, imports exhibited a pattern mirroring exports (Figure 2.3). They were subject to a declining trend from the late 1950s to the mid-1970s. Because of a payment from Great Britain for its contribution to the Second World War, India had available to it some sterling balances during the decade immediately following independence. These balances allowed its imports to exceed exports by a small margin. Imports as a proportion of GDP especially declined after 1957/58, when the sterling balances dried up. During the 1960s and the first half of the 1970s, imports remained in the neighborhood of 5 percent of GDP. The fortuitous appearance of remittances by workers migrating to the Middle East following the oil price hike gave imports some boost in the second half of the 1970s, but they did not return to the 1950s peak of 10 percent until after the liberalizing reforms of 1991.

During 1951–65, GDP grew by 4.3 percent annually. This was a significant acceleration in growth over the first half of the twentieth century. There were two broad reasons this acceleration could be achieved.

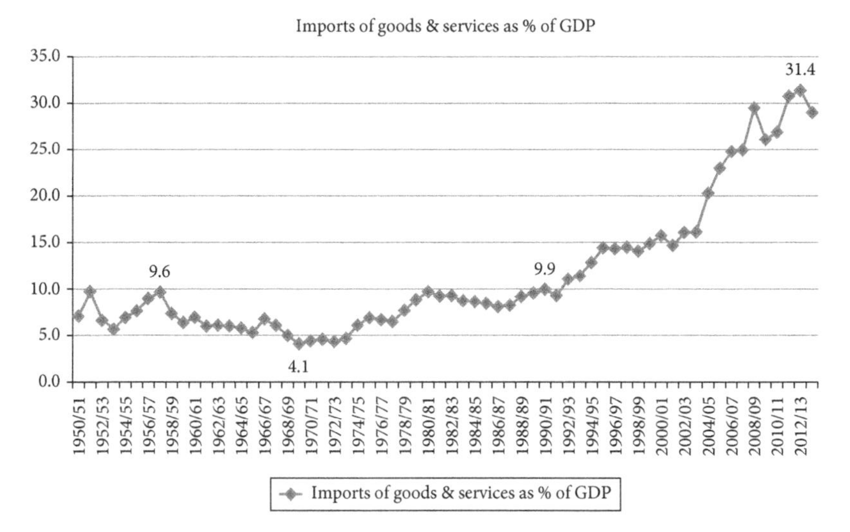

Figure 2.3 Imports as a Proportion of GDP in India, 1950–2012
Source: Author's construction using data from *RBI Handbook of Statistics*, 2014.

First, unlike during the British era, national interest rather than the interest of the colonial power now guided economic policy. All efforts were directed to serving the interests of India rather than Britain. A concerted effort was made to increase investment, build infrastructure, and promote industrial development. This was bound to yield some positive results.

Second, overall, policies during the period 1951–65 were less constraining and their impact less damaging than what was to come. As we have seen, the availability of sterling balances that Britain owed India in payment for its contribution to the Second World War allowed India to maintain a relatively liberal import regime till at least 1957/58, when these balances dried up. Prime Minister Jawaharlal Nehru had inherited a liberal foreign investment regime from the British and liberalized it further. Finally, in the early years when the economy was small, the government had a relatively small number of applications to deal with, so it could make decisions on licenses in a timely fashion.[7] It was only in the early 1960s that the system began to get clogged. Delays became endemic, and recourse to bribes as a means to getting a decision in one's favor and speeding up the process became commonplace. In the following years, both the efficiency of the economy and the moral fabric of the nation suffered.

Government interventions became considerably more ubiquitous under Prime Minister Indira Gandhi, who came into office in 1966. The role of the public sector was expanded not only through public investment but also via nationalization. All major banks, insurance companies, oil companies, and coal mines were nationalized. The SSI reservation was formalized, with the number of industries subject to reservation growing over time. Licensing reigned supreme in virtually all industries. Entry and expansion of firms came to be governed by a series of lists of products subject to a complex web of rules.

The years 1966–76 also saw a significant tightening of rules governing foreign investment. With some exceptions, foreign companies were asked to dilute foreign equity to 40 percent and register in India as Indian companies. Two major foreign companies, IBM and Coca-Cola, exited India as a result. Investments by big business houses and large enterprises were confined to a narrow range of industries. The government also introduced ceilings on urban land holdings and effectively prohibited worker layoffs by factories with one hundred or more workers.

A final set of notable interventions in manufactures concerned price and distribution controls. With imports tightly controlled and licenses issued only to a handful of producers (in view of the existence of scale economies), the government was apprehensive that those lucky enough to get investment licenses would earn monopoly profits. That in turn led the government to impose price controls in many cases. At the controlled prices, demand usually far exceeded the licensed production capacity, forcing the government to introduce distribution controls. Using a set of opaque criteria, the government assumed effective control of who would get to buy the product and who would be excluded from it. Products such as sugar, telephones, cement, scooters, and cars thus became subject to administrative allocation by government via permits. In the case of some products such as telephones and cars, years-long waiting lists formed. Bribes and black markets proliferated in response. The impact of these dirigiste policies was that growth fell to 3.2 percent per year during 1965–81.[8]

Prime Minister Nehru was focused squarely on developing industry, to the neglect of agriculture. After he died in 1964 and before his daughter, Indira Gandhi, came into office, Prime Minister Lal Bahadur Shastri briefly ruled the country. During his short rule (June 1964 to January 1966), Shastri successfully shifted the focus of government policy from heavy industry to agriculture. He sowed the seeds of the Green Revolution and launched several important institutions: the Agricultural Price Commission, the Food Corporation of India (FCI), and the National Dairy Development Board (NDDB). These institutions subsequently played an important role in the development of agriculture and continue to be robust today. Indira Gandhi supported the initiative for the Green Revolution begun by Shastri, which proved extremely important in making India self-sufficient in food.

Hesitant Liberalization: The Transition Decade of the 1980s

By the mid-1970s, some in the government had begun to recognize that the licensing system was becoming a stumbling block to the growth of industry. The industrial sector had experienced annual average growth of just 2 percent during 1970–75, compared with 6.7 percent during 1951–65. This plummeting of industrial growth, combined with pressures from industrialists hamstrung by shortages of inputs, helped create a small constituency for liberalization. Remittances from Indians working in the Middle East became a facilitating factor, since they led to a modest easing of the foreign exchange constraint.

Consequently, India began taking some baby steps toward liberalization of industrial and import controls in the second half of the 1970s. The process saw a slight acceleration in the 1980s, especially beginning in the mid-1980s. But since there was not enough political will to recognize that the command-and-control model was fundamentally flawed, there was no effort to change the policy framework. Instead, small changes were made in rules and regulations within the existing policy framework. Unsurprisingly, liberalization was quite limited and has been rightly labeled as "reform by stealth."[9]

Of course, limited action produced only limited returns. The growth rate during 1981–88 edged up to 4.9 percent. Fiscal expansion and a long-overdue depreciation of the rupee during the second half of the 1980s, which helped boost exports, reinforced the effect of this modest domestic liberalization and temporarily pushed the growth rate up to 7 percent in 1988–91. But the large fiscal deficits, partially financed by borrowing abroad, also carried the seeds of a balance-of-payments crisis. The crisis became a reality in the wake of the First Gulf War in early 1991. An accelerating economy came to a sudden stop. Real GDP at market prices grew just 1.4 percent in 1991/92.

Deeper Reforms During 1991–2004

The 1991 balance-of-payments crisis provided the occasion for more systematic and deeper reforms. In June 1991, Prime Minister Narasimha Rao came to the helm. Within a short period, his government substantially devalued the rupee to make Indian goods competitive on the world markets, abolished investment and import licensing (except on consumer goods imports), and threw open the door to direct foreign investment. It also stabilized the economy macroeconomically, significantly bringing down the fiscal deficit.

Later, the government steadily lowered tariffs, opened civil aviation and telecommunications to the private sector, eased entry of private domestic and foreign banks, and reduced financial repression via reductions in the statutory liquidity ratio (SLR) and cash reserve ratio (CRR). By 1995/96, the highest industrial tariff rate had been brought down to 50 percent (with the exception of some peak tariffs) from 355 percent in 1990/91, personal income tax rates had been unified into three rates, 20, 30, and 40 percent, and the corporate profit tax had been reduced to 40 percent from 50 percent for widely held companies and to 40 percent from 55 percent for closely held companies.

Observers have sometimes described the Rao reforms as the continuation of a process that began in the late 1970s and accelerated in the 1980s. This characterization not only understates Rao's contribution but is wholly misleading. Earlier measures had all been taken within the existing policy framework. In contrast, the 1991/92 reforms entirely abandoned that framework. In a single stroke, the industrial policy statement dated July 24, 1991, did away with investment licensing and myriad entry restrictions on firms. It also ended the public sector monopoly in most sectors and initiated a policy of automatic approval of foreign direct investment up to 51 percent. So robust was this policy framework that to date the government has not had to replace it.

In a similar vein, the entry of the private sector into telecommunications and civil aviation broke new ground. For the first time since independence, the government allowed private players to enter these two sectors, formerly reserved for the public sector. This reform established a precedent for private firms to enter other sectors that previously had been the exclusive preserve of the public sector, and it laid the foundation for yet more reforms and future revolutions in telecommunications and civil aviation.

The government of Prime Minister Atal Bihari Vajpayee, which was in office from March 1998 to May 2004, took the reform process initiated by Rao considerably forward. On the external front, it ended import licensing on consumer goods, brought the top industrial tariff rate down to 20 percent by 2004/5 (the rate was later reduced to 10 percent in 2007/8 by the successor United Progressive Alliance [UPA] government), and opened the door to direct foreign investment much wider, allowing 100 percent foreign investment in a large number of sectors. On the internal front, it made significant progress in dismantling the small-scale industries reservation, abolishing it entirely for firms exporting 50 percent or more of their output in 2000. It brought the corporate profit tax down to 30 percent, included services in the tax net for the first time, rationalized the indirect tax system by compressing the previous eleven excise tax rates into three rates (8, 16, and 24 percent), introduced the principle of a value-added tax in the states, and considerably improved tax administration.

Of particular significance under the Vajpayee government were reforms in the area of macroeconomic policy. The government ended administered interest rates, with one or two exceptions. It continued reducing financial repression by further lowering SLR and CRR. It improved prudential regulation of banks, recapitalized them, and encouraged them to raise their own equity by disinvestment up to 49 percent. It enacted the important Securitisation and Reconstruction of Financial Assets and Enforcement of Security Interest Act (2002). Finally, it enacted the Fiscal Responsibility and Budget Management Act (2001), committing the government to a road map of fiscal consolidation.

The Vajpayee government also gave greater play to the private sector. It undertook genuine privatization of several public sector enterprises (PSEs) leading to a jump in their efficiency and profitability.[10] It opened life insurance and general insurance to the private sector, allowing up to a 26 percent stake by foreign companies. It introduced the open skies policy, giving further impetus to private players in the airline industry.

The New Telecom Policy (NTP) (1999) unleashed the mobile revolution in India. It greatly strengthened the Telecom Regulatory Authority of India (TRAI) and created the Telecom Dispute Settlement and Appellate Tribunal (TDSAT), giving the tribunal full responsibility for settling disputes involving consumers and providers. The NTP introduced a revenue-sharing regime, transferred the service provision function of the Department of Telecommunication to the newly created Bharat Sanchar Nigam Limited (BSNL), freed up entry into domestic and international long-distance service, and introduced a unified license for the provision of fixed-line and mobile telecom services. These changes kicked off an unstoppable revolution in the telecommunications sector, with teledensity rising from just 2.8 per 100 persons in 1999/2000 to 78.7 in 2011/12.

In the area of infrastructure, the government broke new ground. It launched the National Highway Development Project (NHDP), under which it undertook the Golden Quadrilateral project to convert two-lane highways connecting Delhi, Mumbai, Chennai, and Kolkata to four lanes. Also initiated was the Prime Minister's Gram Sadak Yojana (PMGSY), which has become a major source of connectivity for rural India today. In civil aviation, domestic private airlines were given entry into international aviation breaking the monopoly of Air India. The 2003 amendment of the 1994 Airports Authority of India (AAI) Act opened the door to entry of private airports, which led to transformational changes under the successor UPA government.[11]

In agriculture, the government introduced a model law for the reform of Agricultural Produce Marekting Committees acts in the states. The purpose of this law, to be enacted and implemented by states, was to free up farmers from having to compulsorily sell their produce in designated government marketplaces. It provided for the emergence of alternative marketplaces that could compete for the farmer's produce. Though implementation of this law by states was unfortunately halfhearted, in some states it contributed to bringing more remunerative prices to farmers. Kisan credit cards were introduced in 1998, and by the end of 2003/4, the government had cumulatively issued more than 40 million Kisan credit cards. The credit cards gave farmers quick and easy access to short-term credit at affordable rates. For the first time, India also introduced genetically modified (GM) seeds in cotton. Subsequently, Bt cotton revolutionized cotton farming in Gujarat, Andhra Pradesh, and Maharashtra.

In the social sector, the government launched the Sarva Shiksha Abhiyan (SSA), a program whose name, literally translated, means "universal education mission." It led to a massive expansion of elementary school enrollments. For the first time, expenditures on education exceeded 4 percent of GDP, and they did not fall below 3.5 percent in any single year under the Vajpayee government. A constitutional amendment making education a fundamental right was also passed. In the area of health, the Total Sanitation Campaign was launched. The Integrated Child Development Services (ICDS) scheme was extended to all 5,652 blocks.[12] A food-for-work program and the Antyodaya Anna Yojana, a scheme to provide subsidized food for India's 10 million poorest households, were introduced. There was also a massive expansion of urban housing during this period.

Miracle Growth and a Major Blow to Abject Poverty

The reforms during the Rao and Vajpayee eras had a major impact on the economy. India's opening to the world was reflected in the rapid growth of exports and imports. From the peak of 7.9 percent in 1951/52, exports of goods and services as a proportion of GDP had fallen below 5 percent in 1958/59 and did not cross the 7 percent mark again until 1989/90. But after 1991 reforms, they rose steadily and reached an impressive 25.1 percent in 2013/14 (Figure 2.2). Likewise, imports as a proportion of GDP, which crossed the 10 percent mark for the first time in 1992/93, rose to a peak of 31.4 percent in 2012/13 (Figure 2.3). From a near-autarkic economy, India came close to being a free trade economy. This openness was accompanied by faster growth. Between 1992/93 and 2002/3, the economy grew at an average annual rate of 5.8 percent. This was significantly higher than what had been experienced during the earlier periods.

A much bigger impact on growth was seen beginning in 2003/4. This was the last year of the Vajpayee government, and that year growth shifted to a new trajectory of more than 8 percent. Although the successor government of Prime Minister Manmohan Singh did not carry forward the process of reforms and the global economy faced a major financial crisis in 2008, the lagged effect of what the Rao and Vajpayee governments had done sustained growth in India at an average level of 8.2 percent for nine years, from 2003/4 to 2011/12.

Accelerated growth in turn helped combat poverty. It did so through two channels. First, it created employment opportunities and raised wages, which helped reduce poverty directly. Increased income allowed the poor better access not only to daily needs such as food, clothing, and shelter but also to quality services in areas such as education and health.

Second, higher growth placed a larger volume of revenues in the hands of the government than would have been possible if growth had been slower. These revenues allowed the government to increase social spending. It was on the strength of a growth rate over 8 percent during 2003–12 that the UPA government was able to introduce the Mahatma Gandhi National Rural Employment Guarantee Act (MGNREGA) scheme, under which the government guaranteed one adult member of every rural household one hundred days of employment each year. Increased revenues also paved the way for the Right to Education Act (2009) and the National Food Security Act (2013). Under the former, all children ages six to fourteen were guaranteed school education, and under the latter, the availability of highly subsidized food grains was extended to 75 percent of the population in rural areas and 50 percent of the urban population.

Empirical evidence on the evolution of poverty during the post-reform era reinforces these analytic arguments. No matter how we dissect the data, there is unequivocal evidence of significantly faster poverty reduction alongside faster growth. For starters, research has shown that during the early decades of development, poverty fell during years of good monsoons but rose during years of drought, with the result that there was no change in long-term poverty trends.[13] Given that India started with an extremely low per capita income in 1950/51 and that the increase in per capita income in the early decades was very slow, this result is consistent with the hypothesis of no poverty reduction at low per capita income without substantial growth.

By 1990/91, per capita income had slightly more than doubled from its 1950/51 figure. Therefore, prospects for poverty reduction with further increases in per capita income had improved. Evidence shows that poverty declined with growth in the post-1991 era and that it declined faster with faster growth. Most remarkably, when we look at well-defined groups within the population, this pattern holds up for all of them.

Figures 2.4 to 2.6 show poverty ratios at the official poverty line at the aggregate level in urban and rural India, across different social groups, and in the twenty-one largest states respectively in 1993/94, 2004/5, and 2011–12. Three observations follow from these figures. First, the reduction in poverty at the national level is larger for all groups shown during the seven years from 2004/5 to 2011/12 than during the eleven years from 1993/94 to 2004/5. Recall that the period from 2004/5 to 2011/12 also happens to be the period of fastest growth. Second, during the period shown, poverty declined for all groups (including Scheduled Castes and Scheduled Tribes) and all areas, rural and urban. Finally, poverty declined between 1993/94 and 2011/12 for all states shown in Figure 2.6. At the group level, growth has not left anyone behind.

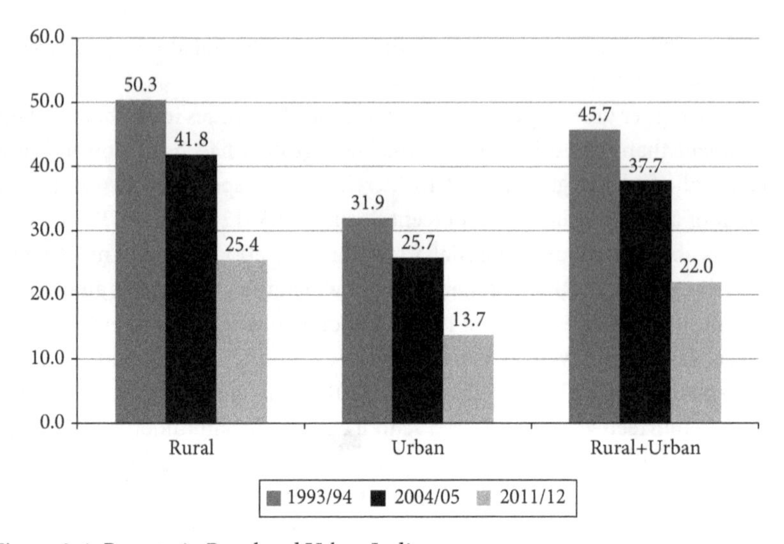

Figure 2.4 Poverty in Rural and Urban India
Source: Author's construction based on estimates in Panagariya and More 2014.

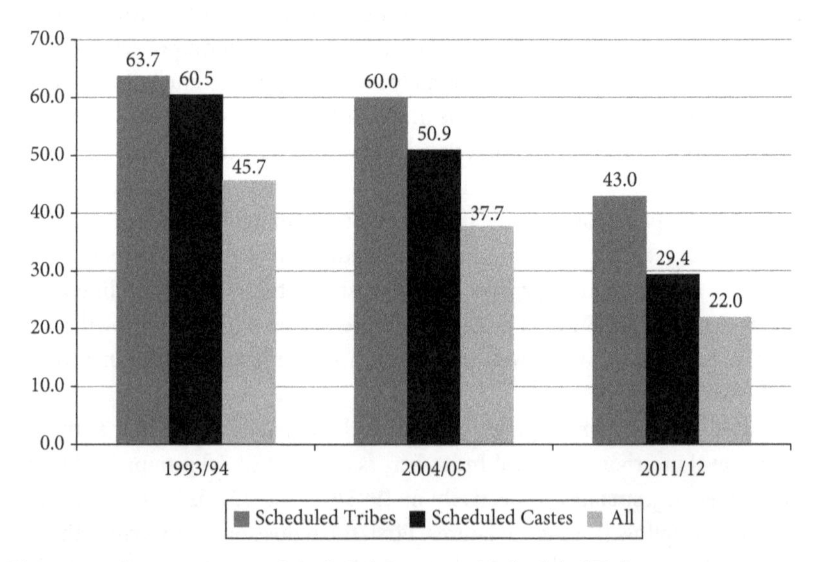

Figure 2.5 Poverty Among Scheduled Castes and Scheduled Tribes
Source: Author's construction based on estimates in Panagariya and More 2014.

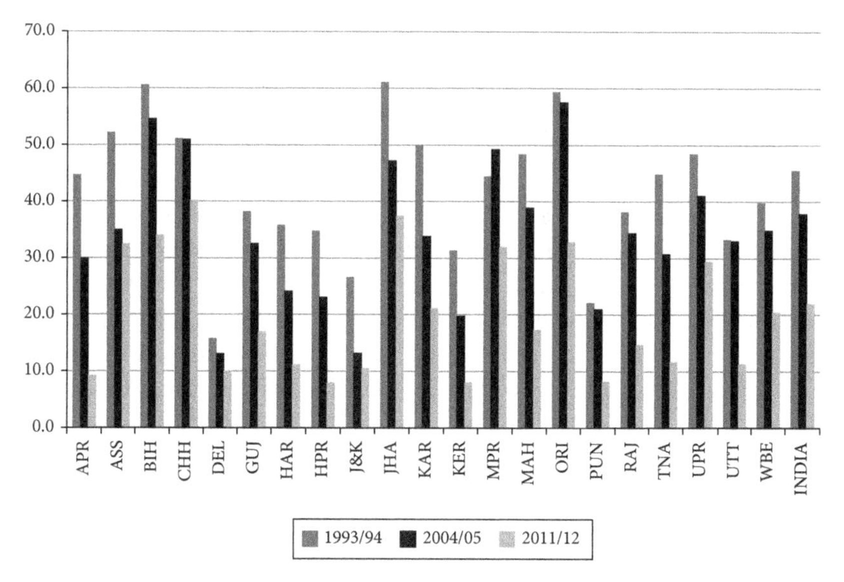

Figure 2.6 Poverty in the Largest 21 States
Source: Author's construction based on estimates in Panagariya and More 2014.

Renewed Policy Mistakes Culminating in a Setback to Growth: 2004–14

The Congress Party–led UPA government of Prime Minister Manmohan Singh, which came to power in 2004, focused principally on social programs. Taking advantage of accelerating revenues that came with high growth, it initiated new programs while also expanding those it had inherited from the previous government. Programs in the former category included the MGNREGA scheme and compulsory education for children six to fourteen years of age under the Right to Education Act (2009). Programs in the latter category were numerous, with the notable ones being rural electrification, the Prime Minister's Rural Roads Program, and the public distribution system (PDS), which provided highly subsidized food grain to the poor.

Unfortunately, however, the Singh government did not maintain the pace of reforms necessary to sustain high growth. The main reforms by the UPA over the ten years of its rule included a reduction in the highest non-agricultural tariff rate from 20 percent to 10 percent (with some sectors retaining higher rates) by April 2007, further liberalization of foreign direct investment, further liberalization of the financial sector, trimming of the SSI reservation list, pension reform, allowing entry to private players in the construction and running of airports, deregulation of petroleum prices, and, most importantly, the launch of a biometric identity project, Aadhaar.

Apart from the slowdown in reform, the UPA also made some decisions that were detrimental to growth, especially during its second term, from 2009 to 2014. It introduced retrospective taxation, which hit a number of multinationals particularly hard and sent a chill down the spines of foreign investors. It also enacted the Land Acquisition Act (2013), which made land acquisition both time-consuming and financially very costly. One part of the Right to Education Act (2009) established standards for schools that were based solely on inputs. Many of these standards had no relationship to the quality of education, and they threatened the survival of low-budget private schools that were providing better education than their public counterparts in the same geographical area. Finally, through the passage of the Food Security Act, the UPA extended a corrupt and leaky public distribution system to 75 percent of the rural population and 50 percent of urban dwellers. This spread the available resources for transfers to the poor thinly over a large population, which included many who did not suffer from any deprivations identified in the Socio-Economic Caste Census.

During the last year of the UPA's first term and the early years of its second term, the UPA also abandoned fiscal discipline, incurring large fiscal deficits. The deficits eventually fueled inflation and widened the current account deficit to alarming levels. In response, the Reserve Bank of India (RBI) raised the interest rate on thirteen consecutive occasions between March 19, 2010, and October 25, 2011. At the same time, environmental clearances for large projects came to a standstill, and decision-making in the central government suffered a general paralysis.

These factors led to a decline in the growth rate from 10.3 percent in 2010/11 to 6.7 percent in 2011/12 and then to 5.5 percent in 2012/13. With the macroeconomic situation relatively weak, anticipation that the United States would be returning to tighter monetary policy during the summer of 2013 led to large capital outflows and depreciation of the rupee by a wide margin. Although there was some recovery in 2013/14, with the growth rate rising to 6.4 percent, the economy remained fragile. These were the circumstances under which Prime Minister Narendra Modi took charge of the government.

Putting the House in Order and Back to Reforms: 2014–18

In May 2014, having won a landslide victory in parliamentary elections on a development platform, Prime Minister Narendra Modi came into office. His government immediately took several measures to restore confidence. It credibly committed to initiating no new cases of retrospective taxation (though it stopped short of repealing the measure altogether). It speeded up environmental clearances and ended the paralysis that had characterized the decision-making process in the central government. The government also made a concerted effort to improve the ease of doing business, both at the central government level and at the level of the states. A large number of projects that had been stuck for a variety of reasons were unblocked. Above all, the government revived and invigorated the process of reforms.

Key reforms by the Modi government included the introduction of a much-needed modern bankruptcy law through the Insolvency and Bankruptcy Code; the replacement of myriad indirect taxes by a single nationwide uniform goods and services tax (GST); the replacement of fragmented and leaky chains for the distribution of government social benefits by direct benefit transfers (DBTs) that relied on the Aadhaar identity system and the near universalization of bank accounts; a systematic assault on corruption in the central government; the provision of fixed-term labor contracts, resulting in greater flexibility in employment; an end to the subsidy on diesel; autonomy for highly ranked universities and colleges; adoption of inflation targeting; stricter rules governing defaults by bank borrowers; the creation of cost-effective digital payment platforms through the Unified Payments Interface (UPI) system; and the near universalization of toilets in rural households.

Improved decision-making and reforms helped return India to a path of higher growth. During the first four years of the Modi government, India clocked an annual average rate of growth of 7.7 percent. It is a fair assessment that the full impact of many of the reforms by the Modi government has yet to be realized. As such, barring serious policy mistakes (such as those made during the period 2009 to 2014), India's growth rate is likely to accelerate further.

Summary Remarks

Historically, India has been among the world's largest economies. Until as late as 1820, it contributed 16 percent of world GDP. But over time, especially under the British rule, it lost the prime place in the global economy that it had enjoyed for more than one and a half millennia. With the Industrial Revolution concentrated in the West, India lost even more ground in relative terms. Happily, in recent years India has begun to regain its position among the large economies. Between 1990 and 2005, it was entirely absent from the top ten countries of the world, ranked by GDP. But in 2010, it became the ninth-largest economy in the world, and it quickly climbed to seventh position in 2015 and sixth in 2017.

In 2017/18, India's GDP was $2.6 trillion in 2017 dollars. If India grows 8 percent in real dollars—a perfectly plausible assumption—it can more than double its GDP in less than ten years. If the Japanese economy remains as tepid as it has been in recent decades, this would comfortably make India the third-largest economy in the world by 2027.

But achieving 8 percent or faster growth would require avoiding the mistakes of the past and staying the course on reforms. An analysis of how other economies have grown rapidly and India's own past experience points to the critical importance of openness to trade. Ultra-tight control of investment and imports in the past, especially during 1951–81, held back India's growth. Releasing controls on the economy, both internally and externally, has allowed India to more fully realize its potential. India must build on this success to transform itself into a prosperous and modern economy. The remainder of this volume is about the reforms India must undertake to achieve this objective.

Notes

1. Fields 1980, 204.
2. In Table 2.1 and the remainder of the book, a period such as 1951–81, when used in the context of India, refers to the period spanning fiscal years 1951/52 to 1980/81, with the endpoint years included. In the context of other countries, unless otherwise specified, data usually relate to the calendar year, and a period such as 1951–81 refers to the period 1951 to 1981.
3. Until 2011/12, growth rates in Table 2.1 are calculated as simple averages of annual growth in GDP at constant 2004/5 market prices. Beginning in 2012/13, India began measuring growth using a new series based on 2011/12 as the base year and incorporating several methodological improvements. Growth rates from 2012/13 onward are calculated using this new GDP series.
4. Panagariya 2008, ch. 1.
5. Khatkhate 2006, 2204.
6. The review here is kept deliberately brief. Readers interested in details should consult two of my earlier books, Panagariya 2008 and Bhagwati and Panagariya 2013.
7. For a more detailed account of policies during the period 1951/52 to 1964/65, see Panagariya 2008, ch. 2.
8. For details, see Panagariya 2008, ch. 3.
9. For details, see Panagariya 2008, ch. 4.
10. Economist Nandini Gupta compared PSEs privatized under Vajpayee with similar PSEs that had been identified for privatization but not privatized. She found that the former outperformed the latter by a wide margin along key dimensions. See Gupta 2013.
11. See https:// www.civilaviation. gov.in/sites/ default/files/ moca_000719_0.Pdf.
12. For administrative purposes, each state in India is divided into several districts and each district into several blocks. In May 2020, the country as a whole had 734 districts and 7096 blocks. See https://lgdirectory.gov.in/.
13. Panagariya 2008, 131–36.

PART II

UNDERSTANDING THE CHALLENGE OF TRANSFORMATION

3
Underemployment in Agriculture

Agriculture is where the largest proportion of India's workforce is employed. Therefore, any analysis of policy reform in India must begin with this sector. The analysis cannot end with prescriptions aimed at improving farm incomes, however. For a significant part of the answer to the puzzle of improving the lives of today's farmers lies in helping a large proportion of them to take more productive jobs in industry and services.

Much public policy discussion on agriculture in India implicitly assumes that this sector is synonymous with the rural economy. This may have been approximately true during the early decades following independence, but it is not so anymore. One would think that politicians who seek rural votes would appreciate the difference and equally address the needs of farmer and non-farmer populations in rural India. But at least in their public pronouncements, they continue to focus disproportionately on farmers and neglect the non-farm rural population.

In 1977/78, the earliest year for which sectoral employment shares are readily available, agriculture had a share of 80.6 percent in the male workforce and 88.1 percent in the female workforce in rural India. At these shares, the assumption that rural workforce was largely agricultural could be defended. But in subsequent years, these shares steadily fell. In 1993/94, they were estimated at 74.1 and 86.2 percent for the male and female workforces, respectively. By 2017/18, the latest year for which we have estimates, the shares had fallen to 55.0 and 73.2 percent.[1] In that year, the employment share of agriculture in the total rural workforce was 59.4 percent.[2] The assumption that the rural workforce is all about agriculture could no longer be defended.

A further complication is that though agriculture is predominantly a rural activity, some agricultural activity also takes place in urban India. The proportion of the urban workforce in agriculture was 10.6 percent for males and 31.9 percent for females in 1977/78. These proportions fell to 5.38 and 9.07 percent, respectively, in 2017/18.[3] The share of agriculture in the total urban workforce stood at 6.14 percent in 2017/18.[4]

These employment estimates imply that though there is a large overlap between agriculture and the rural economy, the two are far from synonymous. As a matter of approximation, we may say that agriculture is a wholly rural activity. But it would be a stretch to say that rural economic activity is all about agriculture. As of 2017/18, two-fifths of the rural workforce was employed in non-agricultural activities.

Unfortunately, National Accounts Statistics of India does not separate sectoral GDP data by rural and urban areas. Therefore, it is not possible to analyze agriculture separately as a rural or urban activity. Likewise, we lack GDP data associated with non-agricultural employment in rural India. Therefore, strictly speaking, the following analysis is purely sectoral in nature, applying to rural and urban areas taken jointly. The most we can say is that what happens in agriculture largely impacts the rural population. But agriculture does not tell us the full story of rural India's economic fortunes. These nuances must be kept in mind throughout this chapter.

A Brief Overview of Agricultural and Rural Policies in India

The Bengal famine of 1943, subsequent food shortages, and repeated bouts of food inflation were foremost on the minds of policymakers following independence. Therefore, the key objective guiding agricultural policy at the time was the achievement of self-sufficiency in food grains. During the years that Prime Minister Jawaharlal Nehru ruled, the government sought to achieve this objective through an institutional approach that consisted of land reforms and farm and service cooperatives.[5]

In the event, both land reform and cooperative movements were largely unsuccessful, and as the population rose, food shortages became more acute in the 1960s. India came to depend heavily on food aid from the United States. Nehru died in 1964 and Prime Minister Lal Bahadur Shastri succeeded him. Around this time food shortages became sufficiently serious that Shastri called upon the nation to forgo at least one meal every week. After Shastri passed away in 1966 and Prime Minister Indira Gandhi came to the helm, India faced virtual humiliation at the hands of U.S. president Lyndon B. Johnson for becoming dependent on food aid from his country. Partially irked by India's lack of support for his Vietnam policy, Johnson vowed to keep India on a "ship-to-mouth" policy, whereby he would release ships carrying food grain only after food shortages reached a point of desperation. An episode reported by Ravi V. Prasad, son of Sharada Prasad, press secretary to Gandhi, captures the anguish Gandhi felt when dealing with Johnson in these terms:

> My father was present when she [Indira Gandhi] was on the telephone with Lyndon Johnson regarding the food shipments when India was living from ship to mouth. She was clenching her fists in anger while she was all sweetness over

> the phone with Johnson in a gentle voice at her persuasive best. She then vowed in fierce determination that she would see to it that India became self sufficient in food, and that no Indian leader would ever have to beg for aid again.[6]

By this time, India had switched from its earlier institutional approach to agricultural policy to one that was based on technology and remunerative prices for farmers. At the center of this policy were imported high-yielding varieties of seeds. Thanks to the new policy's resounding success, India was able to usher in the Green Revolution, which led to fulfillment of the objective of self-sufficiency in food. By the mid-1980s, India's food grain imports had dropped to zero.

With self-sufficiency achieved, the implicit goal of India's agricultural policy became improving the lot of farmers. Regardless of which party or coalition ruled, this objective has guided agricultural policy since the mid-1980s. Accordingly, over the years the government has launched an impressive array of schemes and programs aimed at benefiting the rural population, of which farmers are the largest group. Among the more important of these schemes and programs in force today:

- Under the National Food Security Act (NFSA), a nationwide public distribution system provides 5 kilograms of wheat at 2 rupees per kilogram or rice at 3 rupees per kilogram per person per month to 75 percent of rural households. The poorest of the poor among these 75 percent households receive 35 kilograms of wheat or rice per household at these subsidized prices. With 75 percent of rural households covered, the program has the potential to benefits all poor farm households.
- The government has a massive procurement program under which it buys a substantial proportion of wheat and rice at the minimum support prices (MSPs), which are set well above corresponding market prices. Food grain so procured is then distributed through PDS shops to beneficiaries at subsidized prices. Therefore, as sellers, farmers can receive high prices, and as buyers, they need pay only nominal prices for food grains.
- The Mahatma Gandhi National Rural Employment Guarantee Act scheme offers guaranteed employment up to one hundred days per year to one adult per rural household at specified wage. MGNREGA serves as a source of employment during the lean season. Workers hired under the program help build public assets at the local level.
- Under the government's fertilizer subsidy scheme, farmers can purchase urea at a prespecified below-market price. In 2017/18, this subsidy amounted to 700 billion rupees. Farmers in most states also receive free electricity. A separate scheme provides crop insurance to farmers at highly subsidized premiums.

Finally, the government runs a variety of schemes and programs that benefit farmers directly or indirectly. Following is a partial list of these programs:

- Under the Prime Minister's Housing Scheme, the government provides 120,000 rupees and ninety days of free MGNREGA labor to build pucca houses (strong houses made of materials such as bricks, cement, iron rods and steel) to households living in kuctcha houses (weak or fragile houses made of mud, wood and straw).
- Under the Ujjwala scheme, 1,600 rupees are given to poor households so that they can obtain a connection for cooking gas.
- Under the Prime Minister's Rural Roads Scheme, the government has been building rural roads since 2000/1 to link previously unconnected habitations, with 570,000 kilometers of roads already constructed.
- A rural electrification program has brought electricity to all villages and nearly all households.
- Under the Prime Minister's Irrigation Scheme, massive sums have been spent on expanding the cultivated area under irrigation.
- There are separate schemes to promote the White (milk) and Blue (fisheries) Revolutions.
- Free primary education is provided under the SSA.
- Since the 1960s, the government has built a network of subcenters, primary health centers, and community health centers to provide free primary healthcare services in rural India.[7]
- During elections, governments have waived massive amounts of farm loans, at the expense of the exchequer.

Perpetual Farmer Distress

Notwithstanding these numerous programs aimed at addressing different aspects of the lives of farmers and others in rural India, it is common to come across stories of distress in rural India, especially relating to farmers. There remains a sharp contrast between the resources and efforts successive governments have put into bringing relief to farmers and the dominant narrative in the media and among intellectuals. How is this contradiction to be explained?

There are two hypotheses. First, since stories of distress grab public attention more easily, the media has a vested interest in exaggerating them. Being overly critical of the government of the day, the media also disproportionately focuses on the negative stories. And television, because it is a visual medium, has a great advantage in translating an isolated story of suffering into an account of generalized distress across the length and breadth of the nation. In contrast, hard data are costly to collect, require specialized skills, and often do not get traction with viewers.

Second, it is possible that stories of recurring, even perpetual, distress afflicting the rural population, especially farmers, on a large scale are real. Despite a significant reduction in abject poverty, overall the level of income in India remains low. Indeed, going by the 2011/12 National Sample Survey Office (NSSO) expenditure survey, which is the latest such survey available to date, per capita expenditure of 80 percent of the rural population was 59 rupees per day or less (at prices prevailing that year). The corresponding expenditure in urban India was significantly higher at 111.5 rupees.[8] In all likelihood, the expenditure in urban areas is greatly underestimated because the wealthiest households are unrepresented in the sample from which the estimates are derived.

I would argue that reality lies somewhere between these two hypotheses, though probably closer to the latter. It cannot be denied that the media exhibits a tendency to pick episodes of distress and depict them as representing generalized conditions across the entire nation. For example, just as suicides cannot be eliminated entirely from the non-farmer population, they cannot be eliminated from the farmer population. But many journalists and non-governmental organizations (NGOs) use the existence of farmer suicides by itself as compelling evidence of widespread distress among farmers. Anyone who subjects such an argument to critical scrutiny runs the risk of being labeled as insensitive and oblivious to ground-level reality. As a result, serious analyses of the phenomenon remain confined to journal articles, with the general public protected from being exposed to them.

This being said, to make progress, the first thing we need to do is recognize that rural incomes, including those of farmers, remain low. Rapid growth over the past two decades has most surely helped reduce abject poverty on a significant scale, but this is not the same as saying that the rural population has achieved comfortable levels of income. The per capita expenditure data cited earlier testify to this fact. Therefore, the question we must investigate next is why this is so.

Why Agricultural Incomes Have Remained Low

Rural incomes, which are predominantly derived from agriculture, have not done well. The explanation for this phenomenon is as follows. A robust stylized fact of growth and development is that a declining share of agriculture in GDP accompanies rising per capita incomes. India has been no exception. In most countries experiencing rising per capita incomes, a decline in agriculture's share in GDP is accompanied by a commensurate decline in agriculture's share in employment. In India, the decline in agriculture's share in employment has been at best modest. As a result, too many households in India now depend on too small a share of agriculture in GDP. This problem is compounded by the fact that as family farms have been divided with rising population over the generations, land holdings have become progressively smaller. Half of the land holdings today are 0.5 hectare or smaller. To appreciate the magnitude of the problem, let us consider these phenomena in some detail.

Growth in Agriculture Lagging Behind Industry and Services

As a matter of long-term trend, without exception, the share of agriculture in GDP declines as per capita incomes rise. For instance, it fell from 27 percent in 1990 to 8 percent in 2017 in China; from 26 percent in 1970 to 8 percent in 1990 and then 2 percent in 2017 in South Korea; and from 39 percent in 1990 to 15 percent in 2017 in Vietnam. In developed countries, the share stands at extremely low levels today: 1.5 percent in France in 2017; 1 percent in Japan and the United States in 2016; and 0.5 percent in the United Kingdom in 2017.[9]

This pattern is the result of slower growth in agriculture than in industry and services as the country's economy expands. The impetus for acceleration in growth invariably originates in industry and services. As a result, the faster the rise in per capita income, the faster the decline in the share of agriculture in GDP.

The process of decline in the share of agriculture in GDP has been under way in India since at least independence. In the initial decades, industry and services grew slowly, so the decline in the share of agriculture was also slow. But once growth in industry and services accelerated, the process sped up. Table 3.1, which shows growth rates in agriculture, industry, services, and GDP from 1951/52 to 2016/17, captures this feature of India's post-independence experience. The

Table 3.1 Growth Rates in Agriculture, Industry, and Services, 1951/52 to 2016/17

Period	Agriculture	Industry	Services	GDP
1951/52 to 1979/80	2.1	5.4	4.5	3.5
1980/81 to 1999/2000	3.8	6.1	6.8	5.8
2000/2001 to 2016/17	3.0	7.2	8.4	7.1
1951/52 to 2016/17	2.9	6.1	6.2	5.1

Note: Throughout this volume, unless explicitly stated otherwise, agriculture includes allied activities and services include construction.

Source: Author's calculation using CSO data on GDP at factor cost at constant 2004/5 prices until 2011/12 and at constant 2011/12 prices thereafter.

table divides these years into three periods, showing slow, moderate, and fast growth of GDP.

For the present purpose, two key features of the table may be noted. First, the growth rate in agriculture has been consistently lower than in industry and services. This has meant that the share of agriculture in GDP has consistently shrunk over time. Second, while growth rates in industry and services rose successively and significantly in the second and third periods, agriculture experienced a modest acceleration in the second period but lost a large part of that gain in the third period. Acceleration in agriculture in the second period resulted from the Green Revolution, but the momentum could not be sustained.

The result of this pattern of growth has been that the level of GDP in industry and services taken together diverged greatly from that in agriculture in the second and third periods. The divergence was particularly pronounced during the third period because industry and services continued to accelerate while agriculture decelerated. This "growth" effect on divergence has been reinforced by a "level" effect. Once the absolute level of combined GDP in industry and services came to exceed that in agriculture, each percentage point increase in the former resulted in a larger absolute increase than it did in the latter.

Figure 3.1, which depicts the evolution of GDP in the three sectors from 1950/51 to 2013/14, graphically brings out the uneven performance of the agricultural and non-agricultural sectors. The graph ends in 2013/14 because the Central

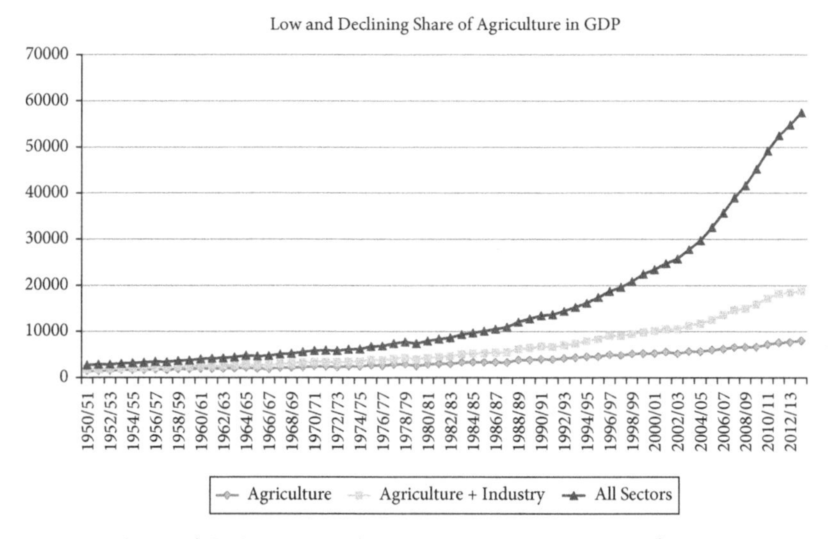

Figure 3.1 Sectoral GDP at Factor Cost in Constant 2004/5 Prices from 1950/51 to 2011/12

Source: Author's construction using CSO data.

Statistics Office (CSO) series on sectoral GDP at constant prices in a common base year is available only up to this year. To emphasize the divergence between industry and services on the one hand and agriculture on the other, Figure 3.1 shows sectoral outputs in stacked form: the middle curve represents GDP in agriculture plus industry and the top one represents GDP in all three sectors combined. As can be seen, the gap between agriculture and other sectors has become progressively larger.

Until the early 1980s, the three sectors saw minimal divergence because industry and services had a minimal lead over agriculture in terms of growth rate and because agriculture had begun with a share of GDP that was over 50 percent in 1950/51. But by the beginning of the second period, not only had the share of agriculture in GDP fallen well below half, but industry and services growth rates acquired substantially greater advantage over it. This process accelerated further in the third period. The result was that the share of agriculture in GDP fell from 53.1 percent in 1950/51 to 36.1 percent in 1980/81 and then plummeted to 14.4 percent in 2011/12.

A More Stubborn Share of Agriculture in Employment

Most countries that have come to enjoy high incomes (and therefore exhibit a low share of agriculture in GDP) have also seen a large decline in the proportion of the workforce employed in agriculture. For example, this proportion stood at 5 percent in South Korea, 3.5 percent in Japan, 2.9 percent in France, 2 percent in the United States, and 1 percent in the United Kingdom in 2017.[10] Low employment share alongside low GDP share in these countries has ensured that output per worker did not fall too far below the average economy-wide output per worker. Even when the gap may have been large, it impacted a tiny proportion of the population. Therefore, compensating this tiny population through transfers from taxes raised from the much larger population in industry and services was a relatively simple matter.

Unfortunately, in the case of India, the process of the movement of workers out of agriculture has not kept pace with the decline in this sector's share in output. Indeed, with the total workforce rising over time, at least until 2004/5, the absolute number of workers in the sector saw an increase. Only after 2004/5 did a sharp decline in female labor participation rates yield a modest decline in this figure.

Estimating the absolute level of employment in different sectors at the national level in a consistent manner requires unit-level observations from what used be called Employment and Unemployment Surveys until 2011/12 and have been rechristened Periodic Labor Force Surveys beginning in 2017/18. They are

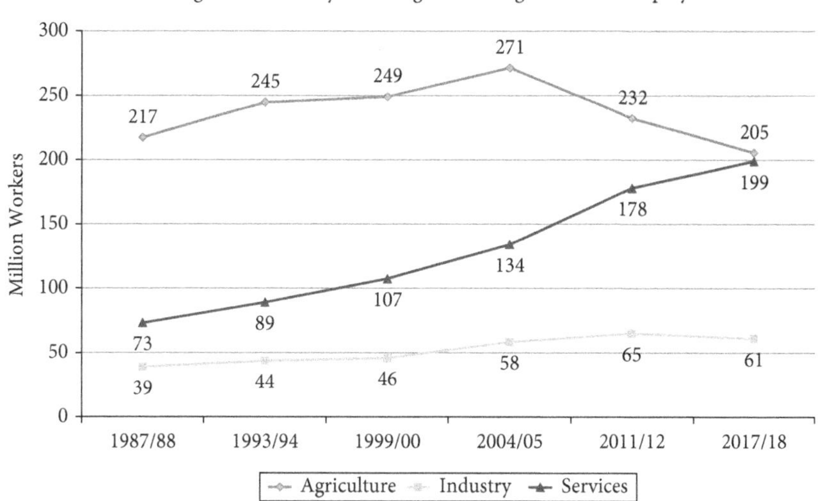

Figure 3.2 Total Number of Workers in Agriculture, Industry, and Services in 1987/88, 1993/94, 1999/2000, 2004/5, and 2011/12

Source: Author's construction based on estimates by economist Rahul Ahluwalia from Employment-Unemployment and Period Labor Force Surveys by National Statistical Office.

available from the National Statistical Office for 1987/88 to 2017/18 at approximately five-year intervals but have become annual since 2017/18. Accordingly, Figure 3.2, which shows the absolute number of workers employed in agriculture, begins in 1987/88 and ends in 2017/18. Between 1987/88 and 2004/5, the workforce in agriculture increased by a hefty 25 percent. This number finally saw a decline beginning in 2011/12, with its level in 2017/18 falling barely a hair's breadth below that in 1987/88.

Table 3.2 shows the evolution of the shares of the three sectors in GDP and workforce to further emphasize the slow pace of change in the composition of workforce relative to GDP. Between 1987/88 and 2017/18, the share of agriculture in GDP fell by more than half, from 30 percent to 14.8 percent. But the decline in the workforce share was far less sharp, falling from 66 percent to 44.1 percent.

A very large part of the decline in the workforce share took place between 2004/5 and 2011/12, when the total workforce grew just 2.6 percent due to a precipitous fall in the female worker participation rate in rural areas. This growth in workforce between 2004/5 and 2011/12 compares with 15.5 percent growth between 1999/2000 and 2004/5. Absent the large decline in female worker participation rate in rural areas, the workforce share of agriculture in 2011/12 would have remained significantly higher than 48.9 percent. Equally disturbing is the

Table 3.2 Shares of Agriculture, Industry, and Services in GDP and Workforce

Year	Agriculture	Industry	Services
Share in GDP			
1987/88	30.0	20.1	49.8
1993/94	28.3	20.1	51.5
1999/2000	23.3	20.4	56.4
2004/5	20.3	20.1	59.6
2011/12	18.5	22.9	58.6
2017/18	14.8	23.5	61.7
Share in Workforce			
1987/88	66.0	11.8	22.2
1993/94	64.6	11.5	23.5
1999/2000	62.0	11.4	26.7
2004/5	58.5	12.6	28.9
2011/12	48.9	13.7	37.5
2017/18	44.1	13.1	42.7

Source: Author's calculations using CSO data on GDP and workforce estimates by Rahul Ahluwalia from Employment and Unemployment Surveys and Periodic Labor Force Surveys.

Note: GDP data are at constant 2004/5 prices until that year and at 2011/12 prices thereafter.

fact that the modest decline in the workforce share of agriculture between 2011/12 and 2017/18 has also been substantially due to a further decline in the female worker participation rate.

Large and Widening Gap in Per-Worker Output Between Agriculture and Other Sectors

To highlight further the implications of a continued high share of agriculture in the workforce in relation to agricultural GDP, Table 3.3 reports per-worker GDP in industry, services, and all sectors relative to per-worker GDP in agriculture. Because of the slow transition of workers out of agriculture even during the decades preceding 1987/88, by that year industry and services had already come to enjoy GDP per worker that was respectively 3.8 and 4.9 times that in agriculture. In subsequent years these multiples rose further, reaching 4.6 in industry and 5.9 in services in 2004/5. Revised GDP estimation methodology

Table 3.3 Per-Worker Productivity in Industry, Services, and All Sectors Relative to Agriculture

Year	Industry	Services	All sectors
1987/88	3.8	4.9	2.2
1993/94	4.0	5.0	2.3
1999/2000	4.8	5.6	2.7
2004/5	4.6	5.9	2.9
2011/12	4.4	4.1	2.6
2017/18	5.3	4.3	3.0

Note: GDP data are at constant 2004/5 prices until that year and at 2011/12 prices thereafter.
Sources: Author's calculation using CSO GDP data and estimates of employment by economist Rahul Ahluwalia.

led to some shift in output proportions in favor of industry over services, but the gap between agricultural and non-agricultural GDP rose steadily. This is reflected in the ratio of output per worker in all sectors taken together to that in agriculture, which rose from 2.2 in 1987/88 to 3.0 in 2017/18. Output per worker in industry and services stood at more than four times that in agriculture in 2017/18.

Low Absolute Level of Per-Worker Output in Agriculture

These per-worker output gaps would not matter much had the proportion of the workforce in agriculture been small or had the overall income per worker been high. But neither of these conditions holds in India. With more than two-fifths of the workforce in agriculture, a very large part of the population is dependent on this sector. Moreover, with overall output per worker remaining low, per-worker output in agriculture is extremely low.

Figure 3.3 illustrates this last point graphically. Per-worker output in agriculture in 2017/18 was just 129,980 rupees at current prices. For a family of five, this works out to just 71.22 rupees per person per day. That is to say, if the entire agricultural output in 2017/18 could be equally distributed among farm workers, it would have given just 71.22 rupees per family member in expenditure in households with only one agricultural worker and no other source of income. Of course, given that the supply chain delivering farm produce from farm gate to the final consumer must be maintained, it is impossible to give the entire farm output to agricultural workers. Likewise, with no history of redistribution

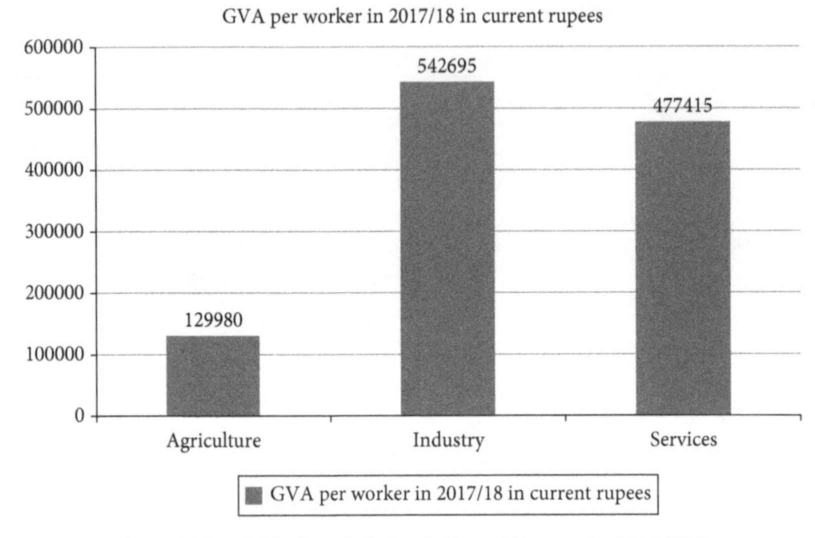

Figure 3.3 Gross Value Added per Worker in Broad Sectors in 2017/18 in Current Rupees
Source: Author's calculations using CSO data on GDP and PLFS data on employment.

of income from rich farmers to poor farmers and agricultural workers, an equal distribution of agricultural income among all agricultural workers is also unlikely. These facts imply that most farmers, who work tiny farms—68.5 percent of Indian farms are smaller than 1 hectare, according to the 2015/16 Agricultural Census—cannot be helped in any significant way through market reforms leading to more remunerative prices.

In comparison, in South Korea, the share of agriculture stood at 2 percent in GDP and 5 percent in employment in 2017. These proportions imply that output per worker in agriculture that year was two-fifths of that in all sectors taken together. But this gap impacted only 5 percent of the workforce. In addition, because the overall level of per capita income in South Korea is high, the absolute level of income in agriculture is high enough to give farmers a decent living standard. Moreover, with high per-worker output overall, the scope for redistribution per farmer is much greater.

Preponderance of Tiny Land Holdings Within Agriculture

The burden of a relatively low sector-wide per-worker GDP in agriculture is made worse by an overly uneven distribution of cultivable land among farmers. The vast majority of farmers in India cultivate tiny farms that are getting tinier

Table 3.4 Size and Operated Area Distributions of Land Holdings

Size groups	1970/71	1990/91	2010/11	2015/16
Percent of all holdings				
Marginal (less than 1 hectare)	51.0	59.4	67.1	68.5
Small (1 to 2 hectares)	18.9	18.8	17.9	17.7
Semi/medium (2 to 4 hectares)	15.0	13.1	10.0	9.5
Medium (4 to 10 hectares)	11.2	7.1	4.2	3.8
Large (10 hectares or more)	3.9	1.6	0.7	0.6
All sizes (in thousands)	71,011	106,637	138,348	145,727
Percent of operated area				
Marginal (less than 1 hectare)	9.0	15.0	22.5	24.2
Small (1 to 2 hectares)	11.9	17.4	22.1	23.2
Semi/medium (2 to 4 hectares)	18.5	23.2	23.6	23.7
Medium (4 to 10 hectares)	29.7	27.0	21.2	20.0
Large (10 hectares or more)	30.8	17.3	10.6	9.0
All sizes (thousands of hectares)	162,318	165,507	159,592	157,142

Source: Author's calculations using data from Agricultural Census 2015/16.

over time. The point is graphically brought out by Table 3.4, which reports the size distribution and operated area distribution of land holdings over time.

Marginal holdings, which are smaller than 1 hectare, have risen in number from 51 percent of all holdings in 1970/71 to 68.5 percent in 2015/16. In the latter year, 48 percent of all holdings were smaller than 0.5 hectare and averaged just 0.23 hectare per holding. Therefore, even within marginal holdings, tiny holdings of 0.5 hectare or less dominate. The area cultivated under small and marginal holdings has risen from 20.9 percent in 1970/71 to 47.4 percent in 2015/16. The share of large holdings, on the other hand, has declined in terms of both number and the area cultivated. In number, they have fallen from 3.9 percent in 1970/71 to 0.6 percent in 2015/16. In area cultivated, their share dropped from 30.8 percent in 1970/71 to just 9 percent in 2015/16.

This size and operated area distribution of land holdings has serious implications for both efficiency and the plight of farmers. As regards efficiency, small farms have numerous disadvantages. They are unable to use high-capacity machinery and have restricted access to cheaper credit from formal (as opposed to informal) sources. A small farmer is also at a great disadvantage when she sells her produce. For example, large farmers are able to sell their produce at the minimum support prices, which are invariably higher than the market prices.

In what is perhaps the most careful study using panel data from India, economists Andrew Foster and Mark Rosezweig find that profits per hectare rise as farm size increases. Even within the same farm, larger plots are more profitable than smaller ones. Larger farms enjoy a credit advantage and are more mechanized.[11]

The most deleterious effect of the progressive fragmentation and decline in farm size relates to the welfare of farmers. With profitability itself declining with farm size, farms of less than 0.5 hectare scarcely allow a family of four or five to earn a living. Indeed, even farms that are 2 hectares in size barely offer a subsistence existence to a family of four or five. Sadly, a whopping 86.2 percent of land holdings in India are smaller than 2 hectares. Unsurprisingly, nearly 80 percent of India's poor households remain in rural areas and are overwhelmingly dependent on small farms for their living.

The Challenge of Bringing Prosperity to Farmers in the Short Term

The bitter reality of the current situation is that, short of radical reforms, there exists no solution that can bring a decent living standard to farmers. Multiple subsidies that tie farmers and other rural households to their inherited locations and other policies that discourage the creation of attractive jobs for them in industry and services have left too large a population stuck in low-productivity agriculture. None of the avenues for bringing prosperity to this population in the short term *within* agriculture promise to succeed. Consider in turn the main remedies commonly suggested.

Accelerating Growth in Agriculture

If the transition of workers out of agriculture into better-paid jobs in industry and services remains slow, could India bring rapid prosperity to farmers through acceleration of growth within agriculture? Unfortunately, the odds in favor of success through this avenue are minuscule. As Table 3.1 shows, agriculture in India has never grown faster than 4 percent at a national level over long periods. Even during the 1980s, when the Green Revolution was spreading fast, it grew only 4.4 percent annually over a decade. Since then, the growth rate has greatly moderated.

For the sake of argument, suppose India could raise the growth rate of agricultural output to 5 percent. We must then confront the question of where the resulting output will be sold. As of 2011/12, more than 70 percent of the rural agricultural workforce was engaged in growing cereals, pulses, and oilseeds. With the exception of oilseeds, India is already self-sufficient in most of these crops, so any additional output will have to be exported. But this poses two problems.

First, since India provides larger subsidies on these crops through MSPs than it is allowed under World Trade Organization (WTO) rules, it will face stiff countervailing duties in importing countries. Such duties will lead to a substantial decline in the net price received on exports. Second, even absent countervailing duties, any major expansion of exports of these crops would lead to a large decline in price. Once again, output expansion will fail to translate into commensurate income expansion for farmers.

Even if buyers can be found for the extra output, a further problem is ensuring that small farmers receive the lion's share of the price paid by the buyer. Marketing of produce in India remains heavily monopolized by middlemen, who continue to pocket the substantial difference between the price paid by the final consumer and that received by the farmer. The process of marketing reforms began in the early 2000s, but few state governments have succeeded in implementing these reforms because of the enormous political clout middlemen have locally. The state of Karnataka is credited with having carried out the most successful marketing reform through e-auctions, yet it found its farmers in enough distress to announce a large loan waiver worth 340 billion rupees in July 2018.[12]

Diversification of Agriculture

Another solution to bringing rapid prosperity to those currently in farming is increased diversification within agriculture. This would involve moving land and labor out of traditional crops into high-value crops such as fruits and vegetables, other commercial crops such as cotton, fisheries, and animal husbandry. While such diversification can bring some prosperity to some farmers, it is implausible that it can bring genuine prosperity to a large farmer population.

Table 3.5 shows the distribution of cultivated area across various crops from 1980/81 to 2014/15 at intervals of ten or more years. It is remarkable that there has been no exit of land whatsoever from rice and wheat over the thirty-five years covered by the table. All we see is a small shift out of rice into wheat. The main exit has been out of other cereals and millets, which are the healthiest grains but which have lost out in popularity to rice and wheat. In addition, there has been a modest exit out of pulses, which also is an unhappy outcome since it has created a serious shortage of pulses in recent years. The cultivated area devoted to fruits

Table 3.5 Percentage of Area Cultivated Under Major Crops

Crops	1980/81	1990/91	2000/2001	2014/15*
Rice	23.3	23	24.2	22.3
Wheat	12.9	12.9	13.9	16.2
Other cereals and millets	24.6	19.6	16.6	12.8
Pulses	13.2	13.4	11.5	10.9
Total food grains	**73.9**	**68.9**	**66.2**	**62.3**
Sugarcane	1.7	2.1	2.5	2.8
Total fruits and vegetables	2.9	3.6	4.4	5
Other food crops	1.3	1.4	1.6	1.8
Total food crops	**79.7**	**75.9**	**74.7**	**72**
Total oilseeds	9.1	13.5	13.3	14.3
Total fibers (mostly cotton)	5.3	4.7	5.2	6.8
Other non-food crops	5.8	5.9	6.8	6.8
Total non-food crops	**20.2**	**24.1**	**25.3**	**28**
Total area under crops	**100**	**100**	**100**	**100**

*Figures for this year are provisional.
Source: Pocketbook of Agricultural Statistics 2017, table 4.2.

and vegetables has gained 2 percentage points, and that for non-food crops has gained 8 percentage points. Clearly, the shifts in cultivated area across different crops do not offer promising prospects for a rapid movement toward greater diversification. Farmers are generally reluctant to experiment with new crops, preferring instead to go for the safety of what they have grown before.

Employment data do not offer any additional support for the idea that diversification could serve as the driving force of farmer prosperity. In 2011/12, of the 64.1 percent of the rural workforce that worked in agriculture, a hefty 87.25 percent were employed in non-perennial crops, including cereals, pulses, oilseeds, vegetables, sugarcane, and fiber crops such as cotton and jute. In 2017/18, the share of rural workforce in agriculture fell to 59.4 percent, but within that, the share of non-perennial crops remained at 85 percent. Non-perennial crops account for the lion's share of agricultural employment, and movement out of them is extremely slow.

Perennial crops including fruits, spices, and beverage crops (such as tea, coffee, and cocoa) accounted for 3.81 percent of the rural agricultural workforce in 2011/12 and 3.97 percent in 2017/18. The only other substantial employer within agriculture is animal husbandry, which accounted for 5.3 percent of the rural agricultural workforce in 2011/12 and 4.4 percent in 2017/18. Remarkably, forestry/logging and fishing/aquaculture employed just 0.78 percent of the rural agricultural workforce in 2011/12 and 0.81 percent in 2017/18.

The main candidates for increased diversification of the workforce are fruits and vegetables, animal husbandry, and fishing and aquaculture. Can such workforce diversification serve as the instrument of farmer prosperity? The answer to this question relies on the answers to two other questions: how much workforce diversification is feasible within a relatively short period of time, and how much can farmers themselves benefit from such diversification?

Regarding the first question, only 10.1 percent of the rural agricultural workforce was employed in fruits and vegetables, animal husbandry, and fisheries in 2011/12. In 2017/18, this proportion rose to 14.34 percent. From these numbers, it is evident that even doubling this proportion from its 2017/18 level within a short period is unrealistic. Moreover, even if such doubling could happen, it would not go far toward bringing high returns to a large farm population, especially when we consider the effects on the prices of fruits, vegetables, and animal products that would accompany such doubling.

Regarding the second question, high returns in fruits and vegetables, animal husbandry, and fishing and aquaculture arise at the processing stage. To be sure, food processing, the meat and poultry industries, and export-oriented fisheries can generate high returns. But these activities can benefit farmers only if they either undertake these activities themselves or are employed at decent wages in them. However, this takes us to diversification of the workforce into non-farm activities, not diversification within agriculture.

Agricultural Marketing Reform

I have already touched upon agricultural marketing reform, but the issue is sufficiently important to require a fuller discussion. Farmers currently receive a rather small share of the price paid by the final consumer. This low share is the result of undue market power that intermediaries exercise at the government-run marketplaces (mundies) where the farmer is required to sell his produce. There is most surely scope for raising the farmer's income through marketing reform. But this avenue to prosperity for farmers has two limitations.

First, India's experience to date does not offer hope that a dramatic reform in this area can and will happen. The need for such reform has been apparent for at least two decades, and a model act for the reform of agricultural produce marketing committees (APMCs) in the states was floated by the central government in 2003. A large number of states have passed legislation to reform their original APMC acts but have not implemented those laws in earnest. Consequently, at best limited progress has been made toward shifting the share of the price paid by the final consumer in favor of the farmer.

Recently, an alternative effort to achieve this objective has been launched in the form of e-auctions at APMC-run marketplaces. Each farmer can bring her produce to the APMC-run marketplace and auction it, with market agents bidding for it without being able to discuss their bids with one another. Such an auction would give the farmer the highest price any buyer agent is willing to pay. The state of Karnataka has pioneered this model, and the Government of India has adapted it for implementation in APMC-run marketplaces across all India.

From the available information, it is difficult to escape the conclusion that so far this reform too has been unsuccessful in bringing significant improvement in the conditions of the farmers. As noted earlier, while Karnataka state is credited with successful implementation of the model, stories of farmer distress in the state remain ubiquitous, and as recently as July 2018, the state government announced a major farm loan waiver to alleviate the distress.

The second and even more compelling limitation of marketing reforms as the vehicle for bringing genuine prosperity to farmers is that output per worker in agriculture remains low. As Table 3.3 shows, per-worker output in agriculture is just one-third of per-worker economy-wide GDP, itself quite low. Therefore, even if marketing reform could deliver the entire value of agricultural output to farmers, genuine prosperity would remain a distant goal for them. There is just not enough output in the sector to bring prosperity to such a vast workforce.

Larger Redistribution from Urban to Rural Areas

The final possible remedy to bring faster prosperity to farmers is to effect yet larger transfers from taxpayers to farmers. But there are two problems with this approach.

First, the feasibility of yet more transfers is seriously in question. Only one-third of the population of India lives in urban areas. Of this one-third, a small fraction has enough income to pay taxes. Redistribution from such a small population simply cannot bring prosperity to the large population residing in rural areas. This is in contrast to countries such as the United States, the United Kingdom, Japan, and South Korea, where farmers account for less than 5 percent of the workforce, income levels are high, and taxpayers are numerous. Though farmer distress stories in the face of drought, floods, and frost are a feature there as well, those countries are well placed to alleviate their distress because farmers are a small proportion of their workforce.

Second, it is also not clear that it is desirable to massively expand such transfers. Because such transfers are tied to farming as a profession, they discourage migration to non-farm jobs. If India is to complete the transition to an economy that is prosperous and in which all get to share in this prosperity, it is important that the agricultural workforce shrinks and the non-agricultural workforce expands—sooner than later.

What Are the Options?

There is no escaping the conclusion that the only available road to rapid prosperity for the current large workforce in agriculture goes through migration of a substantial fraction of the latter to more productive jobs in industry and services. Such migration will directly bring prosperity to those who migrate. It will also raise per-worker output in agriculture by bringing down the worker-to-land ratio. The more we delay this migration, the longer the period of farmer distress will be.

To appreciate why such migration is crucial, consider that over the next fifteen years, the most optimistic assumption we can make is that agricultural growth rates will be around 3.5 percent annually. By contrast, the most conservative estimates would place average annual growth in industry and services combined at 8 percent. Over a period of fifteen years, these growth rates imply a fall in the share of agriculture in GDP from 14.8 percent in 2017/18 to 8.4 percent in 2032/33. Of course, this scenario is the most optimistic one. Realistically, agriculture is not likely to grow more than 3 percent annually over that fifteen-year period, and industry and services together would probably grow at a rate closer to 9 percent. Under this scenario, the share of agriculture in GDP would decline to just 6.9 percent by 2032/33. Under either scenario, even with a decline of 12 to 15 percentage points in the agricultural workforce over this period, we face the prospect of having to continue to support nearly 30 percent of the nation's workforce on less than 10 percent of GDP. This would still leave a very large number of workers exposed to distress. Policies that accelerate the exit of farmers into other professions are urgently required.

A large part of the policy change needed to effect this migration lies outside agriculture, and I will consider that subject in subsequent chapters. But some bold actions would be worthwhile in agriculture as well. Many of these actions have been widely discussed in the rich public policy discourse that takes place in the Indian media, despite its excessively noisy nature. But even at the risk of repetition, I shall spell out the more important of these actions.

First and foremost, India must replace procurement at MSPs and the provision of subsidized food grains through PDS by an equivalent cash transfer to the relevant beneficiaries. MSP procurement, which is principally limited to wheat and rice, suffers from several shortcomings. First, it encourages wheat and rice crops over others and thus undermines progress toward diversification into other crops and activities. Second, it has perpetuated rice cultivation, which requires vast volumes of water, in Punjab, where water tables have fallen to abysmally low levels. Third, MSPs count as a trade-distorting subsidy under WTO rules and therefore undermine the ability of India to export wheat and rice. And finally, whereas only larger farmers growing wheat and rice benefit from procurement at MSPs, income transfers associated with MSPs and PDS will reach smaller farmers and landless workers and will not discriminate between those who grow wheat and rice and those who grow other crops.

In-kind transfers through PDS continue to suffer from substantial inefficiencies despite some improvements after the introduction of the Aadhaar biometric identity cards. Many beneficiaries complain that the quality of PDS grain is so poor that they prefer to forgo the subsidy and buy grain from private shops. Others say that they have to make repeated trips to government shops to avail themselves of the benefit, either because of the shop owner's intransigence or because of a failure of the identity verification system. Income support provided through electronic transfers to beneficiaries' bank accounts do not suffer from these problems.

If this reform is implemented, one by-product is that the government will be able to carry out a major overhaul of the behemoth that is the Food Corporation of India. With a huge workforce, FCI is a massive organization riddled with inefficiencies. Once cash transfers replace the PDS, FCI would have to fully compete with the private sector in the distribution of food grains. It will have to procure food grains at market prices and recover its costs by selling them competitively to consumers. It would be allowed to maintain only a small part of its operations at taxpayer expense, in order to serve pockets that private retailers do not find attractive.

The second important reform concerns marketing of agricultural produce. This reform can only be effective if state governments successfully dilute the market power of local middlemen, who currently have a near monopoly on local purchases of farmers' produce. Genuine reform of the APMC acts is critical. Organized retail, which brings new and influential buyers of agricultural produce into the marketplace, and e-commerce, which can potentially connect sellers directly to consumers, can significantly complement APMC reform.

The third important reform needed is the removal of restrictions on the use of genetically modified seeds and the introduction of emerging gene-editing technologies. Here the key lesson from the Green Revolution and the success of Bt cotton needs highlighting. The beauty of seed varieties that produce high yields is that they can spread rapidly without the government having to do very much.

Other productivity-enhancing measures such as improved irrigation, mechanization, crop diversification, and the spread of contract farming require large investments and are time-consuming. Today, with the ready availability of fertilizer and irrigation and easy access to information through digital platforms, farmers can take advantage of high-yielding seed varieties at a rapid pace.

The fourth important reform is the introduction of a transparent land-leasing law in each state. The government think tank NITI Aayog has prepared and promoted a model law that seeks to balance the rights of the tenant and the landowner while also providing for greater transparency. Most states could greatly improve tenancy conditions by adopting this model law after modifications that take into account any specific local features such as land ownership patterns and political factors.

The case for a modern land-leasing law cannot be overstated. As noted earlier, 68.5 percent of land holdings are smaller than 1 hectare. Many farmers struggling to make a living for families of five or more on such small land holdings would like to lease out their land and look for superior alternatives. But they are unable to do so because laws in most states do not permit leasing of land—anyone leasing her plot runs the risk of losing it to the lessee. This situation has had two deleterious effects: it has perpetuated the fragmentation of land holdings and prevented their consolidation, and it has discouraged the migration of farmers working tiny plots of land to alternative forms of employment.

A transparent land-leasing law is also necessary to make it feasible to provide direct benefit transfers (DBTs) to actual cultivators. Currently, with no formal record of tenancy, any benefit intended for the cultivator goes to the landowner, since formal records show him as the cultivator. A land-leasing law that provides for the recording of tenancy can overcome this problem, allowing benefits to reach the intended beneficiary.

The fifth and final reform is to end MGNREGA. From the beginning, this was a poorly conceived program and has resulted in enormous wastage of taxpayers' money. Once substantial cash transfers to the poor are put in place, the original rationale for MGNREGA—providing relief work during the lean season, when employment opportunities on farms become scarce—would no longer be valid. Some may argue that MGNREGA employment also serves as a means for building public assets, but they need to be reminded that this argument reverses what was originally seen as an end and what was the means to that end. When MGNREGA was first adopted, provision of employment was the end and building public assets the means. It is a bad use of public money when public projects must be imagined so that an available resource can be used. The process has to be the reverse: identify public projects that would serve important public needs and then find the right mix of resources to implement those projects.

It bears emphasizing that the reforms recommended here constitute a package. Productivity-enhancing reforms such as the introduction of GM seeds and transparent land-leasing laws cannot succeed without MSP reform. This is because—as we have seen—India is already self-sufficient in food grains and any further increase in their output would have to be exported. Exports in turn would face countervailing duties in importing country as long as the subsidy via MSPs exceeds the margin permitted by the WTO, which is just 10 percent. In a similar vein, replacing in-kind transfers in the form of subsidized food grain by cash transfers requires massively cutting back on procurement, since ending the requirement that subsidized grain must be purchased from government-run shops means that many consumers would switch their purchases to private retailers of grain.

Concluding Remarks

It is not possible to bring genuine prosperity to Indian farmers without moving half or more of them out of agriculture. Without such a movement, there are only two ways to raise farmers' incomes: more remunerative prices to them and increased productivity in agriculture. It is easy to see that neither avenue can deliver genuine prosperity.

Today, GDP per worker in agriculture is one-third of economy-wide GDP per worker. But given that economy-wide GDP per worker itself is small, GDP per worker in agriculture is truly small. Therefore, even if the farmer could receive the entire price paid by the final consumer—a rather infeasible proposition, since intermediation is essential to deliver the produce from farm gate to the final consumer—it would be insufficient to bring a prosperous existence to the farmer.

A moment's reflection shows that increased productivity in agriculture cannot go very far either. For example, suppose that a technological advance allows India to double agricultural output overnight. The immediate question then would be where this output could be sold. Because India has already achieved self-sufficiency in most grains (especially rice and wheat), selling it domestically would result in a precipitous fall in prices. What is gained in output will be lost in price received, so farmers' final revenue will not change very much. Alternatively, the extra produce could be exported. But this will incur duties from importing countries, especially since India subsidizes the production of wheat and rice through MSPs.

It is thus clear that as long as the proportion of the workforce in agriculture remains large, India will be unable to bring genuine prosperity to them. Movement of workers into industry and services, on the other hand, not only would make those workers prosperous but also would raise GDP per worker in agriculture, making those left behind better off.

The only feasible path to prosperity for farmers, therefore, is the creation of attractive job opportunities in industry and services. The critical question this raises is whether industry and services can provide gainful employment to a large number of workers migrating out of agriculture. This is the key question we must confront in Chapter 4. As we will see, the answer is not straightforward.

Notes

1. National Sample Survey Office 2019, 65, statement 16.
2. National Sample Survey Office 2019, A-150, table 26.
3. National Sample Survey Office 2019, 65, statement 16.
4. National Sample Survey Office 2019, A-150, table 26.
5. Varshney 1995, ch. 2.
6. Prasad 2015. Author Denis Kux reports the same incident in these words: "The Prime Minister [was] clenching her fingers tightly on the telephone. Talking to Johnson, she was friendly and charming, but when she hung up, she said angrily, 'I don't want us to ever have to beg for food again.'" Kux 1992, 257.
7. Each sub-center covers a population of 5,000 in rural areas and is staffed by one male and one female health worker. It provides basic primary health services. For problems beyond them, sub-centers can refer cases to a primary health center, which covers a population of 30,000 and is staffed by doctors and paramedics. Primary health centers refer the cases beyond their competence to community health centers, which cover a population of 120,000 and provide more sophisticaled health services including simple surgeries and obstratics.
8. National Sample Survey Office 2014a, 18, table T3. Expenditure figures quoted in the text are based on the modified mixed reference period method of measurement, which is judged to provide the most accurate estimates of consumer expenditure.
9. These shares have been taken from the World Development Indicators of the World Bank, available at https://data.worldbank.org/indicator/NV.AGR.TOTL.ZS (accessed on December 17, 2018).
10. These figures represent modeled International Labour Organization estimates as reported in the World Development Indicators at https://data.worldbank.org/indicator/SL.AGR.EMPL.ZS (accessed on December 17, 2018).
11. Foster and Rosenzweig 2009.
12. "Karnataka Government Announces Partial Farm Loan Waiver of Rs. 34,000 Crore," *Times of India*, July 5, 2018.

4
Underemployment in Industry and Services

One reason farmers choose not to exit their current occupation despite the below-subsistence-level income is that many government transfers are available only if they stay where they are. But the failure of industry and services to create sufficiently attractive jobs has also contributed to the phenomenon in a major way. If these sectors created jobs that could pay decent wages to those working small farms (0.5 hectare or smaller), migration out of agriculture would surely take place at a faster pace.

When it comes to low-productivity employment, vast sections of Indian industry and services mirror agriculture. There exist millions of tiny enterprises that employ a small number of workers each. Often the owner and her family are the only employees of these enterprises. Even when enterprises employ hired workers, numbers are small. In 2017/18, a solid 56.5 percent of all workers in industry and services were employed in enterprises with just five or fewer workers.[1] Income per worker in these enterprises is uniformly very low. Enterprises with twenty or more workers, which are able to pay better wages, employed only 15.9 percent of workers.

Politicians in India glorify microenterprises without realizing that they have been paddling in the same place for decades, going nowhere. Own-account enterprises, which employ no hired workers on a regular basis, account for a large part of employment in industry and services but only a small part of their output. If these enterprises were growing larger over time, there would be reason to celebrate them. But such is not the case.

Two characteristics of industry and services have played a critical role in causing the shortage of good jobs at the low end of skill distribution. First, sectors able to pay decent wages, such as autos, auto parts, two-wheelers, machinery, pharmaceuticals, finance, and software, are either capital intensive or skilled-labor intensive. Second, the proportion of the workforce employed in medium and large firms in manufacturing, especially of the labor-intensive variety, is small relative to comparator countries. This means that India has had limited success at best in capturing world markets and therefore creating well-paid jobs in large volumes. Any strategy to create a large volume of well-paid jobs that would help speed up the transition of workers out of agriculture and into industry and services must address these deficiencies in the current structure of industry and services.

Low Unemployment Rates

It is common to come across journalists and analysts who point to the large number of individuals, many of them Ph.D. holders, applying for a small number of the lowest-level Class IV positions in the government (multi-tasking staff, MTS), as evidence of a high rate of unemployment in India. For instance, according to a September 2015 news report, more than 2.3 million candidates, including 222,000 engineers and 255 Ph.D. holders, applied for 368 Class IV vacancies in the state secretariat of the Government of Uttar Pradesh.[2] Similar stories have appeared in the press about positions advertised by the Government of Haryana and by Indian Railways.

The reason for such a heavy demand for MTS positions in the government is not unemployment, however. Instead, it is the high salary, the lifetime job security, and the generous housing, pension, and healthcare benefits associated with these positions that account for the large number of applicants. In the Government of India, salaries for the lowest-level employee begin at 18,000 rupees per month, with excellent benefits, prospects for regular salary increases regardless of performance, and job security. In case of the employee's untimely death, there even exist provisions that give preference for government employment to one of her children. At the same time, the duties of MTS staff are the least demanding and offer plenty of free time on the job.

Many engineers and Ph.D. holders are unable to find such compensation and benefits in private sector jobs, which also require harder work. This makes a MTS position in the government an attractive prospect. Therefore, even if they are employed, many engineers and Ph.D. holders apply for MTS positions whenever the government advertises them. Unsatisfactory employment rather than unemployment is what attracts them to these jobs.

In a country like India, where self-employment and informal employment dominate, overall unemployment can only be measured through large household surveys. Even the most carefully conducted censuses of enterprises fail to cover the workforce exhaustively. Surveys of enterprises, no matter how large and inclusive, remain inadequate for the purpose. For example, even the Census of Industries, which India has conducted periodically, fails to account for a substantial part of the workforce within industry and services. Under such circumstances, we do not know whether what happens to the workforce covered by the censuses or surveys of enterprises is offset or reinforced by changes in the workforce not covered by them.

India has conducted large household surveys since 1972/73 (which, as we have seen, was first called the Employment-Unemployment Survey [EUS] and conducted every five years, and since 2017/18 rechristened the Period Labor Force Survey [PLFS] and made annual). The National Statistical Office, which carries out PLFS, now provides unemployment and related estimates annually for all of India and also on a quarterly basis for urban India.

There has been some confusion in media stories about the comparability of EUS and PLFS. A close review of the two surveys' sample designs leads to the conclusion that at the aggregate level they are comparable, though with one important qualification. Data collection for EUS used to be done using paper schedules, while that for PLFS is done using computer-assisted personal interviewing (CAPI). For EUS, different levels of validation were carried out after data entry; for PLFS, validation is done automatically by the software's in-built validation rules. Unfortunately, NSO did not carry out a validation exercise to check if the two methods lead to differences in measurement. Therefore, some doubt remains regarding the full comparability of EUS and PLFS.

This difference in data collection and validation methodologies assumes significance principally because PLFS has given rise to results that are at substantial variance with those yielded by multiple rounds of EUS. Two examples illustrate this point. First, EUS rarely produced an India-wide unemployment rate exceeding 3 percent. In comparison, PLFS has produced an unemployment rate of 6.1 percent. Second, much of the debate on jobs and employment in India in recent years has taken place in the context of a labor force that adds 8 to 10 million workers each year. But labor force calculations based on EUS 2011/12 and PLFS 2017/18 yield additions of less than 300,000 workers per year to the labor force.

There is no way to know whether these anomalies have resulted from the difference in data collection and validation methods or represent real changes in the economy. Luckily, we need not answer this question to proceed further. Regardless of whether the unemployment rate is 6.1 percent in 2017/18 or lower, an inescapable conclusion is that unemployment in India is low. Even the 6.1 percent rate from PLFS for 2017/18 is close to what is viewed as the natural rate of unemployment in many countries. In effect, given the limited assistance from the state and limited economic opportunities, everyone must do something to make ends meet.

With this in view, Table 4.1 reports estimates of unemployment rate in 2017/18 for males, females, and all persons in rural areas, urban areas, and all India. Predictably, the unemployment rate in rural areas is lower than in urban areas. Agriculture often serves as the employment of last resort. The highest unemployment rate is among urban women. But because the proportion of urban women in the workforce is small, the overall urban unemployment rate is much closer to the rate among urban males.

Table 4.1 Unemployment in Rural and Urban Areas, 2017/18

Area	Male	Female	Person
Rural	5.8	3.8	5.3
Urban	7.1	10.8	7.8
Rural + urban	6.2	5.7	6.1

Source: National Statistical Office 2019, 82, statement 30.

Concentration of Employment in Informal Unincorporated Enterprises

Underemployment is the key problem India needs to target. Doing so will automatically help cut outright unemployment as well. Underemployment manifests itself in low-productivity employment. Some of this low productivity can be observed in daily life. For instance, it is common in India to find two or more workers performing tasks that one worker can perform. If a home appliance such as an air conditioner or television requires servicing or if the plumbing needs fixing, often two or more workers show up. But only one of them actually performs the task, with the others either carrying the tools or simply providing company. In government offices and even private companies, it is common to find workers sitting outside office doors nearly all day with little to do. Even workers in small and informal private enterprises can be seen taking long breaks or simply shirking their duties.

Concrete evidence of the dominance of low-productivity jobs in India can be found in the surprisingly large concentration of workers in small (often tiny) and informal enterprises in both industry and services. India's industry and service sectors are perhaps unique in the world for being populated by such a high number of micro and small enterprises and such a low number of medium and large enterprises. The combination of low per-worker productivity in micro and small enterprises and the heavy concentration of employment in smaller enterprises translates into low overall per-worker productivity in industry and services.

Before presenting the evidence, I note that enterprise surveys, which are the only sources of detailed estimates on the distribution of the workforce, output, and wages by enterprise size, do not provide consistent coverage throughout India. Indeed, even the periodic Economic Censuses, which aim to collect information on a handful of variables from all non-agricultural enterprises, fall well short of covering the entire non-agricultural workforce. For instance, the number of non-agricultural workers reported in the latest Economic Census, conducted in 2013/14, was only 131 million, but the Employment-Unemployment Survey of 2011/12 found 243 million.

There are two sets of enterprise surveys in India: the Annual Survey of Industries (ASI), conducted annually by the Central Statistics Office, and the survey of unincorporated or unorganized-sector non-agricultural enterprises periodically conducted by the National Statistical Office (NSO). The former is confined to manufacturing enterprises registered under certain sections of the Factories Act (1948).[3] The latter covers unincorporated enterprises in both industry and services, with some sectors such as financial services or construction occasionally excluded. It explicitly excludes enterprises covered by the ASI. The two surveys are thus mutually exclusive in their coverage.

The latest NSO survey on unincorporated enterprises is from 2015/16 and covers all non-agricultural sectors except construction. These enterprises account for a total of 111.3 million workers. Keeping in mind that the total number of workers identified by the 2013/14 Economic Census, which also covered incorporated enterprises, was 131 million, it can be concluded with a reasonable degree of confidence that the survey covers 80 percent or more of the non-agricultural workforce identifiable in all non-agricultural enterprises. Therefore, an extremely large part of the workforce in India remains in the informal sector.

To gain further insight into the characteristics of the Indian workforce, consider the nature of the enterprises covered by the survey. These enterprises can be classified according to two criteria: employment of hired workers on a regular basis (or lack thereof) and ownership pattern. Under the nomenclature used by NSO, enterprises that run without employing any hired workers on a regular basis are called own-account enterprises (OAEs) and those employing one or more hired workers are classified as establishments. Using the ownership criterion, the enterprises are classified into proprietorships, partnerships, self-help groups (SHGs), and trusts.

At an all-India level, 84.2 percent of the enterprises in 2015/16 were OAEs. In rural areas, the share of these enterprises was even higher, 91.4 percent. Therefore, the vast majority of the enterprises hired no workers on a regular basis. In terms of ownership, 96 percent of the enterprises India-wide were proprietorships. Of the remaining number, 1.4 percent were partnerships and 1.8 percent SHGs. This, once again, indicates the generally informal nature of employment.

Turning to employment structure in unincorporated enterprises, Table 4.2 shows the composition of the workforce broken down by OAE and establishment enterprises across three broad sectors: manufacturing, trade, and other services. Several observations follow. First, at the aggregate level, 62.1 percent of the 111.3 million workers in these enterprises were employed in OAEs, and only 37.9 percent worked in establishment enterprises. Second, the share of OAEs in

Table 4.2 Shares of OAEs and Establishment Enterprises in the Total Workforce in Unincorporated Enterprises, 2015/16

Enterprise type	Manufacturing	Trade	Other services	All
Rural				
OAE	75.9%	87.9%	65.1%	76.5%
Establishment	24.1%	12.1%	34.9%	23.5%
All (millions of workers)	18.7	16.1	15.1	49.9
Urban				
OAE	49.0%	56.4%	45.2%	50.4%
Establishment	51.0%	43.6%	54.8%	49.6%
All (millions of workers)	17.4	22.7	21.3	61.4
Rural + urban				
OAE	62.9%	69.5%	53.4%	62.1%
Establishment	37.1%	30.5%	46.6%	37.9%
All (millions of workers)	36.0	38.7	36.5	111.3

Source: Author's calculations using estimates in National Statistical Office 2017, 16, statement 4.

the total workforce was consistently higher in rural areas. For all sectors taken together, this share was 76.5 percent, compared with 50.4 percent in urban areas. Finally, services accounted for a little more than two-thirds of the total workforce in unincorporated enterprises, while manufacturing employed slightly less than one-third of it.

The full impact of the concentration of non-agricultural employment in unincorporated enterprises, especially OAEs, can only be appreciated when we see it in conjunction with gross value added (GVA) per worker. Table 4.3 provides the relevant estimates. Three features of the table may be noted at the outset. First, output per worker is consistently significantly lower in manufacturing than in services. In rural areas, the gap is particularly large. Second, predictably, OAEs consistently exhibit lower GVA than establishment enterprises. And finally, there is a large gap in per-worker GVA between rural and urban enterprises. At the aggregate level, urban enterprises exhibit a per-worker GVA that is 1.9 times higher than in rural enterprises. In manufacturing, urban GVA per worker is more than twice that in rural areas.

Table 4.3 Gross Value Added Per Worker in Unincorporated Enterprises in Broad Sectors

	In 2015/16 rupees per worker			
Enterprise type	**Manufacturing**	**Trade**	**Other services**	**All**
Rural				
OAE	36,021	64,103	71,008	55,459
Establishment	86,296	131,947	131,227	114,024
All	48,152	72,338	91,901	69,198
Urban				
OAE	62,822	113,541	104,324	96,718
Establishment	140,639	189,749	169,436	167,627
All	102,523	146,739	139,856	131,811
Rural + urban				
OAE	46,088	87,611	87,498	73,951
Establishment	122,344	180,219	157,554	152,723
All	74,379	115,885	119,947	103,744

Source: Author's calculations using estimates in National Statistical Office 2017, 30, statement 20

To appreciate how low per-worker GVAs are across the board (Table 4.3), we must compare them to the nationwide GVA per worker. In 2015/16, the latter was approximately 244,000 rupees at current prices.[4] This figure is more than twice the GVA per worker at the aggregate level (shown in Table 4.3) and uniformly higher than that in every sector and every form of enterprise. Of particular importance in Table 4.3 are GVAs in rural areas. The average value of this parameter across all rural enterprises is less than 70,000 rupees, which is less than one-third of the nationwide GVA per worker. In the manufacturing sector, rural OAEs exhibit less than one-sixth of the nationwide GVA per worker. This low level of productivity relative to the national average in unincorporated enterprises is almost as bad as in agriculture. Even in urban areas, GVA per worker in manufacturing is less than half of the nationwide GVA per worker. The inevitable conclusion is that too many workers even in industry and services are employed in low-productivity enterprises.

Estimates of the compensation received by hired workers reinforce this picture. Because OAEs employ no hired workers on a regular basis, we have these estimates for establishment enterprises only. Table 4.4 shows the estimates for

Table 4.4 Compensation and Number of Hired Workers in Unincorporated Enterprises, 2015–16

Area	Manufacturing	Trade	Other services	All
Annual compensation in 2015/16 rupees				
Rural	56,001	63,048	94,227	74,871
Urban	85,515	83,371	104,161	92,441
Rural + urban	75,595	80,267	101,094	87,544
Number of hired workers (millions)				
Rural	3.2	1.1	3.8	8.2
Urban	6.4	6.2	8.6	21.2
Rural + urban	9.6	7.4	12.4	29.4

Source: Author's calculations using estimates in National Statistical Office 2017, 32, statement 23.

the three broad non-agricultural sectors in rural and urban areas and for all sectors taken together. It also shows the number of workers employed in each category. Out of a total of 111.3 million workers in unincorporated enterprises, only 29.4 million are hired workers. The remaining 81.9 million workers are self-employed in their own enterprises.

More strikingly, the compensation received by these workers is low by almost any measure. In aggregate, average monthly compensation in the enterprises turns out to be only 7,295 rupees in 2015/16 rupees. Compensation in rural manufacturing is particularly low: just 4,667 rupees per month. Even in urban areas, an average monthly compensation of 7,703 rupees reflects rather low worker productivity.

A More Detailed Picture of Manufacturing

Ongoing research by the economist Radhicka Kapoor provides further insight into the phenomenon of the concentration of the manufacturing workforce in small low-productivity enterprises. Combining the manufacturing component of NSO surveys of unorganized/unincorporated enterprises with the CSO surveys of organized sector enterprises, Kapoor constructs the full distribution of the workforce across different firm sizes in manufacturing. Table 4.5 reports the results.

The estimates show that more than half of the manufacturing workforce in India has remained trapped in tiny enterprises employing five or fewer

Table 4.5 Percent Shares of Firms of Different Sizes in Manufacturing Workforce

Firm Size (Number of Workers)	2000/2001	2005/6	2010/11	2015/16*
1 to 5	67.4	63.6	56.6	58.8
6 to 10	9.4	9.7	8.9	7.6
11 to 20	4.9	5.7	6.2	4.8
21 to 50	3.7	4.0	4.7	4.2
51 to 100	2.4	2.9	3.8	3.3
101 to 200	2.5	2.8	4.1	3.8
> 200	9.7	11.2	15.7	17.4
Total number of workers (millions)	44.9	45.1	46.5	48.9

*For 2015/16, ASI 2014/15 survey, the latest available, has been used for organized sector manufacturing enterprises.

Source: Estimated by economists Radhicka Kapoor using surveys of unorganized, unincorporated manufacturing enterprises by NSO and organized sector manufacturing enterprises, ASI, by CSO.

workers. Though the proportion has seen a steady decline since its peak at a hefty 67.4 percent in 2000/2001, it remained as high as 58.8 percent in 2015/16. Traditionally, firms with fifty or fewer workers are defined as small. The proportion of workforce in these firms has ranged from a gigantic 85.4 percent in 2000/2001 to 75.4 percent in 2015/16. India is unique in having such a high proportion of its workforce in small enterprises. The only silver lining to this otherwise unhappy story is that the share of large firms, defined as those employing two hundred workers or more, has been rising over the years. At 17.4 percent in 2015/16, it still remains small compared with other countries, but the increase from 9.7 percent in 2000/2001 is significant.

WhyLarge Firms Are Critical

Lower average worker productivity in smaller firms relative to larger ones is a common phenomenon and can be observed in all countries. Smaller firms typically employ less capital per worker than larger ones, which is sufficient to result in lower per-worker productivity. What makes India's situation unique and disconcerting is the disproportionately large concentration of employment in small firms. Medium and large firms have at best a limited presence in many

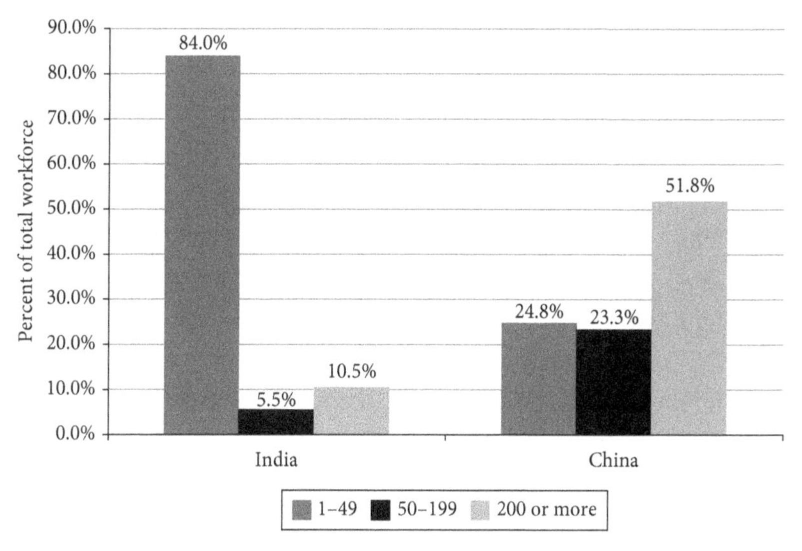

Figure 4.1 Concentration of Manufacturing Employment in India in Small Firms

sectors in India, especially in labor-intensive sectors such as apparel, footwear, and other light manufactures.

A Comparison with China

A comparison of India and China best illustrates the importance of the presence of medium and large firms in significant numbers. Figure 4.1 shows the distribution of workers in manufacturing by firm size in India and China in 2005. Whereas employment in China is predominantly concentrated in medium and large firms, in India it is concentrated in small firms. This difference also translates into a larger wage differential between small and medium firms on the one hand and large firms on the other.

Figure 4.2 illustrates this point: wages in small firms in India are close to 20 percent of the wages in large firms. In contrast, wages in small firms in China are 60 percent of those in large firms. The significance of this wage difference rises yet further when we recognize that wages in large firms in China were themselves significantly higher than the corresponding wages in large firms in India. The work of economists Rana Hasan and Karl Jandoc, on which Figures 4.1 and 4.2 are based, shows that this pattern holds for a wider set of countries.[5]

The pattern just described has serious implications for wages and the process of transformation. With a high concentration of the Indian workforce in small

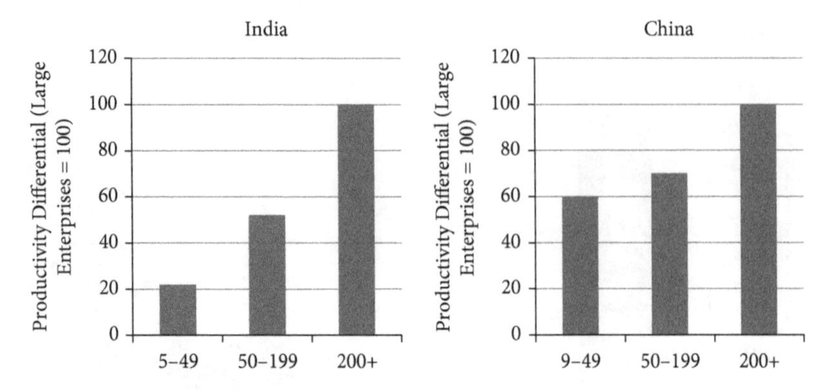

Figure 4.2 Low Wages in Small and Medium Firms Relative to Large Firms in India in Comparison to China

firms, and with small firms paying excessively low wages, India's manufacturing workers remain disproportionately stuck in low-wage employment. At the same time, the vast numbers of farmers dependent on tiny farms of 0.5 hectare or less are unable to find jobs that would give them a better existence, so they remain stuck in subsistence or below-subsistence farming. The transformation from traditional agrarian economy to modern industrial and urban economy advances at a snail's pace.

Large Firms, Productivity, and Exports

Sectoral experience lends further support to the hypothesis that large firms are important to high overall productivity. Nearly all of the sectors in India that have shown significant growth are those in which large firms have a substantial presence. These sectors include autos, auto parts, two-wheelers, machinery, pharmaceuticals, petroleum refining, software, and telecommunications.[6] In parallel, sectors lacking a significant presence of genuinely large firms, such as apparel, textiles, footwear, electrical and electronic products, and other light manufactures, have not done well in India despite the abundance of labor in the country. For example, numerous small manufacturers of mobile phones have emerged in recent years, but none has been able to capture a significant export-market share.

There are many reasons why large firms are crucial to the success of an industry. For one thing, in many industries, the per-unit cost of production declines with rising scale of the firm. Larger scale makes the use of specialized cost-saving machinery viable. Small firms are either unable to deploy these cost-saving machines or unable to utilize them at full capacity. In either case, per-unit cost turns out to be higher than in large firms. Even in a labor-intensive industry such as apparel, larger firms use a lot more machinery per worker than small firms. Additionally, larger scale allows greater specialization, which helps bring costs down through the creation of skills in specific tasks.

Given their large output, large firms must also operate in the global marketplace. This forces them to compete against the best suppliers in the world. Competition compels them to be on their toes all the time so as not to lose their buyers to competitors. They must continuously adopt cost-saving technologies and management practices. Even when large firms sell their product exclusively in the domestic market, they are in direct competition with other global firms.

Furthermore, efficient large firms that operate in the global marketplace define the ecosystem around them and give rise to efficient small and medium firms. Large firms help create a skill pool from which small and medium firms benefit. They also become agents of technological change for small and medium firms, which become either their ancillaries or their competitors. In either case, they are forced to adopt efficient practices and technologies to become competitive in terms of cost and quality.

A comparison of the Indian and Chinese apparel industries best illustrates how the link between the presence of large firms and export performance influences the overall efficiency of an industry. Figure 4.3, also based on the work of Hasan and Jandoc, shows the distribution of employment across small, medium, and

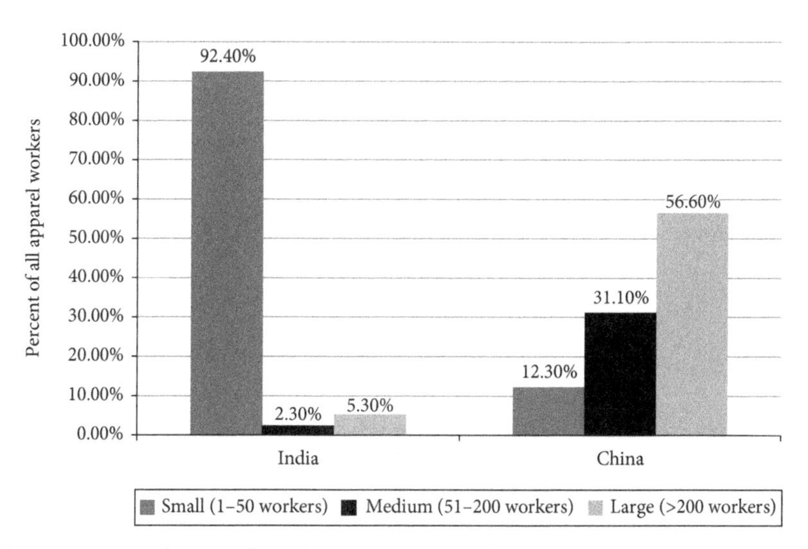

Figure 4.3 Distribution of Employment in Apparel Across Small, Medium, and Large Firms in India and China

large firms in the apparel industry in India and China in 2005. Whereas 92.4 percent of the apparel workforce in India was employed in firms with fewer than fifty workers, only 12.3 percent of the apparel workforce in China was employed in such small firms. The flip side is that India had a very small proportion of the workforce in medium and large firms, while such employment dominated the Chinese apparel industry. Indeed, more-disaggregated data show that the bulk of apparel employment in India (84 percent) was concentrated in tailor shops with seven or fewer workers. Symmetrically, employment in firms with more than five hundred workers was minuscule in India (3.3 percent) in comparison to China (29.4 percent).[7]

These dramatic differences in the distributions of employment across different firm sizes between India and China are matched by differences between their export performances. This is shown in Figure 4.4, which plots the evolution of exports of apparel in India and China from 1999 to 2014. In 1999, exports by China exceeded those by India by just $25 billion. Fifteen years later, this difference had grown to $109 billion. Today, exports of apparel by India have fallen below those by the much smaller countries Bangladesh and Vietnam. Evidence shows that exporting firms in Vietnam are significantly larger than those in India.

The relative export performance of India and China in other labor-intensive industries exhibits a pattern similar to that in apparel. Figures 4.5 and 4.6, which plot exports of footwear and electrical and electronic products,

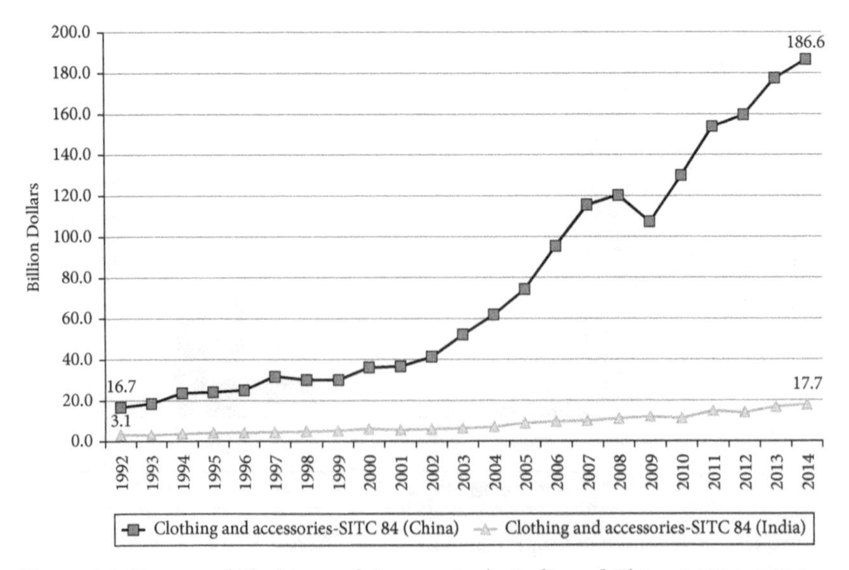

Figure 4.4 Exports of Clothing and Accessories by India and China: 1999 to 2014

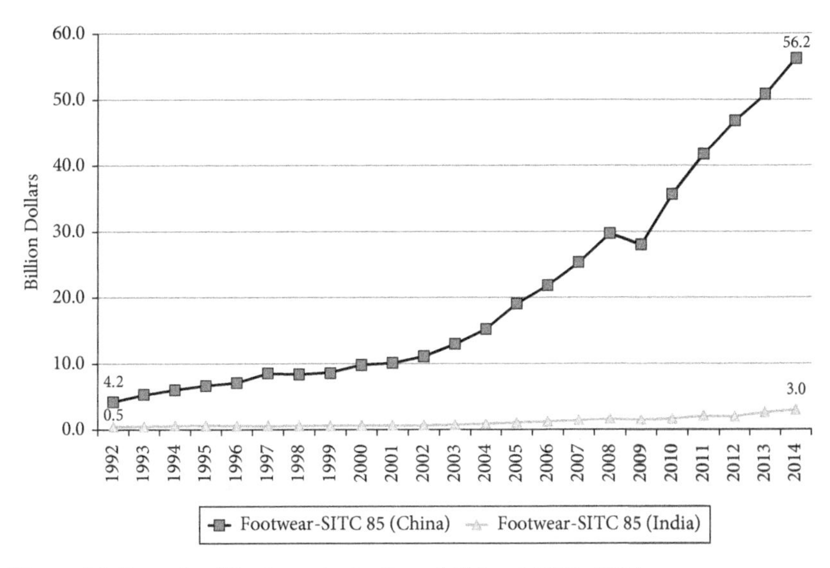

Figure 4.5 Exports of Footwear by India and China: 1999 to 2014

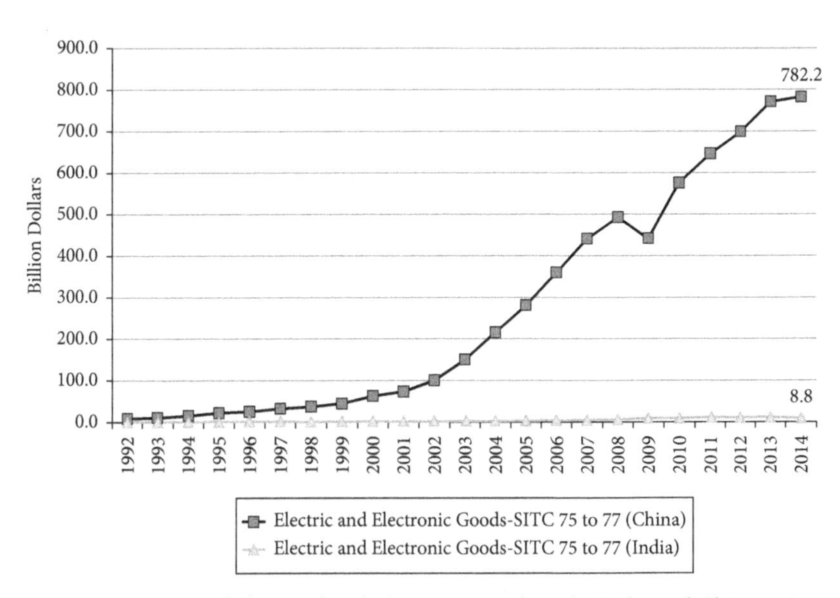

Figure 4.6 Exports of Electrical and Electronic Products by India and China: 1999 to 2014

respectively, by the two countries demonstrate this fact. Larger Chinese firms in these sectors have shown much greater dynamism than their smaller counterparts in India.

Concluding Remarks

Just as there is a preponderance of tiny farms in agriculture in India, tiny firms dominate in industry and services. This feature has resulted in low output per worker and hence low incomes for the bulk of the Indian workforce. India needs to create more productive jobs in industry and services so that workers may exit agriculture.

A key conclusion following from the analysis in this chapter is that creation of high-productivity jobs requires the entry of significantly more large firms in industry and services than is the case presently. It is not merely that large-scale firms themselves are more productive; their presence also helps small and medium firms achieve high productivity. Large firms effectively become agents of change in technology, skills, and management. They also demand high-quality components that small and medium firms may supply.

Therefore, the key policy question we must address is how best to facilitate the emergence and entry of large firms in India. Before tackling this question, though, we need to confront another question that is being asked in the context of current developments in the global trading system and technology: does the manufacturing-fed and export-led growth model that East Asian economies pioneered still offer a feasible path of transformation for a large country such as India? This is the question I address in Chapter 5.

Notes

1. National Statistical Office 2019, 261, table 41.
2. Ali 2015.
3. The sections are 2m(i) and 2(m)(ii).
4. At current prices, India's GVA at factor cost in 2015/16 was 125,666.5 billion rupees. The total number of workers in India was 475 million in 2011/12. Going by EUS 2011/12 and PLFS 2017/18, the workforce actually fell between 2011/12 and 2017/18. Nevertheless, generously assuming that it rose by 10 million workers per year, the total number of workers would be 515 million in 2015/16. Dividing GVA by this workforce figure yields 244,012.5 rupees as the nationwide GVA per worker in 2015/16.
5. Hasan and Jandoc 2013.

6. India's auto sector still remains uncompetitive in the global market because a high level of protection has shielded its inefficiency and permitted the emergence of many small plants. In India, even larger auto firms are smaller than their counterparts in countries such as China and the United States.
7. Hasan and Jandoc 2013.

5
Walking on Two Legs

Can India follow the successful East Asian model of manufacturing-fed and export-led growth, or do changed global market conditions and the impending fourth industrial revolution point to an altogether different approach as being optimal? In discussing this important question, let me reiterate that the approach India adopts must deliver on two key objectives. One, it should accelerate the process of job creation in industry and services to help those sectors absorb new workers who have been joining the workforce and those who may migrate out of agriculture to seek better opportunities. And two, the approach India adopts must produce a proportionately larger number of well-paid jobs for those with no or limited skills.

Seizing on the faster growth of services than manufacturing in India in recent decades, some commentators have argued that manufacturing-fed and export-led transformation is not an option for India and that it should simply go for primarily, even exclusively, a services-led development model. I disagree with this view and will consider this subject in greater detail later.

The Case for Manufacturing as the Engine of Growth

Going by the experience of virtually all countries that have transitioned from low to high per-capita incomes, it is clear that manufacturing, especially of the labor-intensive variety, must serve as the initial source of job creation. As manufacturing pulls workers out of agriculture, rising incomes in this sector create demand for services. Because most services must be supplied domestically, acceleration in demand for them via manufacturing growth accelerates their growth as well. Table 5.1 provides some prima facie evidence in support of this proposition. Whenever countries have experienced an upward shift in the growth rate in manufacturing, the growth rate in services has also seen a jump. In the 1960s, when a shift to outward-oriented policies led to accelerated manufacturing growth in South Korea and Taiwan, both countries also saw their services growth accelerate. On a lesser scale, India too had the same experience during its fast-growth phase from 2003/4 to 2010/11. A paper I co-authored with economist Rajeev Dehejia established this link econometrically using firm-level data.[1]

Table 5.1 Faster Manufacturing Growth Leading to Faster Services Growth

Country and period	GDP	Agriculture	Industry	Services
South Korea				
1954–62	4.2	2.6	11.6	4.4
1963–72	9.5	4.7	17.3	10.0
Taiwan				
1951–53 to 1961–63	7.0	4.9	11.5	7.6
1961–63 to 1971–73	10.0	4.4	15.3	10.3
India				
1991–92 to 2002–3	5.6	2.3	5.6	7.1
2003–4 to 2010–11	8.4	4.1	8.0	9.7

Source: Dehejia and Panagariya 2016, table 1.

As the growth process progresses and per capita incomes and wages rise, production begins to shift into more capital- and skilled-labor-intensive industries. In India to date, manufacturing in general and labor-intensive manufacturing in particular have not fulfilled this function well. If India is to follow the well-trodden and only known path to job creation at decent wages in the early stages of development, it must take steps that would enable manufacturing, especially of the labor-intensive variety, to grow significantly faster.

A minority of commentators in India argues, however, that India is different and that it should eschew manufacturing expansion and build on its successes in services alone. These manufacturing skeptics do not offer a road map for the creation of well-paid jobs for hundreds of millions of workers with limited or no skills, however. Presently these workers either labor in agriculture and informal-sector enterprises or are self-employed. Dynamic services sectors such as software and finance generate relatively few jobs for these workers. Tourism, transportation, and construction hold greater promise, but their potential itself greatly depends on the performance of manufacturing. For example, transportation flourishes when the manufacturing sector generates demand for it. Likewise, tourism and construction are spurred by higher incomes generated by manufacturing. Therefore, if the creation of well-paid jobs for some of those currently employed in agriculture and the informal sector is an important objective, reliance on services as the exclusive engine of growth will not do.

If we thus agree that services alone cannot carry the day, the natural next question is whether manufacturing continues to offer the potential to create the kind of jobs India needs. Two arguments have been offered recently in support of a negative answer to this question: rising protectionism around the world and automation. Let us examine the validity of each of these arguments in turn.

Does Rising Protectionism Pose a Threat to Export-Led Growth?

The first argument says that when South Korea, Taiwan, and China transformed, markets were relatively open. Therefore, these countries could take advantage of scale economies in manufacturing by exporting their products in large volumes. The same option is not available today due to rising protectionism around the world.

This argument greatly overstates the problem. Notwithstanding the current trade tensions, largely bilateral between the United States and China, the global economy is far more open today than in the days when South Korea and Taiwan transformed. Indeed, it remains more open than even during the 1990s and early 2000s, when China transformed. Much of the liberalization under the Uruguay Round agreements was implemented between 1995 and 2005 and remains intact except for tariffs imposed by the United States and China on each other, tariffs on steel and aluminum imposed by the United States, and retaliatory tariffs imposed by a handful of the affected countries.

Total merchandise exports stood at $17.7 trillion in 2017 and have been exhibiting a growing trend. India's share in these exports was only 1.7 percent compared with China's 12.8 percent share in 2017. Even if the export market shrinks to $15 trillion in the coming years—an unlikely prospect—India could more than double its exports by raising its share in the world market to just 4 percent. To put the matter in perspective, global merchandise exports in 2002 were only $6.5 trillion. Yet China managed to export $325.6 billion worth of merchandise goods that year by capturing a 5 percent share in total world exports. India's problem is not a small or shrinking global merchandise export market; it is raising its own share in that market to a respectable level.

Does Impending Automation Render an Export-Centered Strategy Infeasible?

The second argument says that with advances in technology, manufacturing is becoming highly automated and that this would lead to its move back to the developed countries. This argument too has been grossly overstated. It is true that automation is on the increase and perhaps moving at a faster pace than in the past. Yet for many labor-intensive tasks, automation remains technically infeasible. And for many tasks for which automation has become technically feasible, commercial viability remains a distant dream.

Nothing illustrates the limits of automation better than the efforts by Adidas to automate its production of footwear, traditionally one of the most labor-intensive activities. At the end of 2015, the company opened its first high-tech factory in Germany, which produces sneakers using intelligent robotics technology. More recently, it has opened a shoe factory that uses 3-D printing technology. Yet Kasper Rorsted, CEO of Adidas, says that full automation of sneaker manufacturing is unlikely in the next five to ten years. Currently, Adidas produces only 1 million pairs out of its total production of 360 million pairs in automated factories. When asked whether manufacturing is poised to return to the United States and Europe, Rorsted says, "I do not believe, and it is a complete illusion to believe, that manufacturing can go back to Europe in terms of volume."[2] He adds that despite political interest in the United States in bringing back manufacturing, it is financially "very illogical" and unlikely to happen.

What is true of shoe manufacturing is even truer of apparel, where we are still to see the appearance of the first factory that automates manufacturing to the extent the German Adidas factory has done for shoes. And the global apparel market is huge. In 2017, total world exports of clothing and accessories amounted to $810 billion. Of this, India exported only $18.3 billion compared with China's $157.5 billion. With high and rising wages, not only will China see the current trend of declining apparel exports accelerate, it will eventually become a large importer of the product. And with its population of 1.3 billion, its potential apparel imports are large. Put another way, the world population is predicted to reach 7.3 billion in 2030. A nation that becomes the dominant supplier of apparel to this population would be able to create a vast number of good jobs in this one sector alone. If each individual buys just two new shirts each year, that translates into 14.6 billion shirts every year. India can scarcely afford to pass on such an opportunity.

Even as we move beyond shoes and apparel toward more capital-intensive manufacturing, use of human labor is not about to disappear. Tesla recently tried to automate the assembly of its Model 3 electric car and found that it backfired. Elon Musk, CEO of Tesla, had to concede, "Excessive automation at Tesla was a mistake. To be precise, my mistake."[3] Experts say that automation in final assembly has been tried by many in the past and failed.

Mechanization and a shift toward greater capital and skill intensity have been ongoing processes. Even when South Korea, Taiwan, and Singapore industrialized, the capital intensity of production processes was higher than when Europe and the United States industrialized. When China industrialized, the capital intensity of production processes had risen relative to what had been the case when the three East Asian countries industrialized in the 1960s and 1970s. Moreover, China was a significantly larger country. Yet by capturing the vast world market, it successfully created hundreds of millions of well-paid jobs for its workers. Over time, what has been lost for job creation by way of increased capital or skilled-labor intensity has been offset by rising demand due to accompanying higher incomes.

Start-ups and Micro, Small, and Medium Enterprises as Sources of Jobs

Those skeptical about the value of manufacturing sometimes vaguely claim that millions of start-up enterprises, with each employing five to ten individuals, would open up job opportunities to hundreds of millions. But to date such critics have provided no evidence showing that this process is under way. True, a few hundred start-ups, perhaps even a few thousand, have emerged in India recently, including such successful ones as Flipkart, Ola, Paytm, OYO, and Rivigo. But taken together, they probably do not employ more than 5 million workers.

More importantly, it is not clear that such enterprises can be any more successful in creating well-paid jobs for workers on the lowest rung of the skill ladder than more conventional capital- and skilled-labor-intensive enterprises. The mass of the Indian workforce has hardly any skills and is surely not employable in tech start-ups. Recognizing this, some manufacturing skeptics point to micro, small, and medium enterprises (MSMEs) in services sectors as a perpetual source of jobs. But these commentators do not clarify whether the bulk of these jobs will be in micro and small enterprises or in medium enterprises. If it is the former, how will they be any better at generating high-productivity jobs than the current own-account enterprises and small establishment enterprises? All evidence shows that industries that are dominated by enterprises that begin small and stay small are almost certain to suffer from low productivity and low-wage employment. Enterprises that are highly productive and able to pay steadily rising wages grow bigger over time. They then define the industry within which other smaller enterprises must shape up in order to compete.

If the advocates of the hypothesis that services would serve as the primary engine of growth wish to make the case that jobs can still come from medium enterprises, they have not outlined how this will be achieved. All existing evidence shows that medium enterprises are few and far between in India. To date, most services jobs in India at the low end of the skill ladder have been of the self-employment variety or in small enterprises.

Factors Favoring Manufacturing in India

Two factors make the current timing for the expansion of labor-intensive manufacturing opportune for India. First, wages in manufacturing in China are on average three times those in India. Due to China's demographic transition, the Chinese workforce has begun to shrink and will continue to do so in the next one to two decades. This would mean a further rise in manufacturing wages. This change is bound to shift China into higher-value-added activities, including those in the services sector. Low-end manufacturing will move to other locations.

Second, by all indications, the trade war between the United States and China is likely to endure for some years to come. While President Donald Trump may have started this trade war, some of the issues underlying it enjoy a surprising amount of consensus across the political spectrum in the United States. So even if the leadership changes, the stance of the United States is unlikely to change by much. At the same time, China has emerged as an aggressive, belligerent power in recent years and is unlikely to yield the concessions the United States seeks. This situation offers India opportunities to expand its trade with both the United States and China. Each will import less from the other, opening opportunities for India.

Another aspect of the trade war is that it makes China a less attractive production base for multinationals supplying the United States market. Therefore, many export-oriented multinationals currently active in China will be looking for alternative locations. Multinationals making new investments will also be considering China less favorably than in the past. With its vast workforce, India can emerge as the new manufacturing hub, especially at the low end of the spectrum.

In response to high wages in China, some manufacturing multinationals are already moving out of China to other lower-wage locations. India can become the host to many of these multinationals. At the same time, its small and medium domestic firms can capture the market from their Chinese counterparts, which also will find it difficult to compete in low-end manufacturing due to high wages and the outmigration of multinationals, which are often buyers of their products.

Walking on Two Legs: Industry and Services

If the creation of well-paid jobs for those with limited skills is an objective, accelerated growth in manufacturing with special attention paid to labor-intensive products remains an important component of the strategy for economic transformation of India in the forthcoming decades. Yet it would be too much to expect that India's path to transformation would be approximately the same as that followed by Singapore, Taiwan, and South Korea from the 1960s through the

1980s and by China during the past three decades. The unusual success achieved in several capital- and skilled-labor-intensive sectors at a relatively low level of per-capita income already distinguishes India's path from that followed by these other countries. Unlike them, India has also achieved substantial success in some key modern services, such as information technology (IT), IT-enabled services (ITES), telecommunications, and financial services. Accelerated growth in these modern services sectors has also helped spur faster growth in a number of traditional, non-traded services. For its level of per-capita income, India is also poised to achieve a high level of digitalization of the economy.

Therefore, even as India needs a course correction in favor of manufacturing, especially of the labor-intensive variety, it must simultaneously continue to build on its strength in services. In other words, as the Indian economy transforms, it must walk on two legs, manufacturing and services, with agriculture progressively modernizing and releasing workers. It must endeavor to create an ecosystem in which large-scale, high-productivity firms may emerge and capture world markets in both manufacturing and services.

Concluding Remarks

If India is to succeed in creating a significantly larger volume of high-productivity jobs that offer decent incomes to workers, there is no escaping the traditional, well-trodden path of manufacturing-led growth. Those who argue that services can serve as the exclusive or even primary engine of growth for India have provided no road map of how such a growth process would create jobs paying decent wages to those exiting agriculture or currently employed in tiny enterprises at meager wages. I have also offered arguments why the path through manufacturing is not closed by any means. Despite episodes of increased protectionism, the world economy is more open today than during the years when South Korea, Taiwan, and China transformed their economies. Likewise, the threat from automation, what I have sometimes called "robophobia," is greatly exaggerated. In many labor-intensive manufacturing activities, automation is not yet technologically feasible. And in some activities where it is technologically feasible, it will take a few decades for it to become commercially viable.

My bottom-line conclusion is that, having already achieved some degree of success in a number of key services sectors, India must walk on two legs by promoting a healthy atmosphere for the growth of both manufacturing and services. To the extent that the policy regime in India has been particularly unfriendly to the growth of labor-intensive manufacturing, special attention must be paid to the removal of bottlenecks in this area. Armed with these conclusions, we may now turn to a detailed discussion of reforms aimed at facilitating rapid growth of manufacturing and services.

Notes

1. Dehejia and Panagariya 2016.
2. Quoted in Bain 2017.
3. Quoted in Hull 2018.

PART III

THE ROAD TO REFORMS

6

Reforms for Export-Led and Manufacturing-Fed Growth

Evidence shows that the bulk of India's non-agricultural workforce is stuck in low-productivity enterprises that either employ no hired workers on a regular basis or employ a few at subsistence-level wages. Specifically, according to the latest available NSO survey, unincorporated enterprises employed 111.3 million workers. Of these, 62.1 percent were in own-account enterprises, which employed no hired workers on a regular basis, and the remaining 37.9 percent worked in establishment enterprises that employed one or more hired workers. The average annual wage in the latter was 103,744 rupees. If spread over a family of five, this amount would allow an expenditure of just 56.85 rupees per person per day in 2015/16 rupees. If converted to U.S. dollars at the average market exchange rate prevailing during the year, the expenditure would amount to just 87 cents.

India needs to create many more jobs that pay better wages to those at the bottom rung of the skill ladder. Experience around the world shows that these jobs will have to come from manufacturing and services. Evidence also points to the fact that the key factor behind the failure of India to create enough well-paid jobs for those with no or limited skills has been the near absence of large and medium firms in labor-intensive sectors. Therefore, before we can identify policy reforms that would help create a larger number of well-paid jobs, we ask why large-scale enterprises have failed to emerge in labor-intensive sectors in India.

Missing Large-Scale Enterprises in Labor-Intensive Sectors

The answer to this question has three parts. First, until as late as 2000, India maintained an effective ban on the entry of medium and large enterprises in labor-intensive sectors. As a result, even though this ban has now been fully lifted, the historical legacy has been a mass of small firms. Firms that have operated in these sectors for decades feel comfort in operating at the same old small scale. Second, decades of exclusion of medium and large firms and business houses from these sectors, along with a history of highly restrictive labor laws, have hard-wired them to keep away from unskilled-labor-intensive sectors. They habitually operate exclusively in capital- and skilled-labor-intensive sectors. Finally, despite lifting the ban against medium and large firms in labor-intensive sectors, the policy regime remains less than friendly to large firms in these sectors. Consider each of these factors in greater detail.

Prime Minister Nehru's original conception was that light manufactures should be produced exclusively by small household enterprises, which can operate with small amounts of capital per worker, thereby freeing up the bulk of available capital for heavier industries, which required some minimum scale to be viable. Initially this policy was enforced by denial of investment licenses—required for all investments beyond a relatively low threshold—in light manufactures. Later, Prime Minister Indira Gandhi formalized the policy via the SSI reservation list, which explicitly reserved light manufactures for small-scale enterprises. By the late 1980s, this list encompassed more than eight hundred items.

Although the government began trimming the SSI reservation list in 1996, the policy remained effective for most products until at least 2000, when SSI sectors were opened to large-scale enterprises that exported 50 percent or more of their output. In principle this change can be viewed as having ended the SSI reservation, but given the history of inward orientation in India, especially in light manufactures, few large-scale enterprises that could export 50 percent of their output emerged. Subsequently the SSI list itself was trimmed in several steps, with the last twenty items removed from it as late as 2015.

It was expected that once the SSI reservation was ended, new, ambitious entrepreneurs would enter light manufactures to take advantage of India's abundant workforce, but this did not happen. The reason is that, as we have seen, the SSI reservation denied large firms and big business houses entry into these sectors, and this exclusion created a culture among large entrepreneurs that shunned the manufacture of products such as apparel and footwear. This culture was reinforced by yet another policy initiative of the government of Prime Minister Indira Gandhi. Beginning in the early 1970s, new investments by large firms and business houses, defined as those with assets worth 200 million rupees or more, were confined by law to a set of highly capital-intensive "core" industries. Initially, the list of these core industries contained only nine narrowly defined items. Though the list was expanded subsequently, it remained highly restrictive. Over time, as the assets of other firms crossed the 200 million rupee threshold, more and more of them came under the purview of the regulation.

Another factor contributing to large firms' and business houses' aversion toward labor-intensive sectors was the experience of textile firms in Mumbai and Kanpur during the 1980s. In those days, textiles were among the most labor-intensive products. India's labor laws, especially the Industrial Disputes Act (IDA), gave a disproportionately high level of protection to workers over entrepreneurs. An amendment to this law in the early 1980s further strengthened this protection by effectively making it impossible to terminate workers in firms with one hundred or more workers. Armed with this protection, worker unions in textile mills in Mumbai and Kanpur went on strike one after another to seek superior terms of employment. Mounting losses from the shutdown eventually led to the exit of nearly all textile mills. That experience left permanent scars on the psyche of Indian entrepreneurs.

Judicial interventions, which asymmetrically favored workers, further contributed to the aversion toward labor-intensive activities among Indian entrepreneurs. In any dispute between workers and management, the judiciary would almost always rule against management, regardless of the merits of the case. This experience left entrepreneurs worried that they had no effective tool for disciplining errant or defiant workers. The problem seemed insurmountable in activities requiring a large number of workers. As a result, entrepreneurs began exhibiting a strong preference for capital- and skilled-labor-intensive manufacturing sectors. And even within these sectors, they often came to lean heavily in favor of the most capital-intensive technology.

The third and final factor, which continues to discourage the entry into light manufactures on a large scale of even those entrepreneurs not hardwired to operate exclusively in capital- and skilled-labor-intensive sectors, relates to the numerous remaining policy and procedure-related barriers. Within this category, restrictive labor laws, to which I have already alluded, stand out. Under the Indian Constitution, labor is a concurrent subject, which means that both the central and state governments can legislate in this area. Consequently, the number of laws to which enterprises are subject have proliferated. There are 33 central laws that apply to all states. In addition, each state has its own laws. Some of the laws even contradict one another, prompting a wit to quip that India cannot enforce 100 percent of its labor laws without violating 20 percent of them!

As already hinted, one highly restrictive labor law is the central Industrial Disputes Act. The provision in this act effectively outlawing the termination of a regular worker under any circumstances by an enterprise employing one hundred or more regular workers was introduced in the early 1980s and remains in effect. With permission from the central government, some states have been able to raise the number of workers triggering the law to three hundred, but this too remains a low threshold. In modern times, when firms in China employ hundreds of thousands of workers to maximize the benefits of scale economies, those in India need to have at least tens of thousands of workers to be competitive. Recently, the central government has sought a halfway solution to the problem by allowing firms to hire workers on fixed-term employment contracts. But this is a less than ideal solution, since such temporary employees do not develop loyalty to their enterprises and enterprises hesitate to invest in skilling them. Another provision in the IDA makes it extremely difficult to assign a worker a task different from the one for which he was hired. In a world in which technology changes rapidly, such inflexibility becomes very costly.

Today, demands for an ever-rising minimum wage have emerged as another threat to the hiring of workers. Larger formal-sector enterprises must abide by minimum-wage laws. But in labor-intensive activities such as apparel and footwear, competition in the global marketplace is intense and profit margins low. As a result, in an environment in which capital- and skilled-labor-intensive enterprises with high profit margins dominate and minimum wages are set with them in mind, a minimum wage greatly undermines the viability of formal enterprises in labor-intensive sectors.

Procuring land in a suitable location at a reasonable price has also turned into a serious constraint on the entry of large-scale enterprises. With no definitive land titles in India, it is difficult for an entrepreneur to purchase a sufficient number of contiguous pieces of land that are all free of disputes. The holdout problem, whereby individual landowners try to extract exorbitant prices for their pieces of land because they know that the large area sought by the buyer cannot be assembled without the purchase of their pieces of land, adds to this difficulty. The only alternative in such situations is for the government to acquire land on behalf of the entrepreneur. Unfortunately, this is a difficult task under the Land Acquisition Act, making both the central and state governments averse to doing it.

Finally, India also has myriad policy and procedural restrictions on the movement of goods both within the country and at the border. These barriers make the cost of exporting and importing products particularly onerous relative to other competing countries. In view of the fact that large enterprises exploit scale economies effectively only by exporting their product and must also import many of their inputs to meet global quality standards for what they sell, these logistics barriers further discourage their entry.

The First Step: A Change of Mindset

If the government sincerely wishes to expand high-productivity jobs for those at the bottom rung of the skill ladder, it will need to make a concerted effort. Marginal changes here and there or subsidy packages without a sea change in policies will simply not do. Fancy capital-intensive, high-tech, and high-end products on which the government's flagship scheme Make in India has focused the bulk of its efforts so far must give way to the less flashy but employment-friendly sectors. Glorification of micro enterprises as fountainheads of job creation must stop. They do employ a large number of workers, but the low-wage jobs and subsistence-level employment they provide is nothing to celebrate. To the extent that the government can offer rewards, they must go to enterprises that move up in size, from micro to small, small to medium, and medium to large. The aim of the policy should be to ensure that firms with 50 or more workers come to employ half or more of the workers in labor-intensive sectors in no more than fifteen years. Achieving this goal requires reforms in multiple areas.

A Clear Focus on Export Expansion

Exports, made possible by effective policies and not subsidies, are a good measure of the competitiveness of a country's products. Rapidly expanding exports testify to rapidly rising productivity. In a country such as India, which has an extremely large pool of workers with at best limited skills, the surest way to achieve rapid export expansion is to shift its production basket toward labor-intensive products in both manufacturing and services. The experiences of South Korea, Taiwan, and Singapore from the 1960s to the 1980s and of China more recently illustrate the success of this approach. As in India, the production structure in China did not reflect its abundance of labor relative to capital till 1980. But as the 1980s progressed, it rapidly reoriented its production structure toward labor-intensive products, which it came to export in large volumes. India needs to reorient its production structure in a similar manner so as to use its vast pool of workers effectively. My recent book *Free Trade and Prosperity* comprehensively shows the critical importance of free trade to the success of all those countries that have achieved rapid transformation in the post–Second World War era.[1]

Export markets are also critical to the growth of large firms. All evidence shows that productivity and scale of firms are positively correlated with export performance. For instance, firms in the apparel sector in China, Vietnam, and Bangladesh, which have performed better than India in exports, are on average larger than those in India. Even the size of the average exporting firm in these countries is larger than in India. Therefore, it is critical that India adopts policies that expand trade. In products in which India is more cost effective, it should expand and export. In products where the opposite is true, it should import.

The timing could not be more opportune for India to make a success of an export-oriented strategy. The large-scale firms that are currently exiting labor-intensive sectors are predominantly located in China, where wages have seen a significant rise in the last two decades—a trend that is predicted to continue in the forthcoming decade on account of the country's shrinking labor force. Given this, and with the trade war with the United States predicted to continue, many multinational firms currently located in China are looking for low-wage locations around the world. With its vast labor supply, India has the potential to become that location.

A major advantage of attracting existing established firms is that they bring their own capital, technology, management practices, and links to the world markets. They create well-paid jobs and also promise to serve as catalysts for the entry of local firms in similar activities. But foreign multinational firms will not move to India only because of its abundant labor supply. They also require an ecosystem that is friendly to manufacturing and export activities.

Genuine success in turning India into the same factory of manufactures for the world over the next two decades that China has been during the previous two decades would require both a complete change of mindset and focused reforms. In what follows, I outline the major steps that are necessary to help India become a hub of labor-intensive manufacturing. I begin with a critique of import substitution. In 1991, India implemented policy reforms that steadily moved the country towards greater export orientation. But, sadly, import substitution has had a comeback recently.

Avoid Falling into the Import Substitution Trap

After almost three decades of reforms aimed at unshackling the Indian economy, including trade liberalization, Indian policymakers have not been able to fully shed their love affair with import substitution. Nothing illustrates this better than a series of tariff hikes by the government during 2018 and 2019. Until about 2007, India had been systematically lowering its tariffs. While liberalization did not progress further after that point, there was no major reversal of it either. But, after a long pause, tariffs have begun to rise again.

This return to protectionism can be traced to at least four factors. First, despite a considerable shift in thinking in the post-reform era, India has not been able to fully free itself of socialist ideas. Many within the current ruling structure do not fully appreciate the damage protectionism did to the Indian economy during the first four decades following independence. Equally, they lack appreciation for the key role that outward-oriented policies have played in the sustained rapid growth that India has experienced in recent years. Many within the top bureaucracy, who have never come to terms with India's turn away from socialism, readily reinforce these convictions of their political bosses.

The second reason, which complements the first, is that the success of trade liberalization in India has led to a considerable expansion of imports as a proportion of GDP. At its peak, this proportion reached 31 percent in 2012/13 and, despite a decline in recent years, stood at a hefty 24 percent in 2018/19. The large share of imports in GDP means that there is now a large scope for import substitution. Under pressure to make a success of the prime minister's Make in India program, many ministries find it convenient to restrict the entry of imports to make way for domestic production. To some degree, the situation is similar to that in South Korea in the early 1970s, when its success in expanding trade and consequent expansion of imports as a proportion of GDP led it to turn to import substitution policies.

Third, India has a large surplus on its invisibles account due to remittances, plus an overall current account deficit. The mirror image of these balances is a very large deficit on the merchandise trade account. This large deficit adds to the temptation to restrict merchandise imports and replace them with domestic output. Unfortunately, restrictions on imports to counteract the trade deficit find approval in many respectable circles.

Finally, higher inflation in India relative to its trading partners combined with a relatively stable nominal exchange rate has led to a loss of competitiveness of many Indian products relative to foreign products. In turn, this situation has led to demands by Indian industry for increased protection. The government, which is favorably inclined toward import substitution in the first place, has readily obliged domestic industry.

If India is to relaunch itself onto a trajectory of growth at an 8 percent rate or more, however, policymakers must disabuse themselves of import substitution ideology. This policy encourages the production of items that are costly to produce at home and discourages the production of products that are cheaper to produce. Trade liberalization reverses this pattern of specialization by expanding output of products the country produces cheaply and contracting output of those it produces at higher cost relative to its trading partners. Many devotees of import substitution erroneously believe that the policy allows the country to boost GDP by replacing imports with domestic output. They fail to understand that such an increase is accompanied by a larger loss in GDP through a decline in the output of export items.

To understand this subtle fact, think of the extreme case in which a country bans imports altogether. This policy would surely allow it to replace all imports by domestic production. But with no imports, why would the country export anything? The only reason to export is to earn foreign exchange that can be used to import products that are cheaper abroad. Extreme import substitution would lead to complete autarky, eliminating all gains from trade. That is more or less what India experienced during the first four decades following independence.

In international trade theory, there is a powerful proposition that goes by the name of the Lerner symmetry theorem, so named because it was first propounded by economist Abba Lerner in a paper published in a leading British journal in 1936. According to this remarkable theorem, the effect of an across-the-board 10 percent import duty is identical to that of an across-the-board

10 percent export tax. Both interventions reduce imports as well as exports and lead to a loss of the gains from trade.

While the precise logic behind the Lerner symmetry theorem is somewhat involved, its essence can be explained in simple terms. The initial reduction in imports through increased tariffs lowers the demand for foreign currency. This fact leads to a reduction in the price of foreign currency in terms of domestic currency from, say, 70 rupees per dollar to 65 rupees per dollar. A cheaper foreign currency in turn partially reverses the initial tariff-induced reduction in imports. Simultaneously, it lowers the profitability of exports and hence the quantum of exports. Eventually the country finds itself with reduced imports on a net basis and an equivalent reduction in exports, with the gains from trade reduced accordingly. It is thus an illusion that import substitution can make a net addition to income. The sooner policymakers disabuse themselves of this illusion, the better for India.

Drop Insistence on a Strong Rupee

Alongside import substitution, the idea of a strong rupee has also gained currency in the present government. A strong (what economists call overvalued) currency may make a country feel proud, but it has a devastating effect on the competitiveness of the country's products vis-à-vis foreign counterparts. A simple example helps explain this important point.

Consider a strong rupee exchange rate of 70 rupees per dollar and a weak rupee exchange rate of 80 rupees per dollar. Suppose that an imported computer costs $1,000 while a domestically produced computer costs 75,000 rupees. Under the strong rupee rate, the imported computer would sell for 70,000 rupees in the Indian market, outcompeting the domestically produced computer. Under the weak rupee rate, the imported computer would sell for 80,000 rupees, with the domestically produced computer outselling it.

A similar argument applies to exportable goods. Suppose that a particular variety of shirt sells for $10 in a foreign market. Then a shirt costing 750 rupees to produce in India will fail to compete in the foreign market under the strong rupee rate because it would fetch only 700 rupees in Indian currency. But under the weak rupee rate, it will be able to compete because it will bring 800 rupees to the exporter.

In developing countries, inflation is often higher than in the developed countries to which they sell the bulk of their exports. This means that over time, the costs of production in terms of domestic currency rise faster in developing countries than in developed countries. Therefore, if the nominal exchange rate is held fixed, products of developing countries become less and less competitive relative to those of developed countries. A nominal depreciation of the domestic currrency, which weakens it, corrects this differential in cost increases and restores the competitiveness of domestic goods.

When domestic currency is allowed to remain strong in the face of higher inflation at home and domestic products lose competitiveness, producers of goods that compete with imported goods clamor for protection. Democratic governments often end up bowing to such clamor, as has happened in India in recent years. During the five years following 2013/14, depreciation of the Indian rupee has failed to keep pace with India's higher inflation, making Indian goods 10 to 15 percent more expensive relative to many imports. As a result, domestic industry has demanded and received increased tariff protection in many sectors.

Using tariffs instead of exchange rate depreciation to restore the competitiveness of domestic goods with imports has two disadvantages. First, exports still continue to suffer from reduced competitiveness. In principle, exports too can be protected through export subsidies, but such subsidies violate WTO rules. Second, tariffs are very inefficient instruments of protection. They undermine the growth of trade and deprive the country of the gains that accrue with it.

During the decade following 1991, when India became progressively more open, it allowed the rupee to depreciate by a large margin. Between 1991/92 and 2003/4, the average tariff in India fell from 113 percent to approximately 30 percent. Yet Indian goods remained competitive with the current account (exports minus imports), showing a surplus during 2001/2 to 2003/4. This was because the rupee depreciated from 20 rupees per dollar to 46 rupees per dollar over the same time. The depreciation helped exports while also compensating producers of goods competing against imports that had been subject to large cuts in tariffs.

India needs to pay particular attention to the value of the rupee vis-à-vis the Chinese yuan. When the yuan depreciates vis-à-vis the dollar and the rupee does not, Indian goods lose competitiveness against Chinese goods. This has indeed happened in recent years. The result has been a massive expansion of imports from China by India without a parallel expansion of India's exports to China. Given the importance of China in India's trade, the India-China exchange rate is of special importance for India.

Rationalize Tariffs

Tariffs in India remain high and their structure is complex. In many cases, tariffs on inputs are higher than those on outputs, leading to negative protection for the latter. In some cases, tariffs are imposed on items that India does not even produce domestically. Such tariffs hurt buyers of the items, whether they are final consumers or firms using them as input, without benefiting anyone. India's last major effort to compress tariffs in 2007 brought the top tariff down from 12 to 10 percent (with the exception of some tariff peaks applying to sectors such as textiles, apparel, and automobiles, which remained significantly higher than the 10 percent ceiling).

It is now time to resume liberalization and rationalize the structure of tariffs. If the exchange rate is managed prudently at the same time, such rationalization and liberalization can be accomplished while making Indian goods more competitive relative to foreign goods. With this in mind, India should set a goal of adopting a uniform tariff of 7 percent on all industrial products within three years. This will entail raising the tariffs that are currently below 7 percent (except a handful that are bound below 7 percent under India's commitments to the World Trade Organization and therefore cannot be raised) while reducing the higher rates.

A uniform tariff across all products has several advantages over the current highly variegated structure. It will end the current tariff inversion, whereby tariffs on many inputs are levied at higher rates than final products. It will also result in minimal distortion across import-competing sectors (though distortion vis-à-vis exports will remain as long as the tariff rate is positive).

But above all, once the government has committed to a uniform tariff across all imports, demands for higher tariffs by industry lobbies will gradually subside. Once each industry sees that an increase in its tariff would automatically raise the tariff on all other imports, its incentive to lobby will greatly diminish. Symmetrically, commitment to a uniform tariff will also strengthen the hand of the government vis-à-vis lobbies seeking higher tariffs. The government would be in a position to defuse the pressure for higher tariffs from a specific industry lobby by arguing that if it accedes to such demands, it has to raise the tariff on all other products, which is harmful to the economy.[2]

A remaining question is why the recommended tariff rate is 7 percent and not higher or lower. This choice is based on revenue considerations. It will ensure that tariff revenue will not fall below its current level and may indeed rise. The recommendation is not meant to be a rigid number and may be fixed at a slightly lower or higher level than 7 percent as long as it results in some overall liberalization of the regime.

An Alternative Tariff Reform

If the recommendation of a uniform 7 percent tariff is seen as too radical and lacking political acceptance, an alternative would be to bring all tariffs exceeding 10 percent to the 10 percent level. Such tariff compression would be in line with

India's past approach. India needs to pay particular attention to tariff reductions in two areas: textiles and clothing, and the auto sector.

In textiles and clothing, nearly all tariffs range from 20 to 25 percent. This is an area in which India should have the ambition to be the world's largest exporter and should not depend on protection. More importantly, the largest market in apparel globally is in garments produced from man-made fibers. So far, India's exports of apparel not only are small in relation to its size but are concentrated in garments made of cotton fiber.

An important reason for India's poor performance in garments produced of man-made fiber is that it subjects imports of this fiber to a tariff of 20 percent and those of fabric made from it to a 25 percent tariff. Because GST is levied on the tariff-inclusive price, the effective customs duty ends up being even higher than these rates. In addition, India slaps anti-dumping duties on many items falling under the category of man-made fiber or fabric produced from man-made fiber. This fact makes domestic producers of garments made of man-made fiber uncompetitive vis-à-vis their foreign counterparts. This single fact has prevented India from exploiting its comparative advantage in apparel made from man-made fiber, arguably the largest potential source of good jobs for workers with no or limited skills.

India has provided its auto sector an even higher level of tariff protection. According to the 2018 tariff schedule submitted by India to the WTO, applied tariff rates on vehicles meant for ten or more passengers are 40 percent, and rates on those for fewer than ten passengers are 125 percent. These tariffs have produced a highly inefficient auto industry in India, with the result that India's share in world passenger car exports remains less than 1 percent. The industry produces lower-quality cars than their foreign counterparts and often sells them at one and a half times the price charged by the latter. With the industry having been protected by prohibitive trade barriers and the consumer having been punished for the entire seventy-plus years since independence, it is time that the government subjects the auto industry to genuine competition.

Reimburse All Indirect Taxes to Exporters

The second area of border measures requiring correction concerns indirect taxes paid by exporters along the value chain. These must be reimbursed expeditiously and in totality. Such reimbursement is fully consistent with WTO rules. Currently, petroleum products are not integrated into the GST. As a result, taxes paid on them by exporters are not reimbursed. Similarly, duty drawbacks on imported inputs, which are fully WTO legal, end up being partial in some cases.

There are also inordinate delays in reimbursements of indirect taxes and duties paid on inputs, which blocks exporters' working capital.

Free Trade Agreements

Light manufactures, especially apparel and footwear, remain subject to high customs duties in most of India's export markets. In contrast, Bangladesh, a key competitor, has duty-free access to the large European Union (EU) market, with its twenty-seven countries. Recently, Vietnam has also concluded a free trade agreement (FTA) with the EU. The only way India can improve its access to these markets and be at par with competing countries is by forging its own FTAs. Two such FTAs, already under negotiation, could prove especially helpful: the Regional Comprehensive Economic Partnership (RCEP), which is an agreement with the major Asian countries, and one with the EU. In the forthcoming years, the RCEP market in apparel, footwear, and other light manufactures will be huge, so establishing duty-free access to it can bring vast gains for India. Likewise, the EU is already a large market for Indian apparel exports. Duty-free access to it can potentially lead to substantial expansion of India's exports.

These free trade agreements can also prove highly effective instruments for bringing multinationals currently leaving China to Indian shores. The FTAs will give these multinationals duty-free access to European and RCEP markets. They would also allow the companies to import their inputs duty free from these countries. Such a change could be transformational in terms of creating good jobs and reshaping the ecosystem in India.

Trade Facilitation

India also needs to implement trade facilitation in all its aspects. This is a very substantial area of reforms involving many logistical details. I do not venture here into all of those details but will briefly mention the key areas. A recent report by a committee of the Economic Advisory Council to the Prime Minister (EAC-PM) provides a substantially more detailed set of recommendations.[3]

The cost of moving goods into and out of ports remains significantly higher in India than in competitor countries. The EAC-PM report points out that the average time to clear imports at Indian ports varies from six to thirteen days and the average time to clear exports ranges from 3.5 to 6 days. It also notes that port logistics costs at Indian ports average 15 to 16 percent of the total consignment value, compared with 8 percent in developed countries. These costs make exports and imports more costly relative to domestic sales and discourage trade.

Both time and financial costs also exhibit high variability across Indian ports, undermining predictability of delivery costs. Delays in getting imported inputs used in exports can have an adverse impact on the ability to meet export orders on time. Likewise, failure to deliver exports of certain products at the precise designated time due to lack of predictability of clearance time at ports can be fatal to the renewal of orders. Retail stores in the United States and European countries have limited space for inventory. As a result, they require just-in-time delivery for products such as apparel, which have well-defined seasons for sales.

There are similar issues relating to transport links between the point of production and ports. Historically, the economy's inward orientation, forced by poor policy choices in the past, has meant that production agglomerations have developed with domestic markets in mind, and these domestic markets are often far away from the coast and its ports. The problem is exacerbated by the fact that India is a geographically large country. The combined effect of these factors has been poor connectivity between production centers and ports. Efforts to build transport links have taken the form of megaprojects such as the Delhi-Mumbai industrial corridor, which has progressed at a snail's pace. Consequently, the time required and the cost incurred to move goods to and from the ports have remained high. According to the EAC-PM committee report, the time required to move goods on a given route shows fluctuations of 15 to 20 percent around the mean time.

Autonomous Employment Zones

Perhaps the most important initiative India can take today to better integrate itself with global supply chains and become the world's manufacturing hub is to launch half a dozen Autonomous Employment Zones (AEZs). These zones would be along the lines of Shenzhen in China. Unlike the Special Economic Zones (SEZs) with which India experimented during the past one and a half decades with mixed results, AEZs would be spread over large areas (in excess of 500 square kilometers), with the early ones located close to a deep-dredge port, such as those in Gujarat and Andhra Pradesh. They will also be far fewer in number than SEZs—no more than half a dozen in the beginning, and perhaps only two or three. Since suitable unused land areas of this size are unlikely to be available, especially near the coast, the zones may include existing habitations and establishments.

The key feature of AEZs would be to give virtually all powers to frame the rules of economic engagement within the zone's defined boundaries, including labor and land laws and administration of customs, to the local administration. The zones will offer a highly flexible environment, allowing rapid reallocation of land

and labor from one activity to another. They will also allow exporters to import inputs with minimum friction, process them, and export. But there will be no export requirement for firms located in the zones.

In the initial phase—say, during the first ten years—the government may provide a waiver of either GST or corporate profit tax to any single employer employing ten thousand workers or more. This will incentivize early entrants to the zones, who must function within an area that would still be developing. Later entrants would be entering a well-developed area and therefore would not require a similar benefit. In the early phase of the zones, the government must proactively court multinationals currently active in China and other countries, especially in labor-intensive manufacturing.

The government's other contributions to the zones may be limited to building first-rate infrastructure and dormitory housing, which migrant workers can rent. When seen in a national context, the resources needed to build infrastructure and dormitory housing in these AEZs are relatively small. They can be drawn out of the general pool of resources devoted to infrastructure and urban housing.

Once success is demonstrated in a handful of AEZs, more of them may be considered. What is important, however, is that the numbers are kept in proportion to the resources available to build such zones. A key flaw of many government initiatives in India is that they are multiplied too rapidly, which spreads limited resources too thinly to produce any successes.

Tax Simplification and Tax Predictability

India also needs to reform and simplify its tax laws. Complex tax laws with their myriad exemptions create uncertainty for investors. Frequent changes in the laws and the government's high propensity to engage in tax disputes add to this uncertainty. India needs to clear the existing stock of disputes and take measures that would discourage the creation of frivolous tax disputes in the future. Unjust demands for taxes can render profitable investments unprofitable and drive away future investors. The introduction of retrospective taxation in the year 2012 during the second term of the United Progressive Alliance government had a chilling effect on investors. The relevant law still remains on the books and may be invoked by a future government. Therefore, it is best to repeal it.

The goods and services tax is an important step in the direction of simplification and transparency. But the GST too has been subject to considerable uncertainty during its short life, with tax rates on many items being revised. The necessary adjustments to the rate should be done relatively fast and then maintained. It will be best to quickly move the system to two rates, 12 and 18 percent, with no exception other than zero-rated items.

The government has insisted on maintaining the 28 percent tax rate on certain items, on the grounds that luxury items should be taxed at a punishing rate. But it is unwise to pursue the objective of equality through every instrument on which the government can lay its hands. Instead, it is best to design the tax system so that it minimizes efficiency loss; the government should pursue equality principally through expenditures targeted at favored groups. Super-high tax rates may undermine even the objective of collecting revenue by discouraging the purchases of highly taxed items.

Finally, historically India has maintained extra-high tax rates on corporate profits. In the early years of reforms, some rationalization of this tax was done, but that process was not taken to its logical end. Indeed, the effective rate saw a rise through the imposition of a surcharge on the tax. Luckily, the government has recently taken a big step by knocking down the corporate profit tax for domestic companies to 22 percent, with the effective rate (inclusive of surcharge) amounting to 25.2 percent. For new manufacturing firms starting production before 2023, the government has reduced the effective tax rate to 17 percent. In conjunction with this reduction, it has ended all exemptions and incentives. This is a reform worthy of applause. Similar reforms must also be undertaken in the area of personal taxation to incentivize work by professionals and minimize evasion through bribery.

Labor Market Reforms

Labor market rigidities have asymmetrically hurt the manufacturing sector. The result is that the manufacturing sector has responded much more tepidly than the services sector to product market liberalization, on which the reforms have focused to date. As Table 6.1 shows, during the first three decades of development ending in 1979/80, services grew more slowly than industry. During the transition decade of the 1980s, they almost caught up. But following the launch of the reforms in 1991, which principally focused on product market liberalization, growth in services decisively outpaced the growth in industry.

In India, manufacturing firms can choose to stay small, with fewer than ten workers (twenty if not using electricity to manufacture their products), or to become larger. If they choose the former, they can escape most of the myriad labor laws. They do not have to offer formal employment contracts and benefits such as paid leave, sick leave, pensions, and health insurance. They can terminate workers without notice and need not provide severance pay. The only major labor law that applies to firms with less than ten workers and becomes applicable at seven or more workers is the Trade Union Act (1926). Under this law, seven

Table 6.1 Average Annual Growth in Broad Sectors By Decades, 1951/52 to 1916/17

Period	Agriculture	Industry	Services	GDP at factor cost
1951/52 to 1959/60	2.7	5.8	4.2	3.6
1960/61 to 1969/70	2.5	6.2	5.2	4.1
1970/71 to 1979/80	1.3	4.3	3.9	2.9
1980/81 to 1989/90	4.4	6.4	6.3	5.7
1990/91 to 1999/2000	3.2	5.8	7.2	5.8
2000/2001 to 2009/10	2.5	7.3	8.8	7.3
2010/11 to 2016/17	3.7	7.1	7.9	7.0

Source: Author's calculations from CSO estimated data.

or more workers can form a trade union. Most Indian firms choose to hire fewer than ten workers, often fewer than seven.

Firms choosing to hire ten (twenty if not using electricity) or more workers must register under the Factories Act (1948) and accept obligations that become increasingly demanding as the size of the workforce rises. The Factories Act itself limits the maximum hours of work per week to forty-eight and overtime hours per quarter to one hundred. It also bans the employment of women for more than nine hours per day and forbids them from working between 7 PM and 6 AM. At 150 workers, a lunchroom must be provided; at 250 workers, there should be a canteen on the factory premises; and at 30 women employees, a daycare center must be made available.

At ten workers, firms must offer health insurance under the Employee State Insurance Act (1948). At twenty workers, they must establish a pension fund for the workers under the Employees Provident Funds and Miscellaneous Provisions Act (1952). At fifty workers, the Industrial Disputes Act (1947) makes reassignment of a worker from one task to another excessively difficult. At one hundred workers, the same act makes termination of a worker, though possible in theory, impossible in practice.

Each of these laws has many more requirements than those mentioned, and there are numerous other labor laws that I have chosen not to list. The central government alone has enacted thirty-three labor laws with which larger enterprises in all states must comply.[4] In addition, each state has its own labor laws. Though the central government laws have been amended over time, the original dates of their passage indicate that many of them were already in place under British rule, and the vast majority of them were already in place by the 1950s.

Therefore, India historically has had a very high level of protection for labor in the formal sector. Even in the 1960s, when the license-permit raj regulated investment allocations with a heavy hand, labor legislation was at par with developed countries. Though some leading scholars recognized the deleterious effects of such inflexibility in labor markets at an early stage of development, little was done to get the right balance between the rights of employees and employers. P. C. Mahalanobis, who is regarded as the architect of India's Second Five-Year Plan and was revered by leading economists of the time as "The Professor," expressed his concern in a 1969 article in these terms:[5]

> However, it seems to me that in certain respects, welfare measures tend to be implemented in India ahead of economic growth, for example, in labor laws which are probably the most highly protective of labor interests, in the narrowest sense, in the whole world. There is practically no link between output and remuneration; hiring and firing are highly restricted. It is extremely difficult to maintain an economic level of productivity, or improve productivity. At early stages of development in all countries there has been a real conflict between welfare measure and economic growth. Japan is an outstanding example; the concept of minimum wages was introduced only about 10 or 12 years ago when per capita income had reached the level of $250 or $300 per year; and minimum wages were fixed more or less at actual average levels. In India with a per capita income of only about $70, the present form of protection of organized labor, which constitutes, including their families, about five or six per cent of the whole population, would operate as an obstacle to growth and would also increase inequalities. It is a serious problem not only in India but in other under-developed countries.

The need to make labor laws more liberal had thus been identified even as early as the 1960s. Yet the populist government of the day did exactly the opposite, making them yet more stringent. An amendment to the Industrial Disputes Act (introduced in 1976 and strengthened in 1982) made it mandatory for an enterprise with one hundred or more workers to seek permission from the labor department with jurisdiction over it before terminating a worker. By convention, such permission is never granted. Therefore, the effect of the amendment is to ban termination of workers by enterprises with one hundred or more regular employees.

There is an acute need to both rationalize and liberalize India's labor laws. In this respect, the current effort to replace the central government's existing thirty-three labor laws with four codes (covering wages, industrial relations, social security and welfare, and safety and work conditions) is a welcome move. These four codes must carry uniform definitions of terms such as "worker," "wages," "industrial dispute," and "retrenchment," and they must be consistent with one another. But it is not sufficient merely to remove definitional inconsistencies from existing laws. The labor laws must be rewritten to make them flexible. In this respect, the wage code, which has already been enacted into law, falls short. Rather than provide for a single minimum wage in any given region, it retains the existing provisions for multiple minimum wages depending on the worker's skill level. It also calls upon the central government to fix separate minimum wages for railways and mines. If the code on industrial relations follows the same approach as the code on wages and organizes existing laws into a single code without liberalizing them, the cause of reform will hardly progress.

The new codes must seek a better balance between the rights of employees and employers. They must ensure that protections for those having regular employment are not kept so high that firms are discouraged from hiring workers in the first place. Giving employers the right to terminate workers with generous severance pay is crucial. Employers need workers as much as workers need employers. But when an occasional worker persistently violates the rules, refuses to perform his duties, and negatively affects the work environment, employers need the power to rectify the situation.

The right to lay off workers is also needed so that firms can have the option to exit. No investment is without risk. Therefore, for any entrepreneur to enter on a large scale in a labor-intensive sector, the right to lay off workers with reasonable severance pay is essential. Anyone who fears that once he hires a large workforce, he will have to pay the wages of those workers even if the venture turns unprofitable will not take such a risk in the first place. The option to exit is a precondition for entry.

It is important to appreciate that the power to lay off workers may not mean much to employers in highly capital-intensive sectors. In such sectors, labor costs are a tiny part of total costs. According to the managing director of one leading two-wheeler manufacturing enterprise, the wage and salary bill for his entire workforce, from himself down to the watchman, is just 4 percent of total sales.[6] Such employers have the ability to give workers golden handshakes when they need to trim the workforce. This is the reason entrepreneurs engaged in large-scale capital-intensive manufacturing do not find Indian labor laws burdensome. By contrast, employers in labor-intensive sectors such as apparel and footwear, where labor costs constitute a disproportionately large part of the total cost, do not have this luxury. The only way they can cope with the onerous laws is by simply staying small.

These arguments apply equally to minimum wage laws. On the surface, setting the minimum wage at a relatively high level seems to be an attractive proposition. What could be so bad about ensuring that workers receive a decent wage? The problem once again is that wages that employers in labor-intensive sectors can pay while still remaining competitive in the global marketplace are significantly lower than what those operating in the capital-intensive sector can afford. With the majority of formal sector employers engaged in capital-intensive production, it is tempting to fix the minimum wage based on their capacity to pay. But those minimum wages can make it unprofitable for employers in sectors in which labor costs are proportionately large.

Another important aspect of minimum wages is that the cost of living varies across regions and between rural and urban areas. Therefore, appropriate minimum wages should be different according to region and whether the business is located in a rural or urban area. One option is to anchor the minimum wage to poverty thresholds that vary across states and between rural and urban areas within each state, responding to differences in the cost of living.

Finally, setting different minimum wages for different levels of skills, as India does, goes against both ethics and economic principles. Ethically, the philosophy behind the minimum wage is to set a base wage sufficient to ensure a socially accepted minimum standard of living. How can such a minimum standard vary according to the worker's level of skill? What sense does it make to say that higher the skill level of the worker, the higher the minimum acceptable living standard for her should be? Because the socially acceptable minimum living standard cannot vary according to skill level, the minimum wage in nearly all countries other than India is set to target unskilled workers.

Good economics says that once the minimum wage for those at the lowest rung of skill ladder has been set, we should let market forces do the remainder of the work. For instance, when the demand for a product using a certain type of engineer declines, salaries of those engineers must be allowed to decline as well. If the minimum wage for those engineers interferes with such a decline, it will only make that sector prematurely unprofitable and force it to shrink through layoffs of engineers.

Enterprises also need the flexibility to reassign workers from one task to another. With technological change, enterprises must often reinvent themselves to survive in the highly competitive marketplace. If they cannot reassign workers to tasks other than those for which they were originally hired, as is the case currently, their production costs rise unduly. The difficulty of exit under such circumstances makes matters worse still.

Before leaving the subject of labor laws, let me point out that the Indian government has taken some steps to make complying with the labor laws easier. It has introduced digital filing of compliances for a number of central labor laws, with enforcement done through random inspections. This change has helped ameliorate the historical excesses of the inspector raj. The government has also permitted the hiring of workers for fixed terms, which allows some flexibility in right-sizing the workforce. And some states have exempted firms with a workforce of up to three hundred workers (instead of one hundred workers) from the ban on the termination of workers. While these are steps in the right direction, much more needs to be done to create a transparent labor market regime that balances the rights of the workers and those of employers.

Land Market Reforms

Setting up a large-scale firm requires a large piece of land. Land ownership in India is fragmented and, with no definitive titles in existence, often in dispute. This fact makes the task of assembling a large piece of land through purchases of numerous small parcels a difficult as well as costly task. With low profit margins in labor-intensive sectors, the high cost of land can quickly make an otherwise profitable enterprise unprofitable.

There are only two viable alternatives under such circumstances. First, the government can step in and acquire land for the enterprise under the Land Acquisition Act (2013). Unfortunately, this law makes acquisition of land by the government for private enterprises extremely difficult and costly. The law needs to be amended to make such acquisition at a reasonable cost possible. The enterprise may still be asked to purchase the bulk of the land, but where ownership is in dispute or other encumbrances exist, the government needs to intervene.

Second, to some extent, the enterprise can reduce its need for land by building the production facility vertically up. Modern apparel factories can be and are built on multiple floors. This option requires flexible floor space index (FSI) rules. Cities and states in India have tended to be stingy in setting the FSI, often keeping it below 2, which means that a factory may have only twice as much floor space as the area of the plot on which it stands. With such a low FSI, it is not feasible to build large-scale factories on limited land area.

Logistics Sector

I have already touched on transportation in the context of trade facilitation. But this important factor needs to be considered in a broader context. Insofar as sources of inputs and destinations of final products are different from the locations of production activity, delivered costs depend on infrastructure. Closely associated with transportation are the other components of logistics: storage, handling, inventory, and packaging. All these activities require development in India. A vibrant logistics sector is critical to the smooth functioning of supply chains. Today, with the development of e-commerce, it is possible for even individual customers to order products from almost any location. This makes the role of a well-functioning logistics sector even more critical.

Rivigo, a start-up that began operations in 2014, is bringing about a major change in this sector. Breaking away from the model of small fleets of trucks, which dominates the Indian scene, it has built a fleet of several thousand trucks. Its relay trucking model, which keeps trucks running 24/7 while allowing truck drivers to return to their homes the same day, has cut delivery time by a significant amount. It is also pioneering innovative advances in storage and handling. This model needs to be replicated on a larger scale. In addition, laws, rules, and regulations that restrict the size of trucking fleets in India need to be reformed.

Potentially, railways could play a significantly greater role in low-cost speedy transportation. In principle, costs of transportation ought to be lower on railways than by road. But the railways are saddled with bureaucratic inefficiencies, which result in delays in delivery, and they have progressively lost ground to road transport. Today, roads account not only for a much larger proportion of freight than they did two decades ago but also for a much higher proportion of passengers.

Concluding Remarks

Numerous reforms are needed to encourage the emergence of medium- and large-scale firms in labor-intensive sectors, especially within manufacturing. Because large firms must operate in the global marketplace, exporting a part of their output while also relying on imports for many of their inputs, the recommended reforms are partially aimed at bringing down the costs directly associated with exports and imports. But lowering these costs alone is not sufficient to ensure the emergence of medium- and large-scale firms. There also remain serious constraints related to labor and land markets and to the uncertainty of taxation, all of which work asymmetrically against these firms. These constraints must be addressed as well.

A necessary accompaniment to industrialization is urbanization. As manufacturing expands and creates attractive jobs, workers exit low-productivity employment in agriculture and migrate to these other jobs. In turn, this migration leads to the expansion of existing cities or creation of new cities. If cities are not prepared to accommodate these migrant workers, manufacturing growth may be choked off. Therefore, it is critical that governments pay particular attention to managing urbanization as manufacturing growth proceeds. This is the subject of Chapter 7.

Notes

1. Panagariya 2019a.
2. Panagariya and Rodrik 1993 offers a formal model showing how commitment to a uniform tariff can lead to a less distortionary tariff within a political economy model.
3. Economic Advisory Council to the Prime Minister 2018.
4. A partial list of these other laws includes the Minimum Wages Act (1948); the Payment of Bonus Act (1965); the Payment of Gratuity Act (1972); the Workmen's Compensation Act (1923); the Industrial Employment (Standing Order) Act (1946); and the Contract Labor (Regulation and Abolition) Act (1970).
5. Mahalanobis 1969, 1121.
6. This was stated by Rajiv Bajaj, managing director of Bajaj Auto, in a live interview on CNBC-TV18 on August 22, 2019. The interview can be found at https://www.cnbctv18.com/auto/automobile-slowdown-rajiv-bajaj-says-industry-must-look-at-its-shortcomings-before-asking-for-stimulus-4220291.htm (accessed on August 26, 2019).

7

Urbanization: Making Room for Migrant Workers

The rapid growth of industry and services within the formal sector invariably results in greater urbanization.[1] This happens either because formal industry and services concentrate in existing urban agglomerations and expand by drawing workers out of agriculture or because their growth turns initially rural and semi-urban habitations into urban spaces. Shanghai, China, which has grown rapidly through migration from other regions during the last three decades, illustrates the former phenomenon. Shenzhen, which grew into an urban agglomeration of 12 million people out of a group of fishing villages with a population of just 300,000 in 1980, represents the latter phenomenon. In either event, expansion of urban spaces is a necessary accompaniment to the creation of good jobs.

Consistent with the low level of growth in formal sector jobs, urbanization has been slow in India. The share of urban population in total population was just 17 percent in 1951 and rose to barely 31 percent in 2011. This growth amounts to a paltry 2.3 percentage points per decade on average. Some observers argue that this slow growth reflects the stricter definition of urbanization that India uses compared with other countries. Adjusting for this factor would raise the rate of urbanization to some degree but would not change the basic fact that urbanization in countries such as Brazil and China has been much faster and that these countries are far more urbanized than India today.

In addition to slow growth in well-paid jobs in industry and services, two factors have contributed to the slow rate of urbanization in India. First, with accelerated growth providing larger revenues, the government has introduced benefits that are available only in rural areas. For example, guaranteed employment for one hundred days for one member of every household under the Mahatma Gandhi National Rural Employment Guarantee Act is available in rural areas only. Food subsidy coverage in rural areas far exceeds that in urban areas. Subsidies for water, electricity, seeds, and fertilizer are available in rural areas only. Direct revenue grants to local bodies mandated by the Finance Commission are available only to rural local bodies, called gram panchayats, and not to municipalities in urban areas. These benefits have discouraged workers from migrating out of rural areas. They have also discouraged gram panchayats from agreeing to reclassify their communities as urban settlements even when such reclassification is warranted by economically relevant parameters.

Second, urban areas themselves have done a poor job of providing cheap rental housing for potential migrants, often leaving slums and spending nights on sidewalks as the only residential options. Low-fare public transportation is also often missing, which denies potential migrants the option to live in low-rent housing in the suburbs and commute to the city for work. This has made an already weak pull effect of decent jobs for aspiring rural migrants weaker still.

Unlike China, where rural-to-urban migration has played a very important role, growth in the urban population in India has been largely the result of natural population growth. Three other contributors to urbanization—the expansion of existing urban areas (urban sprawl), the reclassification of previously rural areas as urban areas, and rural-to-urban migration—have been much less important. The contribution of natural population growth to urban growth was a hefty 62.7 percent during 1981–91 and 59.2 percent during 1991–2001; the rate saw a significant decline during 2001–11 but remained substantial at 44 percent. While the bulk of the shift during the decade 2001–11 represents the reclassification of previously rural areas as urban, migration also saw a small acceleration during this decade. From 22.6 and 21.1 percent during the 1980s and 1990s, respectively, the contribution of migration rose to approximately 24 percent during 2001–11.[2]

The urban population in India has become increasingly concentrated in cities with 100,000 or more people. The number of these cities rose from 77 in 1951 to 468 in 2011, with their share in urban population rising from 45 to 70 percent over the same period. The number of cities with populations of 1 million or more has risen from 5 in 1951 to 53 in 2011, with the corresponding shares in the total urban population rising from 18.9 to 42.6 percent. Eighteen cities have surpassed the 1 million mark during the period 2001–11 alone.

Mumbai and Delhi qualify as megacities, defined as cities with populations of 10 million or more. In 2011, these cities were home to 12.4 and 11 million people, respectively. According to Census 2011, India has three urban agglomerations (cities and their adjoining outgrowths) whose populations exceed 10 million: the greater Mumbai, Delhi, and Kolkata areas, with populations of 18.4, 16.3, and 14.1 million, respectively. Together, these three agglomerations represented 12.9 percent of the total urban population in 2011. Despite the fact that population growth in these agglomerations saw a significant slowdown in the 2000s relative to the 1990s, their combined population grew an impressive 14.8 percent during the 2000s.

Given the crucial role of cities and towns as centers of economic activity and engines of economic transformation, the importance of their orderly growth and the smooth functioning of life in them can scarcely be overestimated.

Unfortunately, however, grossly insufficient attention has been paid to either the development of new cities or the maintenance and orderly expansion of the existing ones. Basic urban services such as housing, water, electricity, sewage systems, solid waste disposal, and transportation are poorly supplied in much of urban India. Indeed, with the vast majority of Indians living in rural areas, the democratic political system has resulted in a general neglect of cities, with their development largely governed by short-term responses to the day-to-day pressures of life.

The Indian Constitution vests much of the power to govern cities and towns, including the power to enact laws for them, in the states. Though urban local bodies such as municipalities and municipal corporations must attend to citizens' daily needs, they lack the power to make rules, raise revenues to finance expenditures, design policies, or do long-term planning in areas of local concern. The state government also controls the budgets of local bodies. Though the 74th Constitutional Amendment Act (1992) mandated self-government for municipalities, the devolution of real power has been at best limited.

Therefore, states have a crucial role in undertaking reforms related to urban India. In the following, I discuss the problems and possible reforms in four key areas relating to cities: availability of space at affordable prices; transportation; provision of public goods such as clean piped water, clean air, well-functioning sewage systems, and proper disposal of solid waste; and the preponderance of slums.

Housing at Affordable Prices

Bigger Indian cities suffer from sprawl and an acute shortage of space within a 10- or 15-kilometer radius around the city center. Sprawl creates distance between where people live and where they work and burdens government with large expenditures for urban infrastructure and transportation. If government fails to provide adequate infrastructure, commuting becomes a nightmare for those working in the city center and living on the periphery. A shortage of space in and around the city center results in an extra-high cost of living and crowding out of all but the wealthiest residents and most profitable businesses.

A comparison of Mumbai and Shanghai best illustrates this shortage. In 2009, Mumbai residents on average had just 4.5 square meters of space per person. In 1984, Shanghai suffered from an even worse space shortage, with only 3.65 square meters per person. But then the municipality of Shanghai decided to make increasing the availability of space its top priority and chose to make liberal use of the only option available: permitting taller and taller buildings. By 2010, the city could boast of having raised the available space to 34 square meters per person.[3]

There are at least seven supply-side factors and one demand-side factor constraining the availability of space in Indian cities that must be addressed.

Urban Land Ceilings and Regulation Act

Under the Indian Constitution, land acquisition is a concurrent-list subject, which means that both the central and state govenrments can enact laws on this subject. The Constitution also mandates that state laws on concurrent-list subjects not be in violation of any central laws. In 1976, the central government had passed the Urban Land Ceilings and Regulation Act (ULCRA) (1976) within which the states passed their own laws for the acquisition of vacant lots exceeding a certain size (500 to 2,000 square meters, depending on the size of the city) at the fire-sale price of 10 rupees per square meter. These laws led to the disappearance of large lots from the market. Many owners of large plots tried to use loopholes in the law to claim exemptions from it. That led the government to take the matter to the courts.

Although the central government and most states have repealed ULCRA, many large pieces of land remain tied up in litigation. The government must find ways to quickly settle these disputes so that these pieces of land can become available and put to appropriate commercial use. If possible, these lots could be auctioned at competitive prices and the proceeds placed in an escrow account. Those funds can then be transferred to the party that eventually wins ownership rights.

Land Owned by Public and Private Sector Enterprises

Many public sector enterprises in India own much larger chunks of land than they need. In many cases this situation stems from the first three or four decades of independence, when land was plentiful and states competed for PSEs by offering them generous amounts of land. For example, many ordnance factories today own land that is ten to twenty times larger than what they actually use.

Additionally, through investment licensing, the central government controlled the location of private sector enterprises. Once again, state governments coveted these enterprises and offered them large chunks of land. Eventually, many of these enterprises became perpetually loss making but found it difficult to exit due to the complexity of bankruptcy laws. Instead, they absndoned the enterprises. The government was left with no option but to declare them "sick"and take them over. Now in possession of the government, these sick enterprises also have large expanses of land. The government should systematically hive off extra land owned by functioning PSEs and sell it to the highest bidder. As regards the sick enterprises in its possesion, it must close them down and sell their entire land to commercial users.

Land Owned by Other Public Entities

Central and state governments own substantial amounts of land that is unused or used in commercially unviable activities. For example, India's ministries for railways, civil aviation, and defense own substantial amounts of urban land that is either unused or subject to encroachment, meaning occupation by squatters. Auctioning off this land not only would put it to better use but also would generate valuable revenues for the government. Claims that the land might be needed in the future should not be permitted to get in the way of this process. Should the government need some of this land in the future, it can reacquire it using its powers under the Land Acquisition Act.

Land Acquisition Act

The Land Acquisition Act (2013) has contributed to the high price of land by mandating that the government pay a multiple of the market price for any land it acquires from private owners. This fact contributes to higher costs for public projects such as affordable housing. The act also makes it difficult for the government to acquire land for private industry. This would not be a problem had land rights been clearly defined in India. But this is not the case, and often parcels of land are subject to a variety of encumbrances. This makes purchasing large chunks of contiguous land extremely challenging for private buyers. The government needs to amend the act appropriately to remove these bottlenecks.

Land Conversion Rules

Stringent conversion rules further contribute to the shortage of urban land. Potentially, cities could expand to accommodate the migrant population by extending their boundaries on the periphery. But this is often a challenge because such land is classified as agricultural and must be reclassified for non-agricultural use. The authority to convert land is usually vested in state revenue departments, which are reluctant to grant approval. State governments could overcome this bottleneck by transferring the powers to grant approval for conversion to the departments responsible for urbanization and making the process of conversion transparent and flexible.

Flexibility is also required in the conversion of existing urban space from one use to another. Efficiency requires that as demand shifts, warehouses can be converted into residential spaces and residential spaces into office spaces or parking lots. In many Indian cities, such conversion can be a serious challenge.

Coastal Regulation Zones

For decades, rules defining Coastal Regulation Zones (CRZs) under the Environmental Protection Act (1986) have obstructed the development of coastal areas within 500 meters of the coastline. There are no similar restrictions in coastal cities in other countries, such as New York, Hong Kong, and Singapore. Coastal land is highly valuable for building properties that would attract high-end tourism. It is also a source of high-value housing that can further help relieve the overall shortage of land. Though the stated objective has been preservation of the coastline and its associated ecosystem, in reality these areas have been subject to encroachment and illegal occupation. A new CRZ notification, issued in 2018, has begun to relax the regulation, but there is need to go further in this direction.

Floor Space Index

In addition to a shortage of land, Indian cities also face constraints in trying to expand the supply of floor space vertically. Cities are notorious for fixing the floor space index—the ratio of floor space permitted in a building to the area of the plot on which the building stands—at very low levels. Other things being the same, a higher FSI allows taller buildings, which leads to the creation of more floor space on a given plot of land. When land is scarce, a high FSI also makes it possible to free up space for the construction of wide roads, aboveground rail-based transit systems, and parks without compromising the availability of living and office space.

A related perverse feature of policy in Indian cities has been that—in complete contrast to the world's well-functioning cities—cities fix FSI at a lower level in the central business district and at higher levels in the periphery. This creates a serious shortage of space in the central business district, which forces the cities to reserve that district for commercial activities only. In turn, this pushes residential units to the periphery, leading to a heavy burden on transport systems and a high human cost in terms of time spent commuting between workplace and home.

According to experts, in most large cities of the world FSI varies from 5 to 15 in the central business district and is around 0.5 or less in the periphery.[4] As technological improvements have made it possible to build safe taller structures, the FSI in most large cities in the central business district has risen over time. A high FSI in the city center allows the development of a vibrant central business district in which businesses can interact efficiently without having to tightly fit into small spaces. As business activity expands, a rising FSI allows the central business district to accommodate more and more businesses without creating congestion. Cities with limited space such as New York, Singapore, and Hong Kong have rebuilt their central business districts many times over by raising the FSI in response to increases in business activity.

Oddly, Indian cities have chosen to ignore this simple, commonsense principle and held the FSI in the central business districts exceptionally low. The FSI in the island city area of Mumbai has stood at a paltry 1.33 since 1991, down from 4.5 in 1964, when the FSI restriction was first introduced. In the suburbs, the FSI drops to 1 with exceptions made in small areas, where it is allowed to rise to 4. The FSI in Delhi is 1.2 and in Pune and Maharashtra just 1.

Black Money and the Demand for Real Estate

An important demand-side factor reinforces the effect of the previously discussed supply-side factors on real estate prices in India. Many wealthy Indians do not declare or only partially declare their income and wealth to tax authorities, in order to evade taxes. The resulting "black" income and wealth cannot be parked in banks for fear of discovery by the tax authorities. Until recently, the natural place to park black wealth has been real estate. This flow of funds further contributes to high real estate prices in urban India.

Luckily, recent actions by the government to combat corruption and black wealth have begun to ameliorate the effect of this factor on real estate prices. For example, the demonetization of 500- and 1,000-rupee notes in November 2016 had a significant and immediate dampening effect on real estate prices. The measure has also led sellers in real estate transactions to begin insisting on payment via formal instruments such as bank check or electronic transfer instead of cash. If this trend holds up, fresh flows of black wealth into real estate will decline considerably.

Another factor helping to arrest the flow of illicit money into real estate is the tightening and improved enforcement of the Benami Transactions (Prohibition) Act (1988) beginning in 2016. This is also helping to ensure greater transparency in transactions in this sector. Continued efforts by the government to enforce laws against black money are required to keep the effect of black wealth on real estate prices in check.

Shortage of Rental Housing

The shortage of urban land, which makes urban housing overly expensive, prevents all but the wealthy from owning housing, especially in and around the central business district, where many middle-class workers have jobs. Unfortunately, these high prices also contribute to a shortage of rental housing. Sadly, given the difficulty of converting agricultural land into urban land, high land prices lead to a shortage of rental housing for middle-class and poor residents even on the periphery of Indian cities.

High housing prices and the limited purchasing power of the middle class and poor lead to low rental yields (return on rental property investment). Rental yields in Mumbai offer an extreme example of this phenomenon: already low at 6 percent of the investment in 2006, they fell to 3.5 percent in 2009 and 1.5 percent in 2011.[5] Today they are perhaps lower still. Such low yields make investment in commercial rental property a losing business. Census data show that the share of rental housing in total housing fell from 54 percent in 1961 to 28 percent in 2011. The problem hits the migrant population hardest, since that group has no accumulated wealth with which to purchase dwellings outright. The outcome is encroachment of publicly owned unoccupied land and creation of slums on it.

Apart from ultra-high land prices, the absence of market-friendly rental laws has also undermined the development of competitive rental markets in India. Traditionally, rental laws in Indian states have been overly friendly to tenants and neglectful of the interests of owners. They cap rents at low levels, eliminating the incentive to properly maintain existing rental units and to invest in new units. With rental leases having no legal standing in most states, eviction of tenants can be a challenge. Worse yet, since India has no ownership titles for dwellings, owners are often afraid that tenants would claim ownership of their units. The result has been that a large number of units remain vacant despite a severe shortage of rental housing. According to Census 2011, 11.09 million units (12.3 percent of the total) were lying vacant with owners unwilling to rent them.

A handful of states including Delhi, Rajasthan, and West Bengal have introduced reforms lifting rent controls for units that rent for more than a given figure, with this threshold rising with the cost of living. Among these states, the law in Rajasthan best balances the rights of tenants and owners. This law was originally introduced in 2001 and applied to divisional headquarters only. It was amended in 2017 to apply to all cities. With the exception of units with rents below a threshold level, the law allows the potential tenant and owner full freedom to determine the rent. The threshold level for excluded units varies between 2,000 and 7,000 rupees per month, depending on the city in which the unit is located. Within this range, the threshold rises with the cost of living in the city. The law also provides for eviction of the tenant upon failure to pay rent for four months. Laws in Delhi and West Bengal are less liberal, linking permitted rent to the market value of the property, but they are steps in the right direction.

Introduction of liberal tenancy laws that protect the lessor's ownership rights and allow her to charge market rent would bring many currently empty dwelling units onto the market. This will go some distance toward easing housing problem in urban India. But solving the problem fully, especially creating low-rent housing for the poor, will require the expansion of urban land, a generous floor space index, and brakes on the flow of black money into real estate so that land prices and, consequently, rental yields come to be better aligned with interest rates.

To avoid the creation of slums, it is also important to establish conditions under which dormitory housing can be created for migrant workers. Many states treat such housing as commercial hotels and subject them to water and electricity tariffs and property taxes at commercial rates. This leads to high rents on dormitory housing, pushing its cost out of the reach of most migrants, who then seek cheaper alternatives in slums. States that serve as significant destinations for migrant workers should consider adopting more rational policies toward low-end dormitory housing.

Urban Transportation

Poorly functioning transportation networks contribute to inefficient use of valuable space. Absent well-functioning transportation networks, workers must live close to their workplace. This leads to the use of a sizable amount of scarce space in the city center and around it for housing. Ceteris paribus, the outcome is slums and a very small amount of space per individual in the city center. The problem becomes progressively worse as development proceeds and the demand for office space in the city center rises. In cities with low-price public transportation networks such as New York City and London, workers are able to live in spacious homes in the suburbs and commute to work in the city center.

Designing transportation systems for cities is a specialized field. Therefore, the following discussion is limited to some basic issues in urban transportation. I divide it into two parts: transportation services for the existing urban population and using transportation as a tool for future urbanization. In the first part, transportation follows urbanization; in the second, it leads urbanization.

Transportation for the Existing City Population

In a nutshell, the urban transportation problem has two aspects. The first is building a rapid transit system that connects distant points of urban agglomerations to the city center and with each other. The second is providing last-mile connectivity, especially in and around the center. In India, basic transportation service in and around city centers has existed in most major cities for a long time. But rapid transit systems are of more recent origin.

Rapid transit systems have deployed both buses and rail. A successful example of a bus-based rapid transit system is the Bus Rapid Transit System (BRTS) in Ahmedabad. By the end of 2017, it had 89 kilometers of dedicated corridor and a daily ridership of 350,000 passengers. The most successful example of a rail-based system is Delhi Metro. As of early 2019, it was 373 kilometers long, connected Delhi to its satellite cities, and had a daily ridership of 2.5 million. While bus-based systems are significantly less costly for major cities, riders find rail-based systems more comfortable. Bigger cities in India, including Delhi, Mumbai, Kolkata, Chennai, Bengaluru, and Hyderabad, have opted for rail-based systems.

In-city transportation remains a challenge in most cities in India. Traffic jams and delays on roads in major cities are endemic. While a high volume of traffic and a limited number of lanes are partially to blame, lack of enforcement of traffic rules also makes a significant contribution to these delays. Drivers do not follow traffic rules, especially those relating to staying in and changing lanes, which slows down everyone. Stricter enforcement of traffic rules can yield significant gains in speeding up movement. This would also help cut carbon emissions, since traffic congestion ends up contributing substantial volumes to such emissions.

One further challenge of urban transportation in India is the design and maintenance of city roads. Roads are often pedestrian-unfriendly, narrow, and poorly surfaced. Frequent and prolonged digging up of roads to resurface or repair them adds to delays. One factor contributing to the narrowness of roads is the highly restrictive floor space index in most Indian cities. This has meant that every inch of available land is coveted for some use, with space for public projects, mainly roads, becoming the main victim. Cities need to adopt more generous FSIs and use those increases to negotiate the freeing up of some land for road infrastructure. There is also a need for better planning and design of roads, with standardized lane widths, sidewalks for pedestrians, and utilities routed under sidewalks, along with better coordination between utilities providing electricity, water, and cable services and those responsible for building city roads.

Transportation Network to Promote Urbanization

Transport infrastructure, in particular roads, can play a critical role in promoting future urbanization. There are three major ways to accomplish this objective. First, cities can build roads and related infrastructure on their outer peripheries in advance to attract industrial and commercial activity. In addition to catalyzing industrialization and urbanization, such infrastructure may also help relieve congestion along major arteries passing through the city. An example of this approach is the 159-kilometer-long Hyderabad outer ring project, which connects the existing townships around the city. It has created the potential for growth and the development of new satellite townships focused around business parks and technology clusters along a growth corridor of a kilometer on each side of the road. The ring road also connects to various state and national highways, which allows through traffic to avoid having to enter the city and deal with congestion.

The Delhi-Mumbai Industrial Corridor (DMIC) project illustrates the second approach to catalyzing industrial growth and urbanization. This is a far more ambitious approach and requires cooperation between the central government and multiple state governments. The project involves the construction of a 1,483-kilometer-long dedicated freight corridor passing through Delhi, Haryana, Rajasthan, Uttar Pradesh, Gujarat, and Maharashtra. In addition to the freight line, the DMIC project includes nine enormous industrial zones of 200 to 250 square kilometers each, three ports, six airports, and a six-lane intersection-free expressway connecting Delhi and Mumbai.[6] The main shortcoming of this approach is that it requires massive investment, and any positive return may take decades to appear. It is perhaps wiser to break up such projects into multiple smaller projects and implement them in such a way that returns do not have to wait till the entire project is complete.

Building all-weather rural roads that connect villages to nearby urban centers is the third and final approach to using transportation as a means to promote urbanization. Road connectivity allows village residents to exploit urban markets more fully as buyers as well as sellers. Increased exposure to city life may eventually lead some village residents to begin locating their business and commercial activities in the cities and migrate to them.

Clean Piped Water, Clean Public Spaces, and Clean Air

With the share of urban population predicted to increase significantly over the next decade, India needs to address three key problems associated with urban life. First, after more than seventy years of independence, most Indian cities still lack a continuous supply of piped water. Second, poor management of solid waste, sewage, and drainage means that the threat of the spread of communicable diseases remains omnipresent, becoming especially acute in the rainy season. Finally, with increased industrialization and the growth in the use of fossil fuels that accompanies rising incomes, the air in most cities is polluted to dangerous levels, posing a serious threat to health, especially for children.

There are four problems associated with piped water. First, not all households receive piped water. According to Census 2011, only 71 percent of urban households had drinking water taps located within the premises. Going by the findings of a 2012 NSO survey, a significant minority of these households had piped water coming to their yards or plots but not the dwelling.[7]

Second, most households with water pipes in their homes do not receive a continuous supply of water. In most cases, local utilities supply water for a few hours per day, and on some days they may not supply it at all. As a result, households that can afford it keep water tanks that they fill during the hours when water is supplied. This means that even if local utilities supply properly treated water, it may get contaminated while stored in the tank.

Third, often water pressure in taps is low. This leads households to install booster pumps, which is a socially wasteful use of resources—both an unnecessary investment in equipment and a waste of energy. Additionally, when a few residents install booster pumps, water pressure for the remaining residents drops further, forcing them to install booster pumps as well.

Finally, most urban households in India are leery of drinking water straight out of the tap for fear that it is contaminated. The result is that households that can afford it get costly filtering and treatment devices installed in their kitchens to ensure that water they drink and use in cooking is safe. Many choose to drink exclusively bottled water. Those unable to afford either filtering equipment or bottled water end up drinking tap water directly; they risk becoming sick more frequently, for which they must pay later in terms of the cost of medical treatment and lost workdays.

According to newspaper reports, the government has made the bold decision to bring piped water to all households in rural and urban areas by the year 2024. This is an ambitious goal but one that the present government is capable of achieving. What will also be necessary, however, is to improve water governance to ensure that households receive an uninterrupted water supply seven days a week. Supply interruptions result in the contamination of even a treated water supply, for two reasons. One, when the water supply is interrupted, contaminants get into the water supply due to low pressure, backflows, and physical faults in the pipeline. And two, when the water supply is intermittent, households resort to storing water in tanks for use during hours when water is not supplied, and water stored in tanks is prone to contamination. Governance of the water supply remains one of the most difficult problems, and few developing countries have solved it satisfactorily in the early stages of development. India, therefore, is likely to continue to face major challenges in this area.

The level of cleanliness in public spaces in Indian cities remains poor along nearly all dimensions. The Swachchh Bharat Mission (SBM), or Clean India Mission, has made a major push toward improving cleanliness in public spaces, with some success. But this remains a work in progress. Achieving greater cleanliness would require efforts in three areas: sewage systems, drainage, and solid waste management. According to the 2011 Census, 19.6 percent of urban households lacked toilets within the premises and had to use public facilities. This proportion has perhaps fallen considerably in the wake of SBM, but continued progress in this area would still be required. Many public toilets lack a water supply, and many are not connected to the city's sewage system.

A related problem in Indian cities is drainage. Only 44.5 percent of urban households are connected to closed drainage, and another 37.3 percent are connected to open drainage. This still leaves 18.2 percent of the households without any connection to drainage. Following the launch of SBM, these indicators have likely improved, but there can be little doubt that much progress will be needed if Indian cities are to be made healthy places to live.

Even when drainage and sewage systems exist in India, they are poorly maintained. With rising consumption levels, the amount of solid waste is rising, and its poor management has the serious side effect of clogging drainage systems. Solid waste littered in public spaces gets into drains during rains and blocks them. The result is that raw sewage often overflows into the open, creating unsanitary conditions on roads and sidewalks and around residential areas. With clogged drains, even minor rains result in standing bodies of water everywhere, bringing cities to a standstill. Cities such as Hyderabad and Mumbai have been well known for these problems.

Per capita solid waste in India remains low even in comparison to many developing countries. But this is changing rapidly with rising incomes and consumption levels, and waste management is failing to keep pace. Often households and businesses dump garbage at nearby dump sites from which collection is infrequent. There has been at best a limited effort to instill a sense of civic responsibility, so individuals often feel free to dispose of small pieces of trash outside their homes, shops, and businesses. As a result, piles of trash, which are an eyesore, are common in Indian cities.

Solid waste management is almost entirely a local issue, with municipalities and municipal corporations having primary responsibility for it. Arguably, this is the most important function with which these bodies are entrusted. Unfortunately, few municipalities have enough finances, managerial capacity, and technical knowhow to carry out this function effectively. Within the context of overall management of services in local jurisdictions, waste management also gets lower priority than water and sanitation.

The third cleanliness-related challenge in Indian cities is air pollution. Major Indian cities are among the most polluted in the world. Air pollution is measured by the average annual concentration of particulate matter in micrograms per cubic meter of air. Particles whose concentration is commonly measured to gauge pollution are those smaller than 2.5 micrometers and those between 2.5 and 10 micrometers and are referred to as PM2.5 and PM10, respectively. Particulates can penetrate deep into the lungs and bloodstream and cause permanent DNA mutations, heart attacks, and respiratory diseases. Studies show that there is no safe level of particulates, and even starting from low levels, increases in them can raise the risk of lung cancer by a proportionately large amount. The smaller PM2.5 particulates are particularly deadly.

According to the latest available data compiled by the World Health Organization and released in 2018, going by the annual mean PM2.5 concentrations, nine of the ten most polluted cities in the world are in India. Arranged from most to least polluted, these cities are Kanpur, Faridabad, Gaya, Varanasi, Patna, Delhi, Lucknow, Agra, and Gurgaon. Another four cities are among the next ten most polluted. According to declining pollution levels, they are Muzaffarpur, Jaipur, Patiala, and Jodhpur.

The four most important sources of air pollution in India are industries, transportation, construction, and agricultural stubble burning. Each of these factors is directly related to economic growth. Industrialization is an essential element in rapid growth. Rising incomes lead to increased demand for both personal and business transportation. Enhanced construction activity is both the source and consequence of growth. Finally, with growth, cities expand their boundaries, and the distance between them and the countryside, where most farming takes place, declines. In countries with rising population and incomes, the need for agricultural production rises as well. Both factors work toward making cities more vulnerable to pollutants released by stubble burning, which is the lowest-cost means for preparing the farmland for the next crop.

Technical solutions to the problems of clean water, clean public spaces, and clean air have been widely discussed, and we need not go into them in detail here. The real challenge is efficient management and governance. The challenge is multiplied by the fact that within the Indian federal system, city administration is principally under the jurisdiction of the state and to a lesser degree municipal governments. The central government can play at best the role of catalyst for change. For instance, the central government has decided to bring piped water to every household in the next five years, as previously noted. While it may successfully lay down the pipelines connecting water sources to individual households, maintaining water reservoirs and pipelines, ensuring the continuous flow of water, and monitoring water quality will remain the responsibilities of state and possibly municipal governments.[8]

Slums: Rehabilitation and Redevelopment

Slums have been a feature of all major cities during the early phase of urbanization. A quick search on the Internet yields photographs and descriptions of nineteenth-century slums in London, Paris, and New York that would make many modern-day slums in the developing countries look like palaces by comparison. Indian cities are no exception. A sizable proportion of the population of most major Indian cities lives in slums.

There is no standard definition of slums in India. They go by different names in different regions such as "Jhuggi-Jhonpadi" in Delhi, "Jhonpadpatti" and "Chawl" in Mumbai and "Cheris" in Chennai. At the national level, the Slums Area Improvement and Clearance Act (1956) defines slums as residential areas where dwellings are unfit for human habitation by reasons of dilapidation, overcrowding, narrowness of streets, lack of ventilation, light and sanitation or a combination of these factors that are detrimental to health and safety. In addition to this central legislation, many states have their own legislations with their own definitions of slums. Based on these defintions, states, union territories or local governemnts recognize certain residential areas as slums and list them in a register. Eventually, many of these "registered" slums are formally "notified" as slums under some slum act.

Fo purposes of counting slums and individuals and families living in them, Census 2011 adopts this classification and augments it by identifying an additional category of slums that states have not yet recognized. Accordingly, it divides slums into three categories: notified, registered, and identified. Slums in the first category are areas that a state, union territory, or local government has notified as slums under a slum act. Those in the second category are areas that one of these same entities has recognized but not notified as slums. An identified slum is a compact area "of at least 300 population or about 60–70 households of poorly built congested tenements, in unhygienic environment usually with inadequate infrastructure and lacking in proper sanitary and drinking water facilities."[9] Slums in this last category are identified by Cesnus of India staff and require inspection by an officer nominated by the Directorate of Census Operations. The census data reported below include slums in all three categories.

Generally, slums begin to form in a city with migrant workers hired to work on industrial or construction projects locating themselves in temporary dwellings on nearby empty land, often owned by the government. Once a few workers have located themselves in these temporary settlements, their relatives and friends looking for employment in the city join them. Over time, small settlements grow into slums. In a democratic country, a sufficiently long stay in these settlements leads to the conferment of voting rights that impart considerable political clout to slum dwellers. Of course, slums need not always acquire permanence. If the land on which they are located becomes valuable, its owner, usually a government entity, decides to reclaim it. In such situations, slum residents must relocate, a process that can be complicated and painful for both the government and the residents.

According to Census 2011, 63 percent of 4,041 statutory towns have one or more slums.[10] One-fifth of these slums are in Maharashtra alone. India-wide, 13.8 million households—representing 17.4 percent of all urban households and accounting for 64 million people—live in slums. Among the original fifteen largest states, Andhra Pradesh and Madhya Pradesh have the highest proportion of population living in slums and Assam, Kerala and Gujarat have the lowest proportion of population in slums. Mumbai has a gigantic 41.3 percent of its households living in slums (Table 7.1).

Going by Census 2011 data, differences between the average living conditions of slum-dwelling and non-slum-dwelling urban populations do not appear large. In Table 7.2, we show the distribution of slum households and all urban households across types of housing, by the number of rooms in the house, and by ownership. The most glaring difference is that almost 45 percent of slum households live in dwellings of one room, compared with 32 percent for the urban population as a whole.

Next, consider the distribution of slum households and all urban households according to basic amenities such as the source of drinking water, lighting availability, and type of drainage and toilet facilities. I show the main indicators, as per Census 2011, in Table 7.3. With respect to drinking water, the main difference is that proportionately far fewer slum households have a water tap on the premises. Access to electricity for lighting is remarkably similar. Availability of drainage is also similar, with the difference that slums have greater exposure to open drains. Even access to banking is not alarmingly different. The key area of significant difference with serious health implications is access to proper toilets. Here slum dwellers lag by a good 15 percentage points.

Finally, let me turn to the distribution of some basic assets across households in slums and the general urban population. Table 7.4 provides the relevant data from Census 2011. The pattern previously observed carries over to these assets. Slum dwellers lag behind their non-slum counterparts, but not dramatically so. Every tenth slum household (as opposed to every fifth urban household) has a computer. Some own a car, jeep, or van. Every fifth slum household has a scooter, motorcycle, or moped.

Table 7.1 Proportion of Urban Households in Slum Areas, 2011

Location	Percentage of urban households in slums
India (entire)	17.4
States with highest proportions of urban households in slums	
Andhra Pradesh	35.7
Chhattisgarh	31.9
Madhya Pradesh	28.3
Orissa	23.1
West Bengal	21.9
States with lowest proportion of urban households in slums	
Gujarat	6.7
Jharkhand	5.3
Assam	4.8
Kerala	1.5
Five largest metro areas by population	
Greater Mumbai (municipal corp.)	41.3
Kolkata (municipal corp.)	29.6
Chennai (municipal corp.)	28.5
Delhi (municipal corp.)	14.6
Bangalore (municipal corp.)	8.5
Cities with populations over 1 million that have the highest proportion of urban households in slums	
Greater Visakhapatnam (municipal corp.)	44.1
Jabalpur (cantonment board)	43.3
Greater Mumbai (municipal corp.)	41.3
Vijayawada (municipal corp.)	40.6
Meerut (municipal corp.)	40.0
Raipur (municipal corp.)	39.0
Nagpur (municipal corp.)	34.3
Greater Hyderabad (municipal corp.)	31.9
Kota (municipal corp.)	31.8
Agra (municipal corp.)	29.8

Source: Author's construction from slides 15, 17, and 18 in Chandramouli 2011.

Table 7.2 Distribution of Households in Slums and Urban Population by Housing Type and Ownership, 2011

Housing type, number of rooms, and ownership status	Percentage in urban areas	Percentage in slums
Type of housing		
Permanent	84.3	77.7
Semi-permanent	11.6	16.0
Temporary	3.2	5.3
Any other	0.9	1.0
Number of rooms		
No exclusive room	3.1	4.4
One room	32.1	44.8
Two rooms	30.6	29.5
Three rooms	18.4	12.3
Four rooms	9.3	5.4
Five rooms and above	6.5	3.5
Ownership status		
Owned	69.2	70.2
Rented	27.5	26.3
Other	3.3	3.5

Source: Author's construction from slides 22, 25, and 28 in Chandramouli 2011.

This bright picture of slums must be tempered by the recognition of potentially large quality differences. A permanent house need not mean a well-built house. Counting rooms may mislead because rooms may differ in size and in the quality of their walls and floor. Electricity brought into the house through an exposed wire is not the same as that brought in through proper wiring and available to run various appliances, including air conditioners. A television may be small and bought used for as little as $100 or a large modern one selling for over $1,000. The same goes for computers, motorcycles, and cars.

Even more important, slums are characterized by the generally poor availability of most public services. Streets are poorly lit, the road infrastructure is not well built and maintained, and connectivity to sewage lines is often missing. Streets and alleys are narrow and dingy. When combined with poor access to

Table 7.3 Proportion of Households in Slums and Urban Population as a Whole with Access to Basic Amenities, 2011

Amenity	Percentage in urban areas	Percentage in slums
Source of drinking water		
Tap	70.6	74.0
From treated source	62.0	65.3
From untreated source	8.6	8.7
Well	6.2	3.0
Hand pump	11.9	12.7
Tube well/borehole	8.9	7.6
Other sources	2.5	2.8
Location of drinking water source		
Within premises	71.2	56.7
Outside premises	28.8	43.3
Source of lighting		
Electricity	92.7	90.5
Kerosene	6.5	8.2
Solar	0.2	0.3
Other oil	0.1	0.2
Any other	0.2	0.2
No lighting	0.3	0.5
Drainage connectivity		
Closed drainage	44.5	36.9
Open drainage	37.3	44.3
No drainage	18.2	18.8
Type of latrine facility		
Latrine within the premises	81.4	66.0
Flush toilet	72.6	57.7
Pit latrine	7.1	6.2
Other latrine	1.7	2.2
No latrine within premises	18.6	34.0
Public latrine	6.0	15.1
Open	12.6	18.9
Banking services		
Available	67.8	53.2
Not available	32.2	46.8

Source: Author's construction from slides 29, 31, 33, 36, 37 and 40 in Chandramouli 2011.

Table 7.4 Proportion of Households in Slums and Urban Population as a Whole Having Various Assets, 2011

Asset	Urban	Slum
Radio/transistor radio	25.3	18.7
Television	76.7	69.6
Computer	18.7	10.4
With internet	8.3	3.3
Without internet	10.4	7.1
Telephone	82.0	72.7
Landline only	5.9	4.4
Mobile only	64.3	63.5
Both	11.7	4.8
Bicycle	41.9	40.2
Scooter/motorcycle/moped	35.2	22.0
Car/jeep/van	9.7	3.6
None of the specified assets	7.0	10.7

Source: Author's construction from slides 42 and 44 in Chandramouli 2011.

toilet facilities and infrequent collection of solid waste, these features make the environment in slums unhygienic.

The policy question that nearly all state governments must confront is what they can do to improve the lot of slum dwellers and city life as a whole. Before considering the policy options, it is perhaps useful to explain the complexity of the problem and the limits of what policy can do. Three points in particular are worthy of mention.

First, it is unrealistic to think that city, state, and central governments can eliminate the slums anytime soon. As of 2011, 64 million people, constituting 17.4 percent of the country's urban population, lived in slums, as mentioned earlier. Moreover, the slum population is concentrated in certain cities, so the proportions in many cities are much higher. The cities with the greatest populations, over 10 million, have 30 percent or more of their households living in slums. Moving nearly one-third of the households to alternative housing within a short period is not a minor task in a country where local governments are often dysfunctional.

Second, slums are not merely places of residence but also centers of economic activity. This is particularly true of larger slums in which households sell the goods and services they produce to each other as well as to outsiders, including customers abroad. In these cases, moving slum dwellers to alternative locations may involve the loss of their livelihood, further complicating such movement.

Finally, if the Indian economy grows at a rate of 7 percent per year or higher over the next two to three decades, as is very likely, there is bound to be massive rural-urban migration. Moreover, such migration will concentrate in the larger cities, including some new ones that will form in the forthcoming decades. As long as migrants are poor and transportation costly, preventing the formation of new slums near the workplace is going to be a losing battle.

This is not unlike the immigration problem in the United States. Conferring citizenship on illegal migrants is often viewed as a solution to the problem of illegal migration. But before the system is able to make a decision and process the existing illegal migrants, more of them arrive from a border that remains porous despite tougher enforcement.

Given these facts, governments at various levels need to take a long-term approach to the eventual elimination of slums. The objective should be to reduce the incidence of slums gradually through their redevelopment for better in-situ housing, relocation of slum-dwellers to alternative locations and measures that would minimize the formation of new slums. The policy needs to be multi-pronged and adaptable to the specific circumstances of each slum. With these observations as the context, in the following I briefly summarize various elements of the policy.

First, various measures discussed earlier to relieve land shortages must form an integral part of the overall policy package. Land shortages (created by such measures as the passage of ULCRA in 1976, complex laws governing the conversion of land from one usage to another, and low floor space index) and building material shortages (created by the license permit raj in such critical industries as cement and steel) have created a shortage of urban housing and encouraged the proliferation of slums. Rental laws and rent controls, which afflicted almost all major cities until recently and remain unduly tilted in favor of tenants despite reforms during the last decade, have worked in the same direction. State governments must take all steps necessary to relieve land shortages to pave the way for a reasonably priced housing supply to emerge.

Second, a well-functioning transportation system, including a rapid transit service, forms an important part of the policy to discourage the formation and growth of slums as well as phase out existing slums through rehabilitation. As their incomes rise, slum dwellers themselves want to move out to better neighborhoods where they can rear their children in healthier surroundings. But this is only possible if they can find affordable housing in locations from which they can commute to work. A well-functioning transportation system can speed up such transitions. The government's own proactive efforts to relocate slum dwellers in alternative locations have a greater chance of success as well if the city has a good transportation system.

Third, it is essential that the ability of local governments to deliver basic public services such as water, sewage lines, electricity, solid waste removal, road connectivity, and streetlights is greatly enhanced. If these services cannot be adequately supplied, any attempts at redevelopment of slums for more attractive in-situ housing or relocation of slum-dwellers to distant locations, cannot succeed. Any alternative housing must have multiple floors and must have adequate provision of water, sewage lines, and electricity. If water pressure is low, residents must install pumps, which is costly, as we have seen. If electricity is not supplied with regularity, elevators will not function and residents on the upper floors will be subject to undue hardships. And, of course, a proper sewage system is essential to improving the quality of slum dwellers' lives. Additionally, the relevant government departments also have to be able to build basic infrastructure, including roads and streetlights, in residential developments.

Finally, a proactive policy of relocation of slum-dwellers to alternative housing and redevelopment of slums is required. When a slum is located on land that cannot be used for housing, whether for reasons of safety or because it must be used for another public project, relocation of slum dwellers is the only option. For instance, when the Gujarat government decided to undertake the Sabarmati River Front Development project, it had no choice but to move slum dwellers along the riverbanks to alternative locations. Similar issues may also arise on safety grounds, such as when the slum is located too close to a road or railway line. Sometimes even when slum land can be used for housing, some residents and the government may find relocation more attractive.

In most cases, however, experience has shown that as long as slum land is available for housing, in-situ redevelopment of hosuing works better. Dwellers do not want to move away from their workplaces, and they predominantly work near the slums in which they live. As a result, efforts during the last two decades have focused on how best to redevelop slum housing. The dominant model in the largest slum in India, Dharavi, has been to build taller buildings, which allows some land to be reclaimed while allowing the builder to recover costs through the sale of some units on the open market. The effort began in the mid-1990s, but success so far has been at best partial because of the inability of the system to effectively provide basic amenities such as water, drainage, and sanitation. There have also been issues with the cost of running elevators in multi-story buildings.

Slum redevelopment will remain a work in progress for some time to come. One thing governments may try is to focus first on smaller slums, where the scale and complexity are less challenging than in a gigantic slum like Dharavi. Additionally, a greater focus on relieving the land shortage, raising the floor space index in general, building transportation infrastructure (including rapid transit systems), and improving the ability of local governments to effectively deliver water, electricity, and sanitation services may go some distance toward offering slum dwellers alternative options.

Concluding Remarks

The growth of industry and services is intimately linked with urbanization. Urban centers are often homes to growth in industrial and service enterprises. At the same time, growth in industry and services promotes urbanization. In part this happens through migration of rural workers to industry and services located in urban centers. But it also happens through the conversion of previously rural areas into urban zones when industrial activity begins to concentrate in rural areas, as has been the case with Shenzhen in China, which consisted of fishing villages in the late 1970s but has become one of the most vibrant urban centers in the world today.

Given the crucial importance of urbanization in the transition from an agrarian economy to a modern industrial one, I have discussed policies conducive to healthy growth of urban centers in this chapter. I have identified four closely linked components of urban development: availability of land; provision of water supply, sewage systems, drainage, and solid waste management; transportation; and relocation of slum dwellers to alternative locations and redevelopment of slums for better in-situ housing. In order for urbanization to proceed smoothly and for urban residents to have healthy lives, economic policy and reforms must be aimed at progress in each of these four areas. Because of interconnections among these components, progress in one area can make progress in another easier. By the same token, a bottleneck in one area can create bottlenecks in others.

States can work on many fronts to alleviate land shortages. These include repeal of the Urban Land Ceilings and Regulation Act in both letter and spirit; raising the floor space index; provision of legal titles to property; rental laws that balance the rights of tenants and landlords; and reform of laws governing the conversion of land and property from one use to another. Of particular importance is for local and state administrations to understand the importance of a floor space index significantly higher than it is currently, administered transparently on a uniform basis . Equally important is to allow rapid conversion of land and property from one use to another. Efficient use of space requires that warehouses and apartment buildings can be converted into office buildings, shops, and parking lots as demand shifts. Likewise, transparent laws must exist for the conversion of agricultural land on the periphery of a city into living and office space.

Transportation infrastructure complements the measures necessary to alleviate land shortages in an essential way. Conversely, the transportation network can expand more rapidly as land shortages are alleviated. A well-functioning rapid transit system means that workers can reside outside the city and avail themselves of cheaper rents and a cleaner environment. For this reason, as cities grow and the demand for offices in the city center grows, the need for a rapid transit system grows. We have described two successful experiments in this area from which other cities can learn: rail-based Delhi Metro and the Bus Rapid Transit System in Ahmedabad.

As many as 64 million individuals, constituting 17.4 percent of the urban population, live in slums in India, according to Census 2011. As living spaces, these slums remain highly deficient. Access to sewage systems is poor, leading slum dwellers to resort to open defecation. Access to electricity exists, but often through exposed wiring. Public services such as roads and streetlights outside living spaces are poorly supplied as well. All these factors point to the need for relocation of slum dwellers to other locations and redevelopment of slums for beter in-situ housing. This chapter has made several suggestions based on experience to date.

There remain complex issues relating to water supply, sanitation, drainage, solid waste disposal, and air pollution. Indian cities are very far behind in each of these areas. Availability of a 24/7 supply of piped water remains a rarity; sanitation and drainage are poor, with even mild rains leading to the flooding of roads and streets; and solid waste disposal is in its infancy. There are important governance issues surrounding each of these services. These problems are often local, while all the decision-making authority rests at the level of the state. Without the states cooperating with local bodies and at least partially devolving financial and administrative powers to them, arriving at satisfactory solutions will remain a challenge.

Ultimately, industrialization and urbanization cannot proceed smoothly without well-functioning financial markets. Medium and large firms, which are critical to rapid manufacturing growth, must necessarily operate in the formal sector and depend on a vibrant financial sector for investment resources. Likewise, as urban populations prosper, their need for finance to purchase houses, automobiles, and other durable goods rises. Government agencies and local urban bodies also depend on capital markets for financial resources. While India has achieved considerable progress in building its financial sector since the launch of reforms in 1991, a lot more remains to be done. Accordingly, Chapters 8 and 9 focus on this important sector.

Notes

1. This chapter adapts and updates chapter 7 of Panagariya, Chakraborty, and Rao 2014. The latter offers additional details on reforms at state and local levels in areas such as piped water supply, sewage and waste management.
2. Planning Commission 2011, chart 1.5, for estimates relating to 1981–91 and 1991–2001. Estimates relating to 2001–11 are from a presentation entitled "India's Urban Demographic Transition" by the National Institute of Urban Affairs, available at http://www.urbanindia.nic.in/UDataResource/CensusResult_2011.pdf (accessed on May 11, 2013).
3. Bertraud 2011.
4. Bertraud 2011.
5. Ministry of Housing and Urban Poverty Alleviation 2015, 12–13.
6. For further details, visit the DMIC website, http://delhimumbaiindustrialcorridor.com.
7. National Statistical Office 2014, 17, table 3.1.
8. For further details on what needs to be done at state and municipal levels, see Panagariya, Chakraborty, and Rao 2014, chapter 7.
9. See http://censusindia.gov.in/2011-Circulars/Circulars/Circular-08.pdf.
10. Statutory towns are places with municipalities, municipal corporations, cantonment boards, or notified town area committees.

8

Investing Productively: The Securities Market

Capital is usually scarcer in developing countries than in developed ones. Given this, the opportunity cost of its misallocation is higher in the former than in the latter. For this reason alone, it may be argued that financial markets are at least as important in developing countries as in developed countries. Yet they tend to be neglected in the former, especially in the early stages of development.

Reinforcing the scarcity factor is the large dispersion in the rates of return on investments in different enterprises within the same narrowly defined sectors in these countries. Rates of return in production units within the same sector show much greater variation in developing countries than in developed ones. Therefore, governments cannot promote high-return investments without simultaneously promoting low-return ones when they protect or subsidize entire sectors.

What is required, instead, is assignment of priority at the level of the enterprise. Within each sector, support must be provided to enterprises and projects with high returns. But this is possible on an economy-wide basis only if financial markets, which can separate projects and enterprises with high return from those with low return, are well developed. In competitive financial markets, lenders can survive only if they lend on high-return, low-risk projects. Therefore, they have a vested interest in developing expertise in evaluating projects and selecting those yielding high-returns. Governments cannot perform this task.

Financial System: An Overview

The subject of financial markets is extremely wide, technical, and specialized. Therefore, I do not venture to spell out detailed reforms in all areas of financial markets. Instead, I pick and choose some key areas while only flagging others. To help the reader understand this technical subject in terms that are as simple as possible, I devote the first half of this chapter to an overview of the financial system. In the second half, I discuss capital markets. I take up the banking sector, the backbone of the financial system, in Chapter 9.

The financial system consists of a set of markets, organizations, and individuals that engage in borrowing or lending funds via different instruments, including bank credit, stocks, bonds, commercial paper, and instruments derived from these. It also includes regulatory institutions that define and implement the rules governing the transactions. The basic function of the financial system is to channel surplus funds from one set of units in the economy to another set of units facing a deficit of funds. Actors in the former category are called savers or lenders, and those in the latter category are called spenders or borrowers.

Figure 8.1 provides a schematic chart to describe the financial system. The chart has deliberately been kept simple, but it provides a useful introduction to the main components of the financial system. In principle, lenders can include households whose current income exceeds their current expenditure; businesses that may generate more profits than they invest in their own enterprises; government entities that spend less than their revenues; and foreign entities that have funds they wish to lend to entities in the financial system. Symmetrically, borrowers include households whose current income falls short of expenditures; businesses that want to invest or spend more than they earn in profits; government entities that run a fiscal deficit; and foreign entities that want to borrow

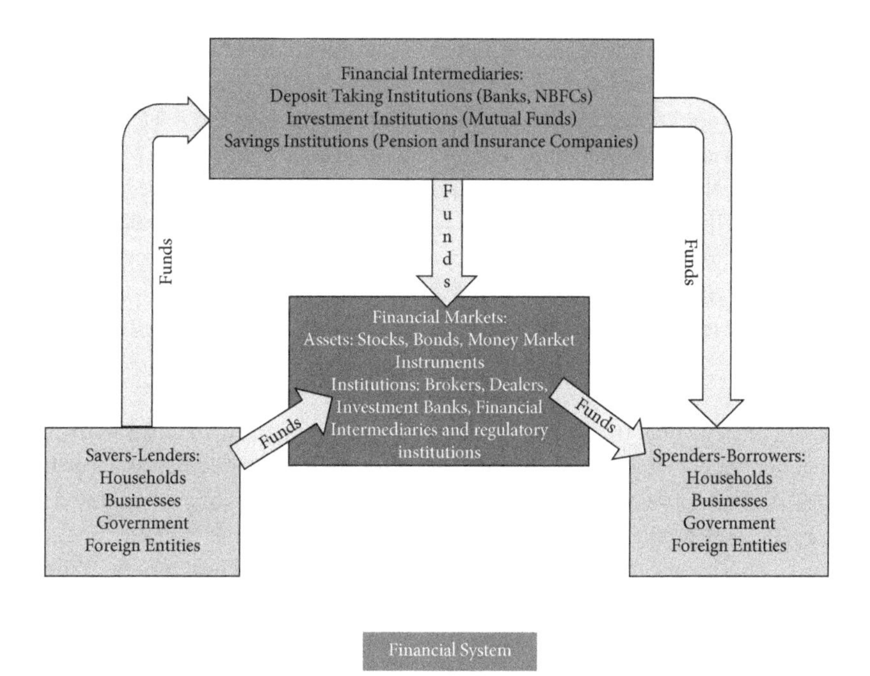

Figure 8.1 A Schematic Representation of the Financial System
Source: Author's construction.

from the financial system. Several aspects of the financial system deserve elaboration.

Indirect and Direct Channels of Transmission of Funds from Savers to Borrowers

Savers have two broad avenues to channel their excess funds to borrowers: an indirect channel and a direct channel. The indirect channel requires financial intermediation by a set of institutions that take the funds from savers and channel them to borrowers either as loans or as investments in securities issued by the borrowers. These institutions include deposit-taking institutions such as commercial banks and non-bank finance companies (NBFCs), investment institutions such as mutual funds, and savings institutions such as pension and insurance funds. When savers opt for the direct channel, they invest directly in the securities issued by borrowers.

Debt and Equity Instruments

Instruments that borrowers issue and in which savers or financial institutions invest can be classified into two categories: debt and equity. The commonest debt instruments are bonds and mortgages. The borrower issues a bond at a certain price, which is also its face value. The bond pays an annual return as a percentage of the face value and has a maturity date. At maturity, the bond is redeemed at face value. The holder of the bond has no claim on the assets of the issuer of the bond. Therefore, the annual return on the bond reflects the prevailing interest rate and the risk of default associated with the issuer of the bond. The greater the risk that the issuer might default at or before maturity, the higher the return she must offer to persuade investors to purchase the bond.

Bonds fall into two broad categories: those publicly traded and those sold as private placements. The former are bought and sold in the financial markets; the latter are not. In India so far, the market for publicly traded bonds has been thin. The bulk of bonds have been issued as private placements. When interest rates rise, new public issues of bonds must offer commensurately higher rates of return. This means that the prices of existing traded bonds, which were issued when interest rates were lower, would fall to ensure that the implicit return on those bonds matches the new, higher interest rate. Bonds with a maturity of one year or less are called short-term bonds, and those with a maturity of ten years or more are called long-term bonds. Bonds with a maturity greater than one year and less than ten years are intermediate-term bonds.

In India, the central and state governments are the issuers of the vast majority of publicly traded bonds. The governments issue these bonds to finance their fiscal deficits. Bonds are also issued by a host of other public sector entities, including All-India Financial Institutions (AIFIs) such as the National Bank for Agricultural and Rural Development (NABARD) and the Small Industries Development Bank of India (SIDBI) as well as public sector enterprises such as the Oil and Natural Gas Corporation (ONGC) and the Steel Authority of India Limited (SAIL). In the private sector, NBFCs account for a significant proportion of bonds.

The second broad form of instrument through which savers can transmit their funds to borrowers directly is equity, commonly referred to as a share or stock. A stock effectively gives its buyer a share in the ownership of the borrower's enterprise. Once again, stocks fall into two broad categories: private equity and public issues. The latter can be bought and sold on the market. If the enterprise that issued the stock performs well in terms of profitability or its future promise, the price of its stock rises. Unlike bonds, stocks do not promise an annual return, but the enterprise issuing it may occasionally choose to distribute a part of its profit to its stockholders in the form of a dividend. Stocks do not have a maturity date and therefore can be bought and sold indefinitely. If a company goes bankrupt, its stock is withdrawn from the market, with the stockholders receiving their share as per the terms of bankruptcy.

Primary and Secondary Markets

Markets in securities—stocks and bonds—can be divided into primary and secondary markets. In the primary markets, borrowers issue and sell new securities. This generally requires the services of investment banks. Once securities have been issued publicly, they become tradable in secondary markets. Most of the secondary trades happen in stock exchanges and nowadays can be carried out through the internet. An alternative to stock exchanges is the over-the-counter market, which represents a dealer network. Stocks and derivatives not listed on any stock exchange may trade on these over-the-counter markets. There is generally less transparency in these markets.

Financial Institutions

Financial institutions are many and varied and do not always lend themselves to an all-inclusive classification. The high frequency of innovation in financial markets makes such classification yet more difficult. At the risk of oversimplification, these institutions may be divided into brokers, dealers, stock markets, investment banks, and financial intermediaries. The first four of these institutions help connect savers directly to borrowers with securities serving as the conduit, while the last ones do so indirectly by collecting the funds from savers by offering them a specified return and lending those funds to borrowers as credit or through purchases of securities.

Brokers only assist their clients in buying and selling securities. They earn their income by charging their clients a fee or commission on the transactions. They do not buy or sell securities for themselves in the hope of making profits through purchases at lower prices and sales at higher prices. Unlike brokers, dealers buy and sell securities for themselves. Rather than rely on commissions, they earn profits by buying the securities cheap and selling them dear.

Stock markets and commodity exchanges offer centralized facilities for purchase and sales of shares in ownership of companies and commodities, respectively. Examples of commodities traded on commodity exchanges include gold, silver, cotton, coffee, corn, and oil. India has four permanent stock exchanges and three permanent commodity derivatives exchanges. The stock exchanges are the Bombay Stock Exchange (BSE), National Stock Exchange (NSE), Calcutta Stock Exchange, and Magadh Stock Exchange. The commodity derivatives exchanges include the Commodity Exchange, Multi Commodity Exchange of India, and National Commodity and Derivatives Exchange.[1] Founded in 1875, BSE is Asia's oldest stock exchange. BSE and NSE together account for more than 95 percent of shares traded in India.

Investment banks such as JPMorgan Chase, Kotak Investment Banking, and Credit Suisse provide a variety of investment services. The most notable of these services is the handling of all aspects of sales of newly issued bonds and stocks of enterprises. At the initial stage, this involves advice on whether to raise the necessary funds through debt, equity, or a combination thereof and the preparation of the necessary papers to fulfill regulatory requirements. At later stages, the bank advises on pricing of the securities, buys a certain proportion of them at a specified price, and helps brings other potential buyers of securities on board. Investment banks also conduct research to predict market trends and identify securities that would yield high returns and those that would do poorly in the future. They use this research to advise their clients with respect to the purchase and sale of securities in the secondary market. They offer broker services and help manage the portfolios of pension and insurance funds and the wealth of individuals and families.

Functions of Financial Markets

Financial markets serve many functions. First and foremost, they channel savings to productive investments. Savers themselves do not know how their funds can be invested to bring high returns. Financial intermediaries such as commercial banks, mutual funds, NBFCs, and pension and insurance funds help bridge this gap. Price movements in securities markets and analyses by investment banks allow savers to directly invest in profitable enterprises. Enterprises present credible business plans to intermediaries, which allows them to obtain the necessary finance.

Financial markets also help diversify risk. Borrowers are able to partially transfer the risks of business to financial intermediaries or savers who offer them funds. Intermediaries who lend funds to many borrowers diversify risk by investing in enterprises with a wide range of risk-return combinations. Savers investing directly can similarly diversify risk by investing in diversified portfolios of securities.

Another function of financial markets is to offer liquidity to owners of assets. In a well-developed financial market, there are many buyers and sellers. This allows asset holders to sell their assets at short notice and convert them into cash should they need it. In a similar vein, credible borrowers are able to raise funds from the market by selling stocks or bonds.

Finally, financial markets serve the critical function of coordination and provision of information. In the absence of financial markets, savers and lenders lack information on borrowers. Financial markets help bridge this gap. In part this information is conveyed by the performance of securities issued by different enterprises. But financial institutions such as investment banks also collect, analyze, and disseminate such information to markets.

Regulation

Regulation and regulatory institutions constitute an integral part of a financial system. There are four key regulatory institutions that actively regulate financial markets in India: the Reserve Bank of India (RBI), Securities and Exchange Board of India (SEBI), Insurance Regulatory and Development Authority of India (IRDAI), and Pension Fund Regulatory and Development Authority (PFRDA). Mention may also be made of the Insolvency and Bankruptcy Board of India (IBBI); strictly speaking, this is not a financial regulatory institution, but it deals with the bankruptcies of companies, which have important implications for the working of financial institutions. Finally, the Financial Stability and

Development Council, a non-statutory body chaired by the finance minister, performs the function of coordinating across different regulatory agencies. The council is also charged with helping strengthen and institutionalize financial stability mechanisms and promote the development of the financial sector.

RBI is first and foremost the regulator of all deposit-taking institutions, and as such, it has the responsibility to ensure the security of hundreds of millions of customers who hold deposits in banks and other institutions. It also regulates the foreign exchange market and the payments system, and it manages the debts of central and state governments. Additionally, it serves as the banker of the central and state governments.

SEBI is the regulator of markets for all securities, including stocks, bonds, and their derivatives. It frames and implements rules for new issues of stocks. It registers and regulates the working of stockbrokers, sub-brokers, share transfer agents, merchant brokers, bankers to stock issues, underwriters, portfolio managers, investment advisers, foreign institutional investors, credit rating agencies, and all other entities associated with securities markets. It also registers and regulates venture capital funds and collective investment schemes, including mutual funds. Its mandate includes the regulation of depositories that serve as custodians of securities. Finally, SEBI conducts inquiries and audits of stock exchanges and regulates company takeovers.

SEBI also regulates trade in commodity derivatives. Until recently this was the task of the Forward Markets Commission. But beginning in September 2015, this function was transferred to the newly created Commodity Derivatives Market Regulation Department within SEBI. SEBI sets policy on trading, clearing, and settlement operations relating to commodity derivatives; approves new commodity-based products; registers and regulates stock exchanges hosting trading in commodity derivatives; and handles investor grievances and complaints relating to commodity derivatives trades.

IRDAI regulates all aspects of the insurance market in India. It registers and regulates all insurance companies, issues licenses to insurance agents, controls and regulates the rates and terms and conditions offered by insurance companies to policyholders, and adjudicates disputes between insurance companies and others in the insurance business. Above all, IRDAI protects the interests of policyholders by ensuring the speedy settlement of legitimate claims and preventing fraud and other malpractices.

PFRDA regulates the National Pension Scheme and pension schemes to which the PFRDA Act (2013) applies. It registers and regulates intermediaries for the purposes of collection, management, recordkeeping, and distribution of accumulations. It also approves schemes, terms and conditions, and norms for management of the corpus of pension funds. Finally, PFRDA settles disputes among intermediaries and between intermediaries and subscribers.

Sources of Commercial Flows in India

Table 8.1 shows the sources of financial flows to the commercial sector for every other year beginning in 2007/8. We can see that a broad pattern emerges in which approximately half of the fund flows are associated with commercial banks. The bulk of these flows take the form of credit. For instance, in 2017/18, 43.1 percent of total flows took the form of bank credit, and 6.5 percent were investments in financial instruments by commercial banks. Of the remaining commercial fund flows, approximately 30 percent came from non-bank domestic sources, including private and public placements by non-financial entities in the forms of stocks and bonds, credit by housing finance companies, and investments in instruments issued by entities such as NBFCs and four AIFIs (namely, NABARD, NHB, SIDBI, and Exim Bank). Approximately 20 percent of the flows come from foreign sources, most notably direct foreign investment.

Table 8.2 provides further details on domestic fund flows to non-bank instruments and entities. It divides them into seven categories and, as in Table 8.1, shows the share of each category in the total fund flows for every other year beginning with 2007/8. The first two of the instruments are public issues and private placements by non-financial entities in the private and public sectors combined. Funds flowing directly to financial institutions in both the private and public sectors are covered by other categories in the table. A key feature of the flows to non-financial institutions is that private placements are significantly larger than public issues. In spite of all the attention that stock markets receive, public issues as a source of new funds remain relatively small in India.

Resources flowing directly from savers to housing finance companies have emerged as a major item in commercial flows in recent years. From 5 percent or less of total commercial flows, they have increased to 8 to 10 percent of the total.

Table 8.1 Sources of Financial Flows to the Commercial Sector (Trillions of Rupees)

Source	2007/8	2009/10	2011/12	2013/14	2015/16	2017/18
Commercial banks (credit plus investments in securities)	44.1	45.0	55.7	54.0	55.4	49.6
Non-bank domestic sources	25.3	34.3	25.3	30.4	27.0	32.1
Foreign sources	30.6	20.7	19.0	15.6	17.6	18.3
Total resources	10.09	10.64	12.16	14.13	13.99	18.47

Source: Author's calculations using data from the *RBI Handbook of Statistics on Indian Economy*, table 68.

Table 8.2 Detailed Breakdown of Shares of Non-Bank Domestic Sources of Commercial Flows in Total Commercial Flows (Percent)

Source	2007/8	2009/10	2011/12	2013/14	2015/16	2017/18
Public issues by non-financial entities	5.1	3.0	1.2	1.4	2.7	2.4
Gross private placements by non-financial entities	6.8	13.3	4.6	9.3	8.1	7.9
Net issuance of commercial paper subscribed by non-banks	1.1	2.5	0.3	1.0	3.7	−1.4
Net credit by housing finance companies	4.1	2.7	4.4	5.2	8.5	10.8
Total gross accommodation by 4 RBI-regulated AIFIs	2.2	3.2	3.9	3.1	3.4	5.1
Large non-deposit-taking NBFCs (net of bank credit)	3.6	5.7	7.5	8.0	−2.0	5.2
LIC investment in corporate debt, infrastructure and Social Sector	2.4	4.0	3.4	2.5	2.6	2.0
Total (as percent of total commercial flows)	25.3	34.3	25.3	30.4	27.0	32.1

*The four AIFIs are NABARD, NHB, SIDBI, and Exim Bank.

Source: Author's calculations using data from the *RBI Handbook of Statistics on Indian Economy*, table 68.

It is likely that the Real Estate Regulation and Development Act (2016) has accelerated the growth of larger real estate companies that raise funds directly from the market. Another form of domestic entity raising substantial funds from the market in recent years is the non-deposit-taking NBFC. To some degree, these NBFCs have filled the void created by slower growth in bank credit, which is due to a rapid rise in the non-performing assets of commercial banks.

Equity and Debt Markets

As in most other countries, bank credit remains by far the largest single source of commercial funds in India. How banks allocate these resources among borrowers has a major impact on the productivity and growth of the country. At the same time, because banks are deposit-taking institutions, they are the key entity helping individuals and households earn a competitive return with minimal or no risk of default. They play an important role in encouraging savings by individuals and households that do not intend to engage in their own business activity. From the viewpoint of resource allocation as well as resource mobilization, it is important that the banking sector be stable, secure and vibrant. Keeping this in view, I devote Chapter 9 to issues in banking reforms.

Here I focus on the securities market. Banks offer individual savers a secure return. On average, this return is lower than what banks charge their borrowers and what the borrowers themselves earn on their investments. Sometimes banks may do a poor job of allocating their resources among borrowers, in which case their earnings are poor and they pay depositors poor interest rates as well. Additionally, large banks may profit from exercising some degree of monopoly power over both savers and borrowers, thereby creating a large spread between deposit rates and lending rates. The existence of a vibrant, transparent, and competitive securities market that offers individual savers the opportunity to lend directly to investors can help counter these factors. In principle, the securities market allows savers to share in the high returns that investors earn (with the concomitant risks of such investments) while subjecting banks to competition for savers' funds.

Securities serve another important function. Valuations of companies on the stock market and the performance of bonds they issue offer valuable corporation-specific information to banks. Banks can use this information in their evaluation of future loans to these companies. The likely result is a lower risk of default on loans and fewer non-performing assets on the books of the banks. The fear of a fall in their valuation in the stock and bond markets can also serve as a check on corporations in terms of meeting their payments to the banks. That is, it encourages them to make payments on the money they borrow from banks on time. A vibrant securities market thus confers many economic benefits.

After reforms were launched in 1991, they reached the equity sector of the securities market rather quickly. As a result, today, India has a vibrant equity market. Beginning in the mid-2000s, India also recognized the importance of the debt market and undertook a series of reforms. These reforms have yielded splendid results, with debt markets quickly outdoing equity markets in terms of new issues. In terms of total size, however, equity markets remain significantly larger.

Data on new issues show private placements dominating in both the equity and debt markets. What is most striking, however, is that private placements in the debt segment have outdone equity placements in public and private placements

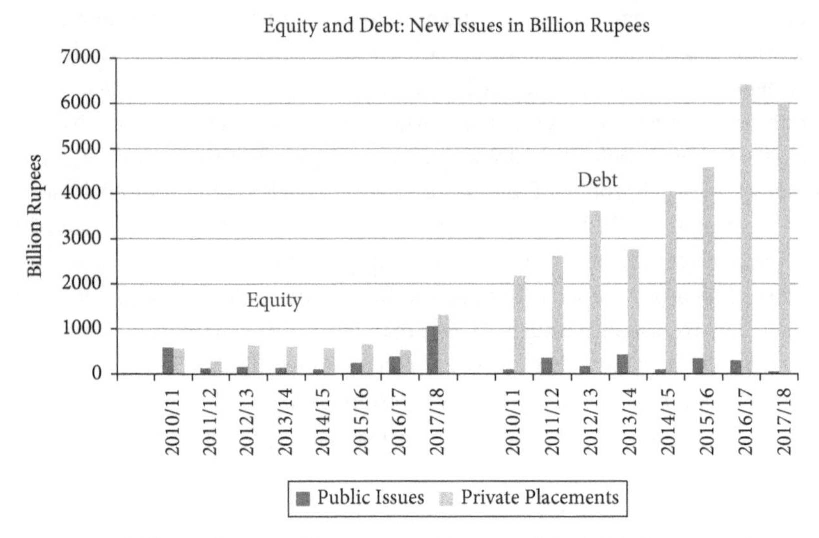

Figure 8.2 Public and Private Placements in Equity and Debt Markets, 2010/11 to 2017/18

Source: Author's construction based on SEBI data.

taken together. Figure 8.2, which depicts public and private placements in the equity and debt segments from 2010/11 to 2017/18, makes the point.

Given that reforms and development efforts targeting equity markets preceded those aimed at debt markets by more than a decade, it makes sense that equity markets are significantly more developed. This is particularly true of publicly traded equities despite their low levels of new issues. Market capitalization of the Bombay Stock Exchange as of March 31, 2018, amounted to 84.8 percent of GDP in 2017/18. In absolute value, it was in excess of $2 trillion. Forbes has ranked the BSE tenth by market capitalization as of April 2018.[2] Daily trade volumes on both the BSE and NSE are large, but publicly traded equity shares are substantially more liquid than their debt counterparts.

Deepen the Corporate Debt Market

Unlike equity shares, whose life is as long as that of the company issuing it, debt is retired at maturity. In a country like India, the maturity period of nearly all corporate debt instruments is five years or less. As a result, building and deepening the corporate debt market takes much longer than it did with the equity market. Given the short history of the efforts to develop the corporate debt market in

India, it remains small and shallow compared to the corporate debt markets in some other countries, where they have had a longer history of development.

At the end of June 2018, outstanding corporate debt in India was 28.4 trillion rupees, amounting to 16.6 percent of GDP in 2017/18. In comparison, outstanding corporate debt at the end of June 2018 as a proportion of GDP in 2017 stood at 114.4 percent in the United Kingdom, 64.7 percent in Japan, 107.4 percent in the United States, 57 percent in China, 59.7 percent in Malaysia, and 60.3 percent in Chile.[3] India still has some distance to go in terms of the development of the corporate debt market.

Indian policymakers recognize this fact, as reflected in the appointment of several committees on this subject beginning in the mid-2000s. Of particular importance is the H. R. Khan Committee, which submitted its report in August 2016. This committee made several specific recommendations, which the government has largely implemented. Some of the acceleration in the issuance of debt instruments by corporations to raise funds in 2017/18 and 2018/19 can be attributed to the implementation of Khan Committee recommendations.

There remains scope for further reforms in this area on both the demand and supply sides of the market. An October 24, 2018, speech by SEBI chairman Ajay Tyagi offers some excellent suggestions.[4] Consider first the demand side. In comparison to equity instruments, corporate bonds are far more complex instruments. The credit rating of a bond depends in large part on the overall creditworthiness of the issuer. In deciding ratings, ratings agencies consider the issuer's assets, debts, income, expenses, financial history, and track record of payments on bonds previously issued. Nevertheless, the risk-return matrix of a specific bond additionally depends on whether or not it is secured, its liquidity, tax benefits associated with it, and whether some form of sovereign support backs it. Because bonds have a specified life, market conditions during that period can seriously impact their riskiness. This is less of a problem with equity shares, since they have an indefinite life, and even if their value slumps at a given point in time, they may recover if they are held long enough.

These complexities, combined with the thinness of public issues of corporate bonds, have meant that so far institutional investors have been the near exclusive customers of corporate bonds in India. Of the shares in outstanding corporate bonds, currently 30 percent are held by non-financial corporations, 25 percent by banks and other financial institutions, 20 percent by mutual funds, 15 percent by trusts, and 7 percent by foreign portfolio investors; retail investors hold a paltry 3 percent.

Several steps can be taken to enhance the demand for corporate debt. First, strengthening the participation of retail customers in the bond market is likely to remain an uphill task in the short term. But the benefits of investment in these assets can still be brought to them through increased participation by pension, provident, and insurance funds. Current regulations on how these funds may invest are highly restrictive. Allowing these funds to invest a higher proportion of their total investments in corporate bonds would boost demand for corporate debt while also bringing the benefits of higher returns to subscribers of these funds. Currently, these bonds are issued nearly exclusively by entities with an AA or higher rating, so the risk of investing in them is minimal.

Second, the market for long-maturity bonds is currently nonexistent in India. Nearly all of the existing corporate bonds have a maturity of five years or less. In cases where projects begin to yield full returns in five years or less, which is true for the vast majority of corporate projects, this maturity period works fine. But most infrastructure projects take much longer to complete. For these projects, bonds of longer maturity are required. Unfortunately, potential issuers of infrastructure bonds are not able to rise above BBB ratings on their own.

Given that banks are typically unwilling to offer loans with a maturity longer than five years, the corporate bond market would seem to be a natural source of funds for infrastructure companies. Here too, allowing large pension, provident, and insurance funds to invest small proportions of their portfolios could help break the ice. Subscribers to these funds need to be able to earn decent returns to support themselves upon retirement; because these funds are relatively large, they are well positioned to diversify risk. In most countries, these funds are an important source of finance for infrastructure companies.

Taking into account the public-good nature of infrastructure, the government can also help boost the ratings of longer-term bonds issued by infrastructure companies through its credit enhancement fund, announced in the 2016/17 budget. Such a fund can either insure or provide collateral for long-range infrastructure bonds. Given India's generally conservative approach to regulation, only truly creditworthy companies will get access to this fund, so the risk that the fund will actually have to be used to repay lenders is minimal.

In this context, it is important to note that the idea of credit enhancement has been widely prevalent in developed countries for five decades. Credit enhancement through third-party guarantees or insurance plays an important role when the underlying sector has strong potential but companies within the sector are unable to obtain high ratings for their issues on their own. At present, the private market in India is not sufficiently developed to provide such insurance or third-party guarantees.

Third, under the current practice, banks get to show their loans at book value on their balance sheets. In contrast, corporate bonds are marked to market, and any loss of creditworthiness for the issuer is immediately reflected in the value of the bonds. Other things held constant, this factor makes loans a more attractive instrument of investment than corporate bonds (and equity) for banks. Removal of this asymmetry through periodic assessments of loans by regulators would help boost demand for bonds.

Finally, the number of dollar-billionaires in India is now over one hundred, and that number will continue to rise at a fast pace in the decades to come. Likewise, small corporations with surplus funds have been growing in number as the economy gets bigger. Potentially, corporate bonds could be attractive investment instruments for these entities. But an inability to borrow against these bonds, while loans against investments in equity shares are routinely available, places them at a disadvantage. Allowing the high-networth individuals and small corporations to borrow against bonds would remove this asymmetry.

While it is demand-side factors that are most constraining, some supply-side measures may also accelerate the development of bond markets. First, limiting the exposure of banks to large corporations, as envisaged in the RBI exposure framework, would cap the access of corporations to bank credit and nudge them toward the bond market. Second, the announcement in the 2018/19 budget that large corporations will eventually be required to raise 25 percent of their funds from the bond market should exert some supply-side pressure in the market. How SEBI will operationalize this mandate remains to be seen, however. Finally, moving to a system of "on tap" bond issuance by corporations may encourage them to rely more on bonds than on bank credit.

Concluding Remarks

The importance of well-functioning financial markets for growth and development cannot be overemphasized. High- and low-productivity enterprises coexist within the same sector in disproportionately large volume in developing countries. As a result, any policy initiatives at the level of the sector end up promoting both high- and low-productivity activities in that sector. Well-developed and well-functioning financial markets can overcome this problem by directing finance to high-productivity activities regardless of the sector.

Security markets, especially in the debt sector, remain a work in progress in India. Though equity markets have deepened, new issues as a source of funds are still not very important. The debt market has had a late start in India. Though it has seen high growth in recent years, total corporate debt remains at only 16.6 percent of GDP. Until new issues of equity and debt take off in a big way, bank credit will remain the most important source of investment funds. Indeed, a well-functioning banking sector, which is the backbone of the financial system of any country, is also critical to the growth of the securities market. Therefore, it is urgent that India take the actions necessary to grow its banking sector and make it competitive, secure and efficient. This is the subject I consider in Chapter 9.

Notes

1. Securities and Exchange Board of India, "Details of Stock Exchanges," https://www.sebi.gov.in/stock-exchanges.html (accessed January 19. 2019).
2. Forbes, "The World's Biggest Stock Exchanges," https://www.forbes.com/pictures/eddk45iglh/the-worlds-biggest-stock-exchanges/#394c58436d2b (accessed January 25, 2019).
3. These percentages have been calculated by taking the data on outstanding corporate debt of financial and non-financial corporations from the Bank of International Settlement and the nominal GDP data from the International Monetary Fund. The former are found at https://www.bis.org/statistics/secstats.htm and the latter at https://en.wikipedia.org/wiki/List_of_countries_by_GDP_(nominal) (both accessed on January 24, 2019).
4. Ajay Tyagi, speech at CRISIL seminar "Expanding India's Corporate Bond Market: Bonds of Growth—Assessing the Supply-Demand Matrix," October 24, 2018, https://www.sebi.gov.in/media/speeches/oct-2018/chairman-s-speech-at-the-crisil-s-5th-annual-seminar-on-expanding-india-s-corporate-bond-market-bonds-of-growth-assessing-the-supply-demand-matrix-october-24-2018_40787.html (accessed January 27, 2018). In the remainder of this section, I draw heavily on this speech.

9

Investing Productively: The Banking Sector

The banking sector is the backbone of the economy's financial sector. Even in advanced economies with highly developed capital markets, banks remain the most critical component of this sector. In part, banks enjoy this key position because individuals and households are risk averse and prefer to keep their savings predominantly in instruments that would be subject to minimal or no risk of default while also earning them a reasonable return. Indeed, even governments and corporates often choose to park significant volumes of funds in banks.

In addition to taking deposits, banks serve several other important functions. One is that they facilitate transactions between buyers and sellers. Until the recent arrival of digital wallets and similar platforms, banks were the only entities clearing non-cash transactions among households, businesses, and governments. Even after the arrival of digital technologies, they remain the key platform for clearing transactions at low cost through transfers from one bank account to another. Banks also intermediate nearly all legitimate foreign currency transactions between residents of two or more countries.

A more challenging function of banks is investing the collected funds into activities that maximize returns, taking into account risks associated with the investments. Ultimately, whether or not a country's banking system makes a significant contribution to growth and prosperity depends on the lending choices it makes. Bank staff must have the ability to distinguish between high- and low-return projects for a given level of risk and between high- and low-risk projects for a given return.

When banks end up investing funds predominantly in projects of dubious quality, which either yield low returns or carry an unduly high risk of default, the banking system undermines growth. Indeed, persistently investing in such projects can undermine the banking system itself. When borrowers fail to make payments, either depositors suffer or the government has to bail out depositors at taxpayers' expense. It is to guard against such outcomes that the central bank must regulate banks in an effective manner. It must ensure that banks refrain from engaging in fraudulent practices while also maintaining a healthy risk-return mix on the funds they lend.

In India, banks have done generally a poor job of selecting high-return, low-risk projects. As a result, there have been two major episodes of large accumulations of non-performing assets (NPAs) following the post-1991 liberalization of the banking sector. In both episodes, the government had to come to the rescue of the banks and infuse substantial equity into them at the expense of the taxpayer. Currently, NPAs amount to more than 10 percent of total loans by the banks. Underlying these large recurrent accumulations of NPAs are serious governance issues that future reforms must address.

Before turning to these reforms, it is necessary to understand the developments that led to the current weaknesses in the banking sector. In turn, this requires tracing the history of banking. To keep the focus on reforms, I relegate a detailed account of the banking sector's early history to an appendix and concentrate here on developments since the launch of economic reforms in 1991. All we need to note here about the early history is that at independence, all banks in India were private. But in 1955, with a desire to expand the bank branch network rapidly to rural areas and bring formal credit to agriculture, the government decided to nationalize the largest bank at the time, the Imperial Bank, renaming it the State Bank of India (SBI). In 1969, political considerations led the government to nationalize all fourteen banks with deposits of 500 million rupees or more. A final round of nationalization using the same criterion brought another six banks into the public sector in 1980.

Two key policies the government pursued during the post-nationalization phase were aggressive bank branch expansion in rural areas and promotion of priority-sector lending, under which up to 40 percent of credit was required to be made available to favored sectors such as agriculture, exports, and small and medium firms. Throughout this period, the government kept tight control on interest rates and credit allocation across various sectors. It also deployed a high cash reserve ratio and statutory liquidity ratio to keep its borrowing costs low.

Reforms and the First Bout of NPAs: 1991 to 2002

Government ownership of all major banks, a minuscule role for private banks, aggressive bank branch expansion, tight controls on credit and interest rates, and financial repression came at a high cost.[1] True, the government had some success in promoting what it considered to be social objectives. But efficiency took a heavy toll. As an acknowledgment of the failure of at least one of its policies, in 1990—a year ahead of the launch of liberalizing reforms—it discontinued its bank branch expansion policy.

India entered the 1990s with a fragile economy. The banking sector was no exception. RBI had introduced a "health code" in 1985, which required banks to classify each loan into one of eight categories based on its performance. Classification in one of the bottom four of these categories meant that the loan was non-performing. Based on this classification, 14.5 percent of total outstanding advances were classified as non-performing at the end of March 1992.

In April 1992, this classification was replaced by a more demanding one that required banks to classify each loan into one of four categories: standard, substandard, doubtful, and loss. Loans classified into any of the last three categories were considered non-performing. The classification was based on objective criteria: the length of time for which payment of principal and interest was overdue. Criteria introduced in 1992 placed non-performing assets at 23.2 percent of total outstanding advances at the end of March 1993.

Criteria defining healthy loans were tightened over time. In 1995, assets with unpaid interest or principal for 180 days were classified as non-performing. By 2004, this threshold was revised to the international norm of 90 days. From that year onward, an asset that remained non-performing for up to one year had to be classified as substandard and an asset that remained non-performing for more than one year as doubtful. Assets considered substantially uncollectable had to be classified as losses. Under "provisioning" requirements, banks were required to set aside a proportion of the loan value out of their incomes to cover any losses that may arise in the event of non-recovery of substandard assets. The provision amounted to 10 percent of the loan value for sub-standard assets, 20 to 50 percent for the secured portion of doubtful assets, and 100 percent for unsecured doubtful assets and all loss assets.

A key objective of the financial sector reforms undertaken during the 1990s was restoration of the banks' health. With liberalization gaining acceptance, the government was able to take several measures that helped restore banks' profitability while also bringing down the volume of NPAs. Four such measures are worthy of note.

First, beginning in 1993/94, the government infused funds into banks to recapitalize them. By the end of 1997/98, its capital contribution to nationalized banks had reached 200.5 billion rupees. In addition, it provided 15.3 billion rupees to two banks to write off losses. Second, the government allowed its stake in public sector banks to be diluted as long as it did not fall below 51 percent. The dilution allowed the banks to mobilize equity funds from the market. By the end of March 1998, nine public sector banks had raised 60.2 billion rupees. Third, RBI reduced the statutory liquidity ratio from the peak rate of 38.5 percent in February 1992 to 25 percent by October 1997 and the cash reserve requirement from 15 percent in October 1992 to 9.5 percent in November 1997. These relaxations went a long way toward rolling back financial repression and releasing funds for credit expansion. Finally, the government freed up all but a small number of deposit and lending interest rates and did away with credit controls except priority-sector lending. This reform allowed banks to better align interest rates and loan amounts with profitability.

Alongside these measures, the government also introduced tighter prudential norms with respect to income recognition, asset classification and provisioning, and capital adequacy criteria. Banks were advised not to post interest on non-performing assets to their income account. Non-performing assets were defined using objective criteria, and new and higher provisioning norms were specified. Finally, a system utilizing a capital to risk-weighted assets ratio (CRAR) was introduced for banks in a phased manner. These measures helped turn around the banks' balance sheets. From −1.1 percent in 1992/93, the return on assets rose to 0.8 percent in 1997/98. The number of loss-making public sector banks fell significantly over the period.

For the first time since the nationalization of fourteen banks in 1969, the government also opened entry to new private banks. It announced the norms of entry in January 1993, and by 1998, ten new private banks had begun operations. The government also liberalized the entry of foreign banks, with twenty-two new foreign banks being set up by 1998. The policy regarding branch expansion was liberalized for both domestic banks and foreign banks. By the end of March 1998, the share of new private banks in total banking assets had risen to 3.2 percent and of foreign banks to 8.2 percent. Competition from new domestic private banks as well as foreign banks helped improve service conditions in public sector banks and old private sector banks.

In the post-reform era, the government also tried to create avenues to recovery of NPAs. The first step in this direction was the passage of the Recovery of Debts Due to Banks and Financial Institutions Act (1993). The act provided for the establishment of debt recovery tribunals (DRTs) and debt recovery appellate tribunals (DRATs). In the following years, 29 DRTs and five DRATs were established.

The pace of recovery under the DRT-DRAT process was painfully slow. Therefore, the government set up asset reconstruction companies (ARCs). To provide legal underpinning to ARCs, it enacted the Securitization and Reconstruction of Financial Assets and Enforcement of Security Interest (SARFAESI) Act (2002). The act provided for enforcement of the security interest for recovery of the amount owed, utilizing the court system. It also permitted banks and financial institutions to seize the assets of defaulting borrowers or sell their bank accounts to ARCs. A third avenue had previously existed for the recovery of small loans in the form of Lok Adalats or "People's Courts." Although these courts had existed since the early 1980s, they were given legal basis in 1987 by the Legal Services Authorities Act (1987). Litigants can take civil cases pending before other courts to these courts for expedited resolution. They can also bring cases to them for settlement before going to regular courts. The decision of Lok Adalats is final and cannot be appealed.

Unfortunately, the three avenues still proved inadequate for recoveries. As mentioned, the DRT-DRAT process was extremely slow. SARFAESI gave banks leverage by empowering them to take over the assets of defaulting borrowers, but they had no expertise in either working the acquired assets productively or liquidating them for recovery. Public sector banks also did not want to sell the accounts of defaulting borrowers to ARCs at less than face value for fear of being investigated by governmental vigilance agencies. Some recoveries were made under all three processes, but recovery rates were invariably low.

Recapitalization by the government, provision for the dilution of government equity, and some increase in profitability due to accelerated economic growth helped reduce NPAs from 23.2 percent at the end of March 1993 to 16 percent at the end of 1998. Though the government did not undertake any significant recapitalization after 1998, NPAs continued to decline at the rate of approximately 2 percentage points each year, with non-performing loans as a proportion of total advances declining to 2.7 percent by the end of March 2007. Unfortunately, however, even as NPAs and other indicators suggested the emergence of a healthy and competitive banking sector, the seeds of the next NPA crisis were being sown.

Rapid Expansion of Credit: 2003 to 2013

Economic reforms under Prime Ministers Narasimha Rao (1991–96) and Atal Bihari Vajpayee (1998–2004) launched India onto a high-growth trajectory. In 2003/4, the economy grew at a rate above 8 percent, with this momentum maintained for nearly a decade. Expectations of high returns in a burgeoning economy led entrepreneurs and business houses to line up for bank credit. From the rapid expansion that followed over the next several years, it would seem that banks successfully accommodated this growth in credit demand.

Figure 9.1 shows the total outstanding advances for public, private, foreign, and all scheduled commercial banks (SCBs) at the end of fiscal years 2004/05 to 2017/18. The total outstanding advances of all SCBs rose from 11.9 trillion rupees at the end of 2004/5 to 68.7 trillion rupees at the end of 2013/14. Indian banks, both public and private, drove this growth in credit. Foreign banks also contributed, but in a limited way. Credit growth slowed down considerably beginning in 2014/15.

Table 9.1 shows the annual growth in credit for each broad group of banks. Three observations may be made on the basis of these growth rates. First, overall credit by SCBs grew very rapidly till 2011/12 and maintained a healthy pace till 2013/14. But after that year, credit expansion rapidly decelerated, with its growth dropping to just 3.6 percent in 2016/17.

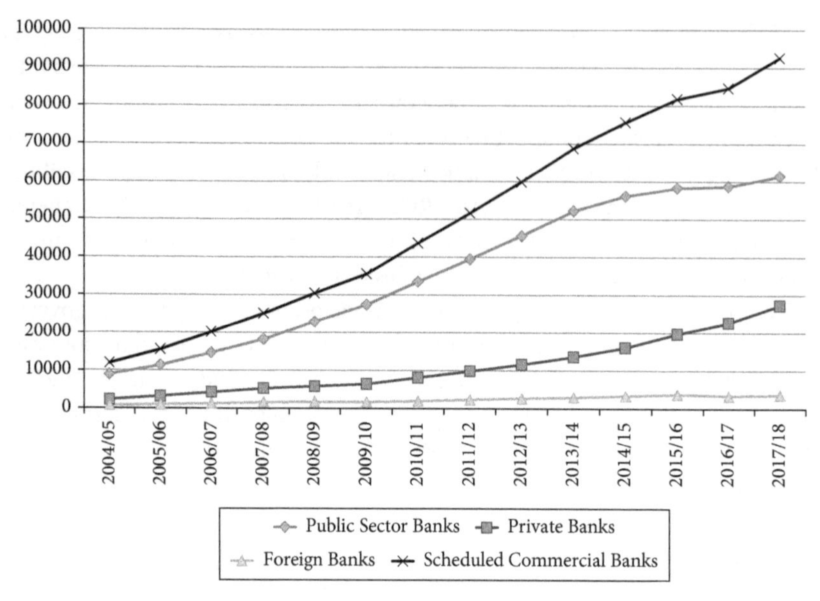

Figure 9.1 Total Outstanding Advances of Broad Groups of Banks at the End of the Fiscal Year: 2004/5 to 2017/18

Source: Author's construction based on RBI data at https://dbie.rbi.org.in/DBIE/dbie.rbi?site=publications#!4 (accessed March 15, 2019).

Second, public and private sector banks behaved similarly until 2013/14 but differently subsequently. Expansion of credit by public sector banks from 2014/15 onward suffered a serious setback, while credit expansion by private sector banks maintained its healthy pace. Foreign banks, which are impacted a lot more by what goes on in the global economy, showed a different pattern. They saw a sharp decline in their credit during 2008/9 and 2009/10 due to the global financial crisis. Again, after interest rates rose in the United States in 2013, their credit growth exhibited a sharper decline.

Finally, overall credit growth remains heavily tied to credit growth by public sector banks. This reflects the disproportionately large volume of deposits held by these banks. Because public sector banks are backed by the government's implicit guarantee, they continue to receive deposits even when they perform poorly.

NPAs Masquerade as Restructured Loans

A progressive weakening of the banking system accompanied the rapid growth in credit from 2005/6 to 2013/14. One would have thought that the adoption

Table 9.1 Percentage Growth in Credit Over the Previous Year by Broad Groups Of Banks: 2005/6 to 2017/18

Fiscal year	Public sector banks	Private banks	Foreign banks	Scheduled commercial banks
2005/6	28.0	40.6	28.4	30.5
2006/7	29.2	32.3	29.3	29.8
2007/8	24.2	25.2	27.5	24.6
2008/9	25.5	11.2	4.0	21.1
2009/10	19.7	10.1	-1.4	16.7
2010/11	22.4	26.0	19.1	22.9
2011/12	17.8	20.9	17.7	18.4
2012/13	15.7	18.1	14.6	16.1
2013/14	14.4	17.4	11.4	14.8
2014/15	7.7	18.2	12.4	10.0
2015/16	3.8	22.7	11.9	8.2
2016/17	0.7	14.5	-8.7	3.6
2017/18	4.7	20.6	5.6	9.4

Source: Author's calculations using RBI data at https://dbie.rbi.org.in/DBIE/dbie.rbi?site=publications#!4 (accessed March 15, 2019).

of international standards in prudential regulation would have protected the banking sector against renewed fragility. It turned out, however, that the government and RBI failed to implement international best practice in regulation in one important respect: treatment of restructured loans. International best practice is to treat restructured loans as substandard. For a long time, RBI chose to treat them as standard. The regime regulating NPAs was thus effectively subverted. Governance problems associated with the ownership of the vast majority of banking assets by public sector banks—most notably, undue government interference in the granting of credit by these banks—added to this subversion.

The restructuring of loans involves adjustment to one or more features of the loan: the payable amount, the payment period, the amount of the installment, and the interest rate. The earliest directives on restructuring in India were issued in the 1970s in the context of flood-affected borrowers and the rehabilitation of sick enterprises. Later, in 1985, the government issued more detailed guidelines for the identification of sick units and parameters determining their viability for purposes of loan restructuring.

In 1992, when the government introduced the system of classification of loans into the four categories of standard, substandard, doubtful, and loss, it also adopted the practice of classifying loans restructured after commencement of production by a unit as substandard for two years. If the borrower performed in a satisfactory manner over these two years, the loans could be reclassified as standard. In 1999, the regulation was weakened, with the reclassification of restructured loans into the standard category permitted after one year of satisfactory performance. A further weakening took place in 2001, when RBI issued revised guidelines permitting restructured standard and substandard loans to retain their original classifications provided they were fully secured.

Until 2001, formal mechanisms for restructuring loans and subsequently reclassifying them were available only on loans extended to enterprises by a single bank. They did not accommodate restructuring of large loans advanced by multiple banks. In 2001, RBI took steps to fill this gap by putting in place the Corporate Debt Restructuring (CDR) framework for standard and substandard accounts. This framework initially applied to loans extended by two or more banks and totaling 200 million rupees or more. It provided for coordinated restructuring of viable standard and substandard corporate loans and allowed them to retain their respective classifications. In 2003, the framework was extended to doubtful accounts, and in 2005, it was broadened to include all consortium loans worth 100 million rupees or more.

In 2005, RBI also issued guidelines for restructuring the debt of small and medium enterprises (SMEs). Different sets of guidelines were issued for non-corporate and corporate SMEs with loans from a single bank and for corporate SMEs with outstanding loans up to 100 million rupees from a group of banks. Therefore, by 2005, formal loan restructuring mechanisms became available to all enterprises, corporate or non-corporate, and regardless of whether the loan was extended by one bank or a group of banks.

In 2008, all restructuring guidelines were aligned to those applying under CDR. These guidelines allowed banks to restructure the accounts of viable entities classified as standard, substandard, and doubtful. They also provided that accounts classified as standard, other than those relating to commercial real estate (CRE), capital market exposure (CME), and personal loans, could retain their classification upon restructuring as long as they satisfied certain conditions.

Both the borrower and the lender found it profitable to restructure a loan that faced the prospect of turning into an NPA. For the borrower, restructuring offered the opportunity to renegotiate the terms of loans and continue business as usual without any loss of reputation that might follow his loan being classified as NPA. For the lender, restructuring came with a substantially reduced provisioning requirement. Whereas the provisioning requirement for a loan falling into the substandard category was 15 percent, the requirement for a restructured standard loan until November 2012 was only 2 percent. The requirement was raised to 2.75 percent in November 2012 and to 5 percent on April 1, 2013, but this still left provisioning requirements for restructured standard loans well below the 15 percent level for substandard loans.

These small tweaks to the rules were done on the recommendation of an RBI working group that had been tasked with offering advice on making changes to the restructuring regime in the light of international best practice. As late as July 2012, contrary to the prevailing international practice of downgrading restructured loans, the working group recommended permitting them to retain their original classification as long as certain conditions were satisfied. The report stated, "The WG [working group] has observed that internationally accounts are generally treated as impaired/downgraded on restructuring. The WG examined the consequences of aligning our restructuring guidelines with this best practice but felt that doing so immediately might act as a disincentive to banks to restructure viable accounts which would severely impact the viable accounts facing temporary challenge and may result in higher provisioning requirement for banks on account of increase in the non-performing assets."[2]

Figure 9.2 shows the evolution of NPAs and restructured standard loans of all scheduled commercial banks taken together from 2004/5 to 2017/18. Between 2004/5 and 2007/8, NPAs saw a decline, with restructured loans staying at

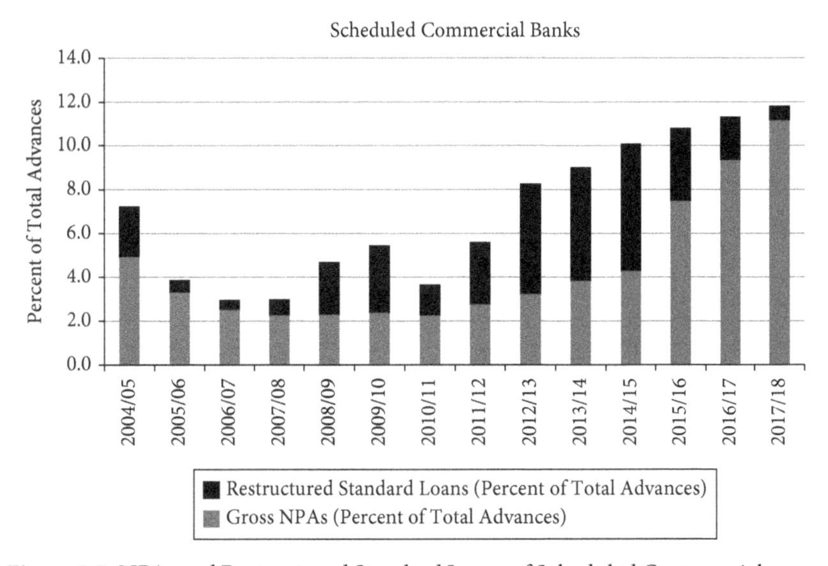

Figure 9.2 NPAs and Restructured Standard Loans of Scheduled Commercial Banks, 2004/5 to 2017/18

Source: Author's construction using RBI data at https://dbie.rbi.org.in/DBIE/dbie.rbi?site=publications#!4 (accessed on March 15, 2019).

relatively low levels. This was the period during which the banking system was still coming out of the first round of NPAs that had carried over from the 1990s and early 2000s. The decline in NPAs as a proportion of advances was substantially driven by the rapid expansion of advances, which grew 30 percent in both 2005/6 and 2006/7 and 25 percent in 2007/8 (Table 9.1). But beginning in 2008/9, the year of the global financial crisis, restructured standard loans began to rise at a fast pace. By 2014/15, they had increased to nearly 5.8 percent from 0.4 percent in 2006/7, while NPAs rose to only 4.3 percent from 2.5 percent over the same period.

Disaggregated data show that though a rising proportion of restructured standard loans characterized all three major groups of banks—public, private, and foreign—the expansion was heavily concentrated in public sector banks. Figure 9.3 shows that restructured standard loans in public sector banks rose from 0.6 percent of total advances in 2006/7 to 7.1 percent in 2014/15. With these banks accounting for two-thirds or more of outstanding advances throughout the period, their health had a determining effect on the health of the banking system as a whole.

The performance of private and foreign banks, depicted in Figures 9.4 and 9.5, respectively, was significantly superior as far as NPAs and restructured standard loans are concerned. Even at their peak in 2014/15, restructured standard loans

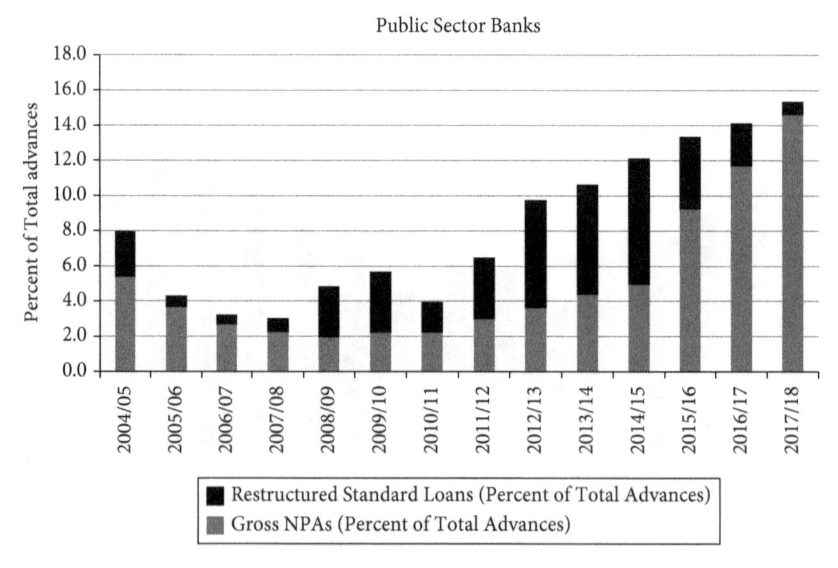

Figure 9.3 NPAs and Restructured Standard Loans in Public Sector Banks, 2004/5 to 2017/18

Source: Author's construction using RBI data at https://dbie.rbi.org.in/DBIE/dbie.rbi?site=publications#!4 (accessed on March 15, 2019).

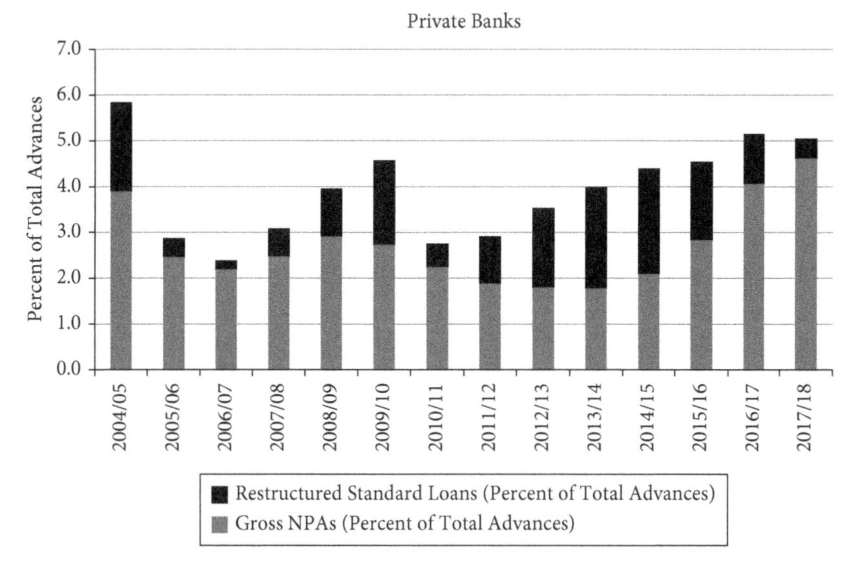

Figure 9.4 NPAs and Restructured Standard Loans of Private Banks, 2004/5 to 2017/18

Source: Author's construction using RBI data at https://dbie.rbi.org.in/DBIE/dbie.rbi?site=publications#!4 (accessed on March 15, 2019).

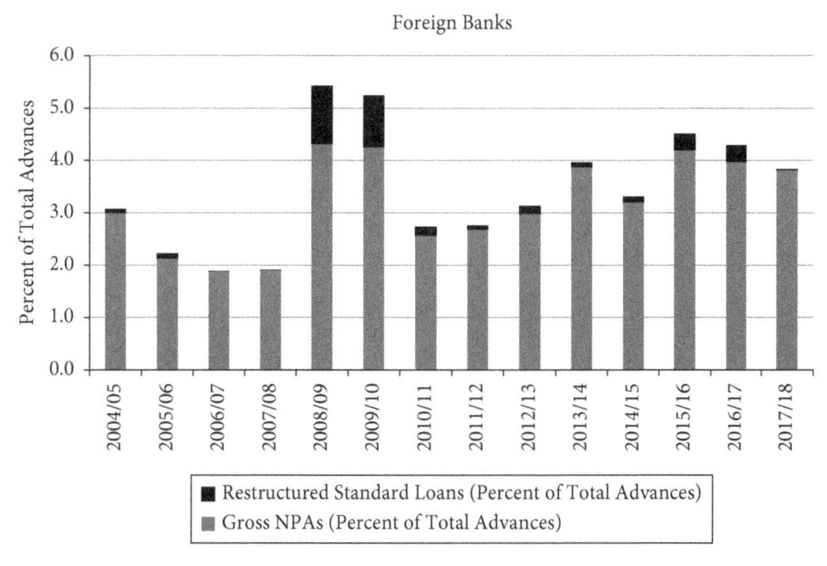

Figure 9.5 NPAs and Restructured Standard Loans of Foreign Banks, 2004/5 to 2017/18

Source: Author's construction using RBI data at https://dbie.rbi.org.in/DBIE/dbie.rbi?site=publications#!4 (accessed on March 15, 2019).

amounted to only 2.3 percent of total advances for private banks. In foreign banks, the peak was reached in 2008/9, the year of the global financial crisis; their restructured loans that year amounted to only 1.1 percent of total advances. Indeed, their NPAs, at 4.3 percent that year, were significantly higher.

Much-Delayed Recognition But No Effort Toward Resolution

To many observers, it was clear by the end of 2013/14 that India had a serious NPA problem. Given that the classification of restructured loans as standard loans under relatively generous conditions was contrary to international practice, their large volume could not be excluded from any realistic assessment of non-performing assets. And the combined value of NPAs and restructured loans as a proportion of total advances had crossed the 10 percent mark for public sector banks by this time. For some individual banks, the proportion was significantly larger. Yet neither RBI nor the government seemed to appreciate the gravity of the situation. The only corrective step RBI took was to raise the provisioning level for restructured loans to 2.75 percent in November 2012 and 5 percent in April 2013, as we have seen. These measures amounted to no more than band-aid solutions.

It was not until April 1, 2015, that RBI finally recognized that lenders and borrowers were abusing CDR by representing many bad loans as temporary problems that would go away if given breathing space through restructuring. At that juncture, it adopted the international best practice of downgrading restructured loans to the substandard category. By this time, NPAs plus restructured loans of public sector banks had reached 13.5 percent, though NPAs by themselves amounted to only 5 percent.

While aligning CDR with international best practice, RBI also offered borrowers several new restructuring avenues to escape the classification of their loans as NPAs. In June 2015, it introduced the Strategic Debt Restructuring (SDR) scheme, under which it provided for the conversion of a part of the loan to an ailing company into equity. Under the scheme, lender banks had to become majority owners with the right to replace management in order to turn around the asset. Though they were not allowed to sell partial equity, they could recover what they were owed by selling the company in its entirety. Under this scheme, RBI relaxed several of its regulations and allowed loans to be reported as standard assets. In case the bank failed to sell the company within eighteen months, the relaxations were withdrawn and the loan was downgraded to substandard.

On June 13, 2016, RBI introduced the Scheme for Sustainable Structuring of Stressed Assets (S4A). Under the scheme, a problematic company's debt was divided into sustainable and unsustainable components. As long as the sustainable component accounted for 50 percent or more of the loan and could be serviced under the original terms, the unsustainable component could be converted into equity or optionally convertible debentures with clearly spelled-out terms. Banks could sell this stake to a new owner.

A third RBI initiative, introduced in July 2014, was the scheme for Flexible Structuring of Long Term Loans to Infrastructure and Core Sector Industries. Commonly known as the 5:25 scheme, it was intended to resolve lending problems in the infrastructure sector, where projects typically take twenty to twenty-five years to complete. Banks normally do not lend beyond ten- to twelve-year terms, creating a mismatch between what is needed and what is available. The 5:25 scheme allowed lenders to offer loans with terms extending to twenty or twenty-five years by refinancing outstanding amounts every five to seven years. The scheme did not permit any haircuts, however, which meant that banks had to protect the net present value of the loans refinanced.

In 2014, RBI also attempted to create a mechanism to coordinate restructuring when multiple lenders were involved. It issued guidelines for the creation of a Joint Lenders Forum (JLF), which would recognize stressed assets early and formulate a Corrective Action Plan (CAP) with the consent of the majority of JLF members within forty-five days. The next year, RBI also directed banks to set up an empowered group that would be tasked with approving the restructuring package.

Predictably, these schemes failed to produce any major successes and were principally used by borrowers and lenders to delay downgrading of loans to non-performing status. The measure that made a major difference was the end of CDR, which finally began to bring bad loans into the open. At the end of 2015/16, just a year after the end of CDR, NPAs of public sector banks zoomed up 5 percentage points to reach 9.3 percent, and restructured loans fell from 8.5 percent to 6.7 percent. This shift continued in the following years, with public sector banks' NPAs rising to 14.6 percent and restructured loans declining to 4.2 percent at the end of 2017/18.

No progress took place, however, on cleaning up NPAs. Defaulting borrowers had a vested interest in maintaining the status quo, since it allowed them continued ownership of their assets. CEOs of public sector banks were reluctant to initiate action that would lead to partial instead of full recovery, out of the fear that this might bring accusations of corruption or lead to investigation by vigilance agencies. They preferred to postpone any action until their term was over and pass the buck to their successor. This remained true even after the Insolvency and Bankruptcy Code (IBC) (2016), which provided a clear, time-bound pathway to resolution of loans in default, had become operational.

Given this situation, any progress toward cleaning up NPAs required intervention by RBI and the Department of Financial Services (DFS) in the Finance Ministry. Unfortunately, neither RBI nor DFS exhibited any interest in the task between 2014 and 2016. RBI remained preoccupied with the introduction of different methods of restructuring loans and carrying out stress tests on them and the DFS with its Indradhanush initiative, which consisted of bend-aid solutions such as the replacement of the appointments board of public sector banks by Bank Boards Bureau, cosmetic governance reforms, and recapitalization of banks by the relatively small amount of 700 billion rupees spread over a period of four years.

Collapse of Credit and Action at Last

By early 2017, the evidence became compelling that rapidly accumulating NPAs were choking credit growth. As Table 9.1 shows, credit growth of public sector banks, which accounted for two-thirds of total credit, dropped to just 0.7 percent in 2016/17. The figure for all scheduled commercial banks fell to 3.6 percent the same year. These growth rates compared with substantially higher growth of credit of 14.5 percent for private sector banks, which enjoyed significantly lower levels of NPAs.[3]

Very likely, it was this breakdown in credit growth that finally led the government to move decisively to tackle the NPAs. In May 2017, it enacted an ordinance amending the Banking Regulation Act (1949). Now the government could authorize RBI to direct banks to initiate an insolvency resolution process in cases involving defaults. It also empowered RBI to appoint committees with the authority to advise banks on the resolution of stressed assets. The first part of the amendment helped ensure that banks would have the backing of the government and RBI in the initiation of bankruptcy proceedings against politically connected and powerful defaulters. RBI-appointed committees, which originated in the second part of the directive, gave them cover against potential charges of corruption on grounds such as excessive haircuts taken. Soon after the enactment of the ordinance, in October 2017, the government also announced its decision to raise the amount to be infused into public sector banks from 700 billion rupees to 2.1 trillion rupees. The period of this infusion was pegged at two years.

Armed with the ordinance, the government moved swiftly to authorize RBI to direct banks to initiate insolvency proceedings against defaulting borrowers. RBI moved equally swiftly and immediately directed banks to begin proceedings under the IBC for all accounts with an outstanding amount of 50 billion rupees or more. Numbering twelve in all, these accounts had an outstanding amount of

3.45 trillion rupees and represented a quarter of all NPAs at the time. The liquidation value of these accounts was assessed at 732.2 billion rupees.[4]

The IBC Process Yields Impressive Outcomes

Though still in its early stages, the IBC process has led to impressive outcomes, with many large accounts reaching resolution faster than ever before and yielding significantly higher recovery rates. By December 31, 2018, resolution plans for four of the twelve accounts had been approved. In another case, a liquidation order had been issued. The four accounts approved for restructuring had more than 920 billion rupees due on them jointly. The recovery rate for them, at 51 percent, was considerably higher than their estimated liquidation value.

Table 9.2 provides a summary of the timeline for all cases admitted under the Corporate Insolvency Resolution Process (CIRP) of the IBC as of December 31, 2018. Of the 1,484 cases admitted, 586, or 39.5 percent, had already reached closure by this date. Another 623 cases or 42 percent had been under resolution for less than 270 days. Cases exceeding 270 days numbered 275, or 18.5 percent of the total. Compared to India's past history, this is a significant jump in the speed of resolution of bankruptcy cases. Given that the National Company Law

Table 9.2 Status of Corporate Insolvency Resolution Process as of December 31, 2018

Status of CIRPs	Number of CIRPs
Admitted	1,484
Closed on appeal/review/settled	142
Closed by withdrawal under section 12A	63
Closed by resolution	79
Closed by liquidation	302
Ongoing CIRP	898
> 270 days	275
> 180 days < 270 days	166
> 90 days < 180 days	202
< 90 days	255

Source: Insolvency and Bankruptcy Board of India, 2018, table 4.

Tribunal, which conducts the proceedings, remains understaffed, these numbers bode well for the future of bankruptcy cases in India.

One criticism of the IBC process has been that it has led to liquidation in a disproportionately large number of cases. According to Table 9.2, a hefty 51.5 percent of the total cases reaching closure resulted in liquidation. This criticism misses the fact that 227 out of 302 cases culminating in liquidation, or 75.2 percent, had been with the Bureau of Industrial and Financial Restructuring earlier and the entities had lost much of their economic value before they were brought into the IBC process.

The reduction of delays in resolution has also translated into increased recovery rates. Under alternative channels such as Lok Adalat, DRT, and SARFAESI, which are subject to long delays, recovery rates have been much lower. Table 9.3 provides recovery rates associated with these alternative avenues to bankruptcy for 2016/17 and 2017/18. In aggregate, recovery rates from the three channels have averaged less than 15 percent. The recovery rate under SARFAESI has been significantly higher than under the other two processes and also saw an improvement in 2017/18. The reason for this may be an amendment to the SARFAESI Act providing for three months of imprisonment if the borrower does not give asset details and possession of mortgaged property by the lender within thirty days. In comparison, based on the results for twenty-one financial creditors during 2017/18, the recovery rate under IBC has been 49.6 percent.

Table 9.3 Recovery in Cases Under Channels Existing Prior to IBC

Amounts involved or recovered	Lok Adalats	DRTs	SARFAESI	Total
2016/17				
Amount involved (billions of rupees)	361	1008	1414	2783
Amount recovered (billions of rupees)	23	103	259	385
Recovery rate*	6.3	10.2	18.3	13.8
2017/18				
Amount involved (billions of rupees)	457	1,333	1,067	2857
Amount recovered (billions of rupees)	18	72	265	355
Recovery rate*	4.0	5.4	24.8	12.4

*Amount recovered as percent of amount involved.

Source: Reserve Bank of India 2018, 64, table IV.15.

Though the cleaning up of NPAs remains a work in progress, there is no doubt that the IBC-RBI process has turned over a new leaf in this area. If this process continues to progress, with RBI leading the way, banks would see steady improvement in the quality of their assets. This improvement would also lead to a return to healthy credit growth.

Combating the Creation of New NPAs

A final question concerns the creation of new NPAs. Even if the current crisis of NPAs passes, how can India be sure that history will not repeat itself? In February 2018, RBI issued a circular specifying a number of measures aimed at early detection of NPAs and their resolution in a timely manner. Unfortunately, the Supreme Court struck down this circular in April 2019 on the grounds that it violated the laws under which it had been issued. Subsequently, in June 2019, RBI issued a new circular that aims to achieve the same objectives, but it is significantly weaker than the February 2018 circular.

During the short time it was in force, the February 2018 circular produced a very encouraging experience. Therefore, it is worthwhile to consider its main provisions. It withdrew the existing restructuring schemes, such as 5:25, SDR, and S4A, and mandated that banks must report a loan as being in default if the borrower misses her payment even by one day. It required that the banks clssify such a loan immediately as a special mention account. The special mention account was to turn into NPA if it remained in default for ninety days or longer. All lenders associated with the special mention account were required to put in place a board-approved resolution plan.

In the case of accounts with aggregate exposures equaling or exceeding 20 billion rupees, the circular applied additional regulations. Resolution plans in such cases had to be implemented within 180 days of the first day of default. If this was not done, lenders were compelled to file an insolvency application under IBC within fifteen days after the 180-day deadline. If a resolution plan was implemented within the 180-day period, the account had to remain free of default at all points during the "specified period," which was the longer of (1) one year from the commencement of the first payment of interest or principal or (2) the period from the date of implementation of the resolution plan until 20 percent of the outstanding principal debt and interest capitalization was repaid.

This added to the IBC regime by making the process of resolution of accounts in default automatic and time-bound in the case of loans worth 20 billion rupees or more. It required that banks either demonstrate the sustainability of loans in default by either implementing a resolution plan that keeps the borrower out of further default during the specified period or filing an insolvency application. The provision meant that borrowers and lenders could not let an account remain in default indefinitely.

The default by Jet Airways illustrates the power of the circular. A story in the newspaper *Economic Times* describes the episode thus: "Indian bankers were never this powerful. . . . A resolution plan for a failed airline, with debt of more than Rs 8,000 crore [80 billion rupees], is in place in less than three months from the day of default. This would have been impossible without the new rules—the Reserve Bank of India's (RBI) February 12 order on the treatment of defaults, and the December 2016 bankruptcy laws."[5] The story goes on to contrast this experience with that of Essar Steel, which managed to delay a takeover of the company for two years after defaulting on a 400 billion rupee loan under the old rules.

The revised RBI circular of June 2019 retains many features of the February 2018 circular but does away with the requirement of compulsory filing for bankruptcy in the event that lenders fail to implement a resolution plan for accounts amounting to 20 billion rupees or more within 180 days; instead, it provides for additional provisioning. This change represents a vast improvement over the situation prevailing prior to April 1, 2015, when RBI did away with CDR. But it is a step back from the RBI circular of February 2018.

The Case for Privatization of Public Sector Banks

The decision to nationalize the larger banks in 1969 was wholly political. Prime Minister Indira Gandhi faced an existential threat from her rivals, who controlled the organizational wing of the Congress Party. Morarji Desai, then finance minister, was one of these rivals. To break loose of the organizational wing, Gandhi needed to fire Desai and take full charge of the government. Desai's opposition to bank nationalization gave her the necessary excuse to get rid of him. She took charge of the Finance Ministry and issued an ordinance nationalizing all banks with deposits worth 500 million rupees or more. The decision led the organizational wing of the Congress Party to separate from Gandhi. But with nationalization proving highly popular, Gandhi came out victorious. Her faction of the Congress Party eventually scored a resounding victory in parliamentary elections in 1971.

Although many commentators have hailed bank nationalization as an important step toward bringing banking to the masses and improving access of the common people to credit, the reality remains that on balance the measure has been costly along many dimensions. I am convinced that it is now time for the government to return public sector banks to the private sector. This conviction is grounded in a number of factors that may be discussed under three headings: efficiency, social goals, and governance.

Efficiency

First, there is overwhelming evidence that public sector banks have performed less efficiently than their private sector counterparts. Much of the earlier evidence gathered by economists is discussed in my 2008 book, *India: The Emerging Giant*. Here it suffices to present four key indicators of efficiency: credit-deposit ratio, return on assets, wages as a proportion of income, and asset shares.

Figures 9.6 and 9.9 depict the relative levels of these indicators in public, private, and foreign banks from 2004/5 to 2017/18. Across all four indicators and all years shown, private banks unambiguously outperform public sector banks. Broadly, foreign banks also perform better than public sector banks. If exceptions arise with respect to foreign banks, they are related to events in the global economy such as the global financial crisis of 2008 and shifts in interest rates abroad, especially the United States, due to the greater integration of these banks into the global economy.

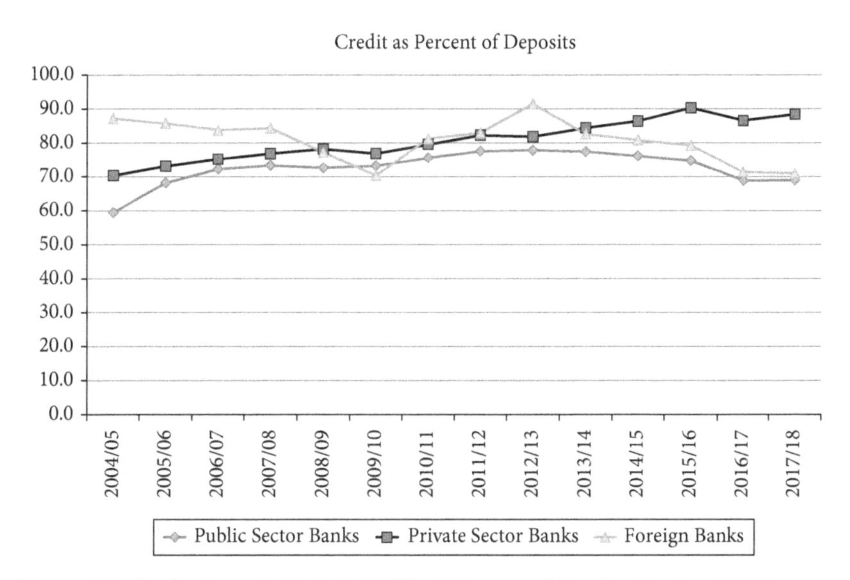

Figure 9.6 Credit-Deposit Ratio in Public, Private, and Foreign Banks, 2004/5 to 2017/18

Source: Author's construction using RBI data.

According to Figure 9.6, the credit-deposit ratio in private sector banks has been consistently higher than in public sector banks. The gap between the ratios of the two sets of banks has seen a sharp widening in recent years—in all likelihood because of the significantly faster accumulation of NPAs in public sector banks. What is remarkable, however, is that even during the years that public sector bank credit expanded rapidly without due diligence, private sector banks maintained a higher credit-deposit ratio and yet did not see their loans convert into NPAs at a rate as high as public sector banks in subsequent years. Foreign banks also outperformed public sector banks in terms of credit-deposit ratio except in 2009/10, the year immediately following the global financial crisis.

Figure 9.7 shows the return on assets in the three sets of banks. This is the single most important measure of bank performance, and here the contrast between public sector banks on the one hand and private and foreign banks on the other could not be sharper. Not only is the return in private banks higher than in public sector banks for every single year from 2009/10 to 2014/15, but private banks saw their return rise, while public sector banks saw theirs decline. During the last three years shown, the return turned negative in public sector banks. Foreign banks have outperformed even private banks in all but three years shown.

Figure 9.8 shows the wage bill as a proportion of income for the three sets of banks. According to this measure, private banks consistently outdo both public

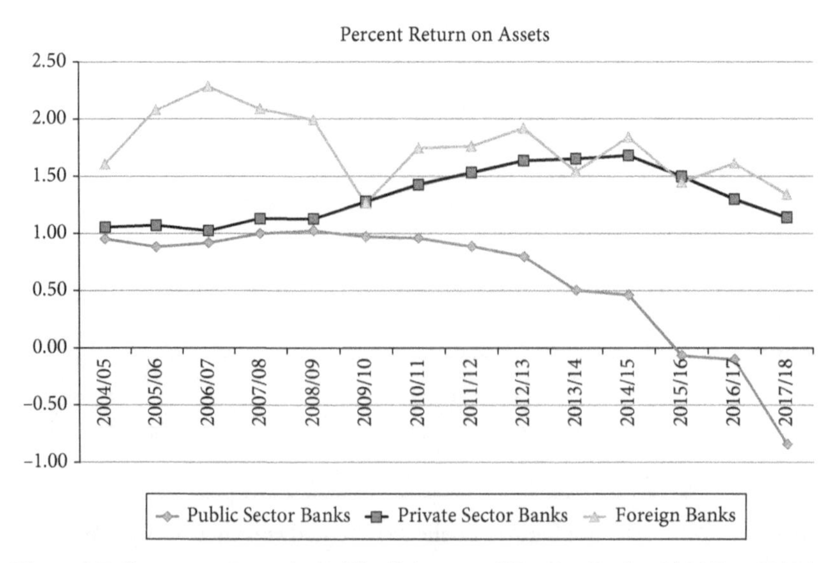

Figure 9.7 Return on Assets in Public, Private, and Foreign Banks, 2004/5 to 2017/18

Source: Author's construction using RBI data.

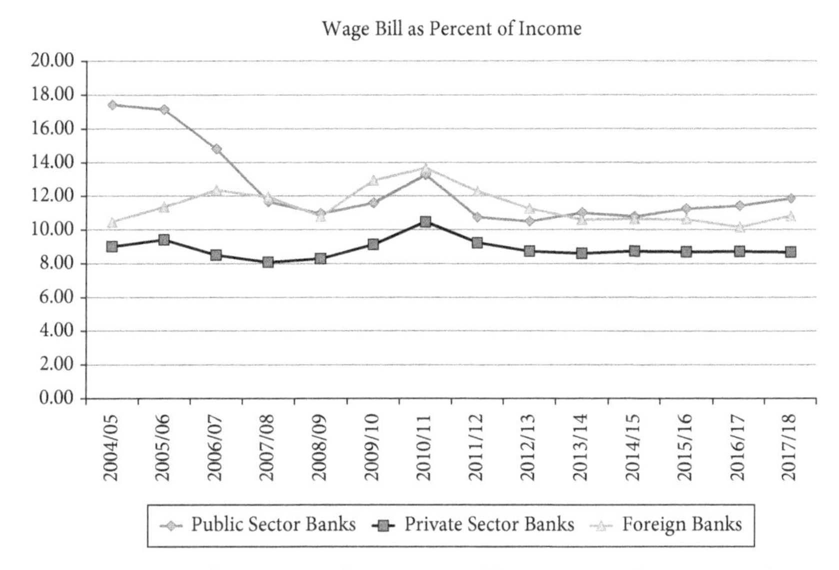

Figure 9.8 Wage Bill as Percent of Income in Public, Private, and Foreign Banks, 2004/5 to 2017/18

Source: Author's construction using RBI data.

sector and foreign banks. They generally use labor more efficiently than the latter. A higher wage-income ratio for foreign banks is not surprising given that their wages are partially linked to international wages. What is surprising is that during the last five years shown, the wage-income ratio in public sector banks has exceeded even that in foreign banks.

Figure 9.9 depicts shifts in asset shares of the three sets of banks. The better performance of private sector banks has resulted in a progressive shift in relative shares in favor of private banks. From around 90 percent in the early 1990s, the share of public sector banks in the total assets of scheduled commercial banks had fallen to 80.2 percent as of March 31, 2000. This share fell further to 71.9 percent by March 31, 2009, and then to 66.0 percent by March 31, 2018. The trend has continued despite large infusions of capital by the government in public sector banks on different occasions.

Social Goals

The second issue that a discussion of privatization of banks must address concerns their role in promoting social goals. It is often argued that the government needs public sector banks to promote desirable social goals that

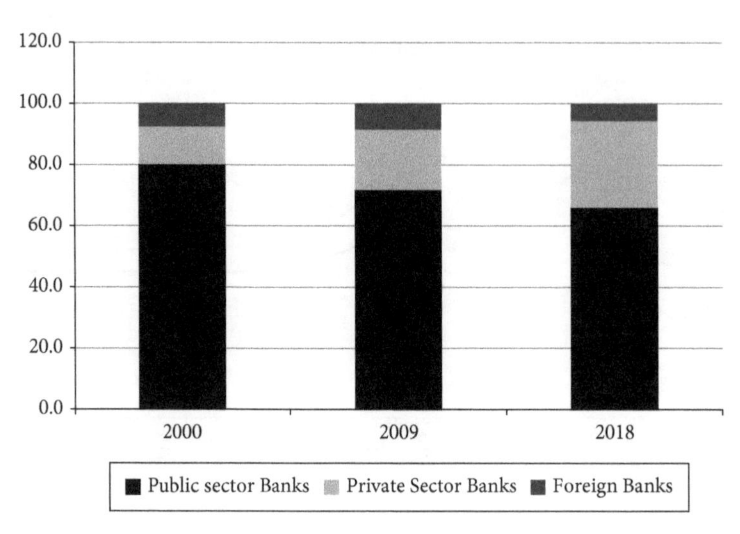

Figure 9.9 Percent Shares of Bank Groups in the Total Assets of Scheduled Commercial Banks
Source: Author's construction using RBI data.

profit-driven private banks will not pursue. Here, the counterargument is that appropriate regulation by RBI can nudge profit-maximizing banks to contribute to social goals as well. Moreover, efficiency dictates that all banks equally share the burden of achieving socially desirable objectives. There is no reason only one set of banks should carry that burden. When the burden is placed only on one set of banks—public sector banks—it creates a distortion in the system. Moreover, it necessitates offsetting action to compensate these banks in some form. This adds to the initial distortion.

In one important area, priority-sector lending, experience shows that it is entirely possible to have a common regime for public and private sector banks to promote social objectives. This can be seen in Figure 9.10, which depicts the share of priority-sector advances in the total advances of different bank groups. While it is true that the share has been higher for public sector banks during many of the years shown, private and foreign banks have also delivered satisfactory outcomes. Indeed, in some years, private banks have allocated a larger share of their advances to priority sectors than public sector banks have.

Regulation by RBI can be used to promote other social goals as well. For example, the burden of expansion of rural banking can be placed equally on all banks through appropriate incentives. Expansion of bank accounts to promote financial inclusion can be similarly spread over all banks. In a similar vein, a non-discriminatory regime can be devised to incentivize the speedy digitization of transactions should that be viewed as a desirable social goal.

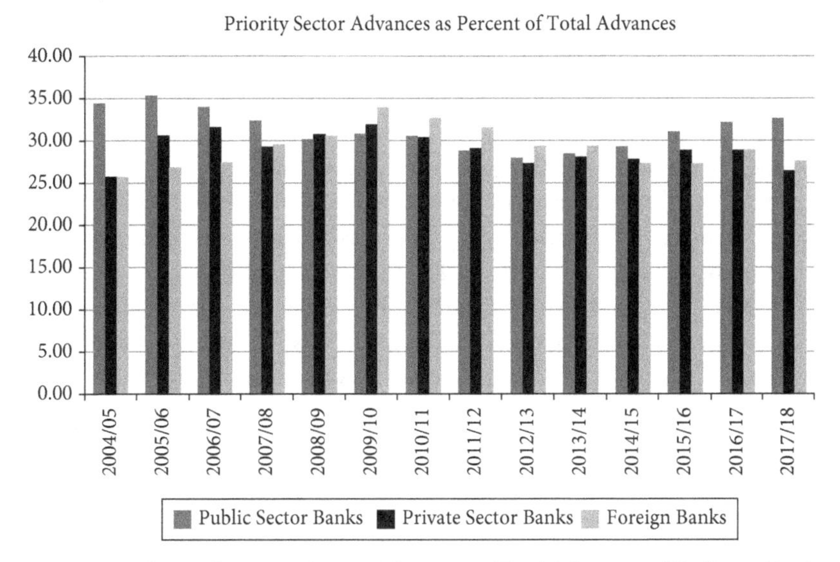

Figure 9.10 Share of Priority-Sector Advances in Total Advances of Different Bank Groups, 2004/5 to 2017/18

Source: Author's construction using RBI data.

Governance

Issues related to governance offer the most compelling case for privatization of public sector banks. A number of factors are worthy of highlighting.

First, government ownership has led to a regulatory regime that is not ownership neutral. RBI can remove directors or management of private banks but not public sector banks. It can force a merger or trigger liquidation of a private bank but not public sector bank. It has legal authority to hold boards of private and foreign banks accountable regarding strategic direction, risk profiles, assessment of management, and compensation, but not public sector banks. Unlike private and foreign banks, public sector banks do not require a license to operate from RBI. This means that RBI lacks the power to halt the operations of public sector banks should the need arise.

Second, as a corollary of the previous point, public sector banks are subject to dual regulation by the Finance Ministry and RBI. The Finance Ministry issues numerous circulars to give formal directives to the banks. When the government launches special programs. such as the campaign to open bank accounts for all under the Pradhan Mantri Jan Dhan Yojana financial inclusion program, it issues special directives to public sector banks that do not apply to private banks. The government also gives verbal, undocumented direction to these banks. At the same time, in matters such as cash reserve ratio, statutory liquidity ratio, capital adequacy ratio, classification of assets into standard and non-standard, and numerous reporting requirements, the banks are subject to regulations issued by RBI.

Under this system of dual regulation, the government appoints all directors of public sector banks other than those elected by shareholders. These directors cannot be considered as independent. This means that when it comes to listing public sector banks on the stock market, they are in violation of the guidelines of the SEBI. Unlike private banks, the boards of public sector banks do not have the power to bring on directors with special skills. The tenures of chairmen and executive directors of boards of public sector bank are short, which greatly undermines their ability and motivation to exercise control over management.

Third, with government ownership come government rules applicable to employees that differ from those applying to employees of private sector banks. Over time, this has led to a significant widening of differences in salaries and other compensation between public and private banks. In turn, this has also led to differences in skills, which has contributed to differences in performance of the two sets of banks.

Equally important, public sector bank employees are under constant threat of being investigated by the Central Vigilance Commission (CVC) and Central Bureau of Investigation (CBI). While even systematic good performance of loans advanced by an employee promises to bring few rewards, failures of even a small number of loans can trigger investigation by CVC and CBI. This situation greatly impacts the risk-taking behavior of bank employees when they are making decisions about loans. At the same time, the short tenures of top management and board members plus the absence of commercial pressures similar to those faced by private sector banks provide fertile ground for fraudulent transactions for private gain by corrupt but enterprising regular employees. A recent episode of a major fraud at Punjab National Bank highlights this problem.

Fourth, ownership by the government leads to political interference in ways that have worked to greatly weaken public sector banks and, given their disproportionate share in total banking assets, the entire banking sector. This interference has typically taken two forms. One, politically powerful private entrepreneurs are able to manipulate the system to obtain loans even when they have no intention of paying them back in full. Two, the government directs public sector banks to advance loans to entities (both private and public) operating in the infrastructure, transportation, and energy sectors even when the projects are not commercially viable. Often the lack of commercial viability is the result of difficulties in land acquisition and slow clearances by various government ministries, most notably the Environment Ministry. Both types of interference have resulted in the accumulation of large volumes of non-performing assets in recent years.

Finally, ownership of banks creates serious conflicts across the various roles that the government must play. First and foremost, the government is the policymaker for the banking sector. But as the owner of public sector banks, it also becomes a service provider. In addition, through various channels, it also acts as a regulator of banks. Therefore, we have a situation in which the policymaker is making policy for itself and the regulator is regulating itself. While few analysts would question the right of the government to give direction to the regulator in a crisis situation, exercising that right on a day-to-day basis leads to conflicts of interest and undesirable interference in the functioning of the sector.

Will There Be Takers for Public Sector Banks?

Skeptics sometimes argue that the government may not find any takers if it tries to sell public sector banks. This fear is based on the assumption that the government will be selling its entire equity in each bank in a single go within a short period. But that assumption is unfounded.

All public sector banks are currently listed on the stock market. What the government will need to do is begin the process by selling just enough shares in a bank to bring its equity below 50 percent. At that stage, after appropriate changes in the law, management of the bank can be transferred to a private board. The government can then further reduce its stake gradually and take advantage of increases in share prices that would follow. A simple path to privatization can thus be laid out.

The assumption that the government must privatize all banks at once or within a short period also lacks basis. It can have a plan extending to three or four years, during which time its share in equity in each bank will be reduced below 50 percent. State Bank of India can be placed at the end of the line. As the government dilutes its equity in more and more banks and transfers control of management to private boards, it will have the opportunity to assess whether this is unduly undermining its ability to achieve social objectives. If the answer turns out to be in the affirmative, it can choose not to privatize the State Bank of India.

An Alternative to Privatization and Toward Bank Consolidation

It is sometimes argued that many of the objectives of bank privatization can be achieved without the government having to give up ownership of public sector banks. The Nayak Committee report, submitted in 2014, has outlined one such plan. Under it, the government would form the Bank Investment Company (BIC) under the Companies Act, which would have the character of a passive sovereign wealth fund for the government's banks. Legislation nationalizing banks would be repealed and ownership rights would be transferred to BIC, which would also become the holder of the government's equity in the banks. In the final stage of reform, BIC would transfer all ownership functions to bank boards and would be left to exercise investor functions only. Public sector banks would be governed the same way as private banks, with the positions of chairman of the board and CEO held by different individuals. RBI would adopt a uniform licensing regime across all board-based banks serving similar functions and ensure that publicly owned and private banks are subject to the same set of regulations. The government would withdraw from regulating banks and pursue all social objectives through RBI regulation that would apply uniformly to the two types of banks.

Theoretically, these reforms can achieve approximately the same outcome as privatization. But I am skeptical that within the complex system of governance that India has, these reforms will reach their logical conclusion. The intent may be there, but as the reforms work their way through the labyrinth of India's political-bureaucratic process, they will morph into something quite different or get stalled altogether. It would be best to repeal the legislation nationalizing the banks, dilute the government's equity below 50 percent in a short period of time, and offload the rest of it over a five-year period. RBI should license the banks as private banks so that any regulatory distinction between them and existing private banks would be eliminated.

India also needs to consolidate its banks. Banking is subject to substantial economies of scale and scope, which means that the existence of too many small banks undermines efficiency. In this respect, recent decisions to merge several public sector banks into a smaller number of larger banks are a very welcome development. These decisions have brought down the number of public sector banks from twenty-seven before 2017 to twelve. The government should work toward bringing this number further down to half a dozen, since creating even larger banks will make the banks more efficient and competitive. Moreover, privatization will be easier to accomplish when the number of banks is smaller.

Government Policies and Private Investment

Three aspects of government policy bearing on the availability of financial resources to private investors through financial markets may be noted. First, taking GDP and private consumption as given, the higher the level of government expenditure, the lower the level of resources available to private investors. The government finances its expenditures principally by tax revenue or borrowing from financial markets. But whether the government raises tax revenue by taxing household income, corporate profits, or consumption of goods and services, it lowers the savings available to private investors. Reduced savings in turn result in reduced private investment. If the government finances expenditures by borrowing from the market, it crowds out private investors, once again reducing private investment. No matter how the government finances expenditures, it has an effect on private investment. This fact must be given due consideration when considering increases in government spending.

Second, India has had a long-standing policy of requiring banks to offer a specified percentage of their credit to a particular set of sectors or entities, including agriculture, renewable energy, education, micro and small enterprises, low-cost housing, and small businesses and service enterprises. This policy of priority-sector lending has an adverse effect on the allocation of available investment funds across sectors. To the extent that a floor on lending to priority sectors results in the diversion of investment funds from higher-return projects in non-priority sectors, there is a loss of efficiency in the use of the funds. In the 1990s, the first Narasimham Committee on banking reforms had recommended phasing out priority-sector lending, but the government did not accept that recommendation. It is time to return to a discussion of this reform.

Finally, despite considerable liberalization, interest rates on many small savings schemes, including the Public Provident Fund, Senior Citizen Savings Scheme, and Sukanya Samriddhi (Girl Child Prosperity) Scheme, continue to be administered by the government. Interest rates paid on savings deposits under these schemes are held well above market rates. To attract deposits, banks have to compete against these schemes, with the result that the connection of lending rates to the policy interest rate of the Reserve Bank of India is weakened. Pass-through of reductions in the latter rate to lending rates is at best partial. In order for monetary policy to work smoothly, the government needs to free up all interest rates and use alternative instruments to protect the interests of the groups currently being helped through above-market interest rates.

Concluding Remarks

Channeling finance to projects with high returns is a highly critical function in any economy. In a developing economy where available funds are limited and high-return projects are spread out and not easily identified, this function assumes even greater importance. Only a well-functioning banking system, manned by staff with skills to identify high-return projects, can satisfactorily solve this problem.

India has a substantial banking sector today. But it is underperforming by a wide margin and has been afflicted by repeated bouts of accumulation of non-performing assets. A key factor in the underperformance of the sector is public ownership of banks accounting for two-thirds of banking assets. This ownership has been justified on the ground that banks must promote a set of social goals. But the argument is flawed. All banks must contribute equally to the pursuit of social goals, as is currently the case with priority-sector lending. Requiring one set of banks to perform functions that another set of banks need not perform does not just create an uneven playing field but also leads to gross inefficiency. RBI must use one set of regulatory rules for publicly owned banks and another set of rules for private banks. In turn, public sector banks must answer to two masters: RBI and the government. Public ownership also means that the banks are not subject to the usual commercial pressures. All these features of the current Indian banking system point to the urgent need for privatization of public sector banks. If the government must retain ownership, it should limit it to one bank, the State Bank of India. If this is done, the government must place the State Bank of India at arm's length with a special-purpose vehicle so that the regulatory anomalies discussed in this chapter can be minimized.

A healthy financial sector is critical to the accumulation of physical capital in high-productivity activities. Equally important, however, is human capital formation. Indeed, it may be argued that with technology taking center stage in all aspects of human life today, human capital formation has become even more important than physical capital formation. A critical element in human capital formation is the availability of first-rate higher education, a much neglected sector in India; a detailed treatment of this issue is in Chapter 10.

Appendix: History of Banking Prior to 1991 Reforms

The history of banking in India prior to the launch of economic reforms in 1991 can be divided into three periods: the pre-independence era (1720 to 1947), the early post-independence years (1947 to 1967), and the nationalization phase (1967 to 1991).

Pre-Independence Era (1720 to 1947)

The first Western-style joint stock bank in India was Bank of Bombay, established in 1720 in Bombay. But it lasted for only sixty years.[6] More substantial activity started later and was located on the eastern side of the country, where the British East India Company was successful in establishing control during its early years. Bank of Hindustan was established in 1770 and General Bank of Bengal and Bihar in 1773. Three Presidency banks with government participation followed: Bank of Bengal in Calcutta in 1806, Bank of Bombay in 1840 in Bombay, and Bank of Madras in Madras (now Chennai) in 1843. Royal charters governed the Presidency banks. The banks also issued currency notes until the enactment of the Paper Currency Act (1861), which transferred the right to issue currency to the government.

Until 1860, banks and insurance companies were subject to unlimited liability. Beginning in 1860, Indian law permitted limited liability, which led to an increase in banking activity. Allahabad Bank, the first Indian-owned bank, came into existence in 1865. Punjab National Bank was established in Lahore in 1895 and Bank of India in Bombay in 1906. The Swadeshi movement of 1906 accelerated the process of establishing joint stock banks of Indian ownership. It led to the founding of Central Bank of India, Bank of Baroda, Canara Bank, Indian Bank, and Bank of Mysore between 1906 and 1913. By December 1913, India had fifty-six reporting commercial banks.

During the First World War, many banks with low capital bases and limited liquid assets failed. Failed banks also included some large banks such as the British-owned Indian Special Bank. In large part the failures were due to imprudent management involving large unsecured advances to directors and their companies. Such lending was possible due to the absence of adequate regulatory safeguards.

In 1921, the three Presidency banks were merged to form Imperial Bank of India. Later, several banks belonging to princely states such as Jaipur, Mysore, Patiala, and Jodhpur were merged into Imperial Bank of India. In addition to functioning as a commercial bank, Imperial Bank also discharged the functions of a central bank until the establishment of the Reserve Bank of India in 1935 via the Reserve Bank of India Act (1934). RBI was assigned four functions: act as a banker to the government, issue notes, act as banker to other banks, and maintain the exchange rate. In its role as banker to other banks, RBI also became the lender of last resort.

In its early years, RBI lacked adequate powers of control and regulation. The Companies Act (1913), which governed ordinary non-banking companies, also governed banks. New banks could be set up under this law without the permission of RBI. In this environment of virtual free entry and exit of banks and no real regulation, small banks mushroomed. At the same time, banks also remained subject to a high rate of bankruptcy. The Companies (Amendment) Act (1936) introduced a separate chapter on banking companies and specified norms with respect to minimum capital and cash reserve requirements, but the provisions fell far short of creating an adequate regulatory regime. It was not until the

Banking Companies Act (1949) that RBI acquired comprehensive powers of supervision and control of the banking system.

Wartime expenditures on defense and supplies led to a rapid expansion of currency. This correspondingly increased the incomes of some sections of the population. With supplies of consumption goods (including through imports) restricted, however, unspent margins expanded and created a large pool of bank deposits. In turn, this led to a rapid expansion of bank branches of scheduled commercial banks between 1940 and 1945. Several banks were spread thin and the risk of failure increased. Luckily, with the sector highly fragmented and interbank linkages missing, failures remained localized with no contagion effect.

Early Post-Independence Phase (1947 to 1967)

At independence, Indian banking was entirely in the private sector. Even the central bank, the Reserve Bank of India (RBI), was not entirely state-owned until its nationalization via the Reserve Bank of India (Transfer to Public Ownership) Act (1948). Imperial Bank of India, created by merging three Presidency banks in 1921, was the largest commercial bank. There were five other large banks with deposits of 1 billion rupees each: Central Bank of India, Punjab National Bank, Bank of India, Bank of Baroda, and United Commercial Bank.

Scheduled commercial banks, numbering 97, dominated the banking system at the end of December 1947. Non-scheduled banks and cooperative banks, though large in number at 557 and 395, respectively, jointly accounted for only 13.6 percent of the total deposits.[7] Scheduled banks had a regional focus, with West Bengal having the largest concentration of them, followed by Madras and Bombay. Madras led by a wide margin in the concentration of non-scheduled banks, with West Bengal and Bombay claiming distant second and third positions, respectively.

The immediate post-independence era saw an acceleration in bankruptcies of banks. This was in part due to disruptions resulting from Partition. The western and eastern parts of the country, which had been impacted heavily by Partition, also witnessed a greater incidence of such bankruptcies. To address the problem and to protect the interests of depositors, the government passed the Banking Companies Act (1949), giving RBI wide powers to regulate banks. This helped slow down bank failures but did not eliminate them. Therefore, efforts were made to force the merger or liquidation of weaker banks. A total of 83 banks were merged with other banks between 1954 and 1960. This process accelerated after the enactment of the Banking Companies (Amendment) Act (1961), which gave clarity to and supplemented the provisions in the original legislation regarding compulsory mergers of banks. Between 1960 and 1966, 217 banks were merged with other banks. The total number of non-scheduled banks fell from 474 in 1951 to 210 in 1961 and just 20 in 1967.

While consolidating banks, India also made it a high priority to use the sector as an instrument to mobilize savings by Indians for economic development. This required both the expansion of bank branches (including in rural areas and smaller towns) and improving the flow of credit to agriculture, which employed 70 percent of India's workforce. According to the All India Rural Credit Survey (AIRCS) Committee, which submitted its report in 1954, commercial banks provided only 0.9 percent of the total credit to farmers in 1951/52, which amounted to 7.5 billion rupees. Therefore, the committee recommended proactive measures to increase the flow of bank credit to agriculture.

A key recommendation of the AIRCS Committee was nationalization of the Imperial Bank of India and merging the former state-owned and state-associated banks with it. Accordingly, an act was passed in May 1955 that led to the constitution of the State Bank of India in July 1955. More than a quarter of the resources of the banking system came into the public sector as a result. In 1959, another act led to the takeover of eight former state-associated banks as subsidiaries of SBI. This brought nearly one-third of the country's banking resources into the public sector. To maintain an arm's-length relationship between the government and SBI, the ownership of the latter was given to RBI. This step was also seen as helpful in preserving the original corporate character of the Imperial Bank of India under its new name.

At the direction of RBI, SBI speeded up branch expansion in general and in rural areas in particular. Other commercial banks also expanded their networks, though their focus remained largely urban India. Between 1952 and 1967, rural branches expanded from 540 to 1,247, semi-urban branches from 1,942 to 3,022, and urban branches from 1,451 to 2,716. Advances to agriculture rose from 120 million rupees in 1951 to 570 million rupees in 1967, but this amounted to only a marginal increase in its share in total bank credit over the period, from 2.1 to 2.2 percent. In 1967, industry had the largest share in total advances at 64.3 percent, followed by commerce at 19.4 percent.

By 1967, two key concerns with the banking sector occupied the attention of policymakers. First, through ownership of banks, a handful of business families managed to concentrate bank deposits in their hands. These families loaned the funds to their own or each other's industrial arms. Second, as far as bank credit was concerned, agriculture remained neglected, with its share in total bank credit remaining minuscule.

In the early years, this situation may well have resulted from the priority that Prime Minister Jawaharlal Nehru gave to industry, especially heavy industry. But after Nehru died in 1964 and his successor, Prime Minister Lal Bahadur Shastri, shifted the focus of policy to agriculture, the concern with the low share of agriculture in bank credit became more acute. Under Prime Minister Indira Gandhi, who succeeded Shastri following his untimely death, Indian socialism turned far more aggressive and populist, with industrialists becoming its direct target. The concern that the nexus between banks and industrial houses had led the latter to hog the bulk of the credit, with agriculture and small enterprises left to starve financially, assumed center stage.

Social Control and Nationalization (1967 to 1991)

During 1967–69, the government tried to address these concerns through social control of banks. In 1966 the government had amended the Banking Companies Act, renaming it the Banking Regulation Act, to require commercial banks to include in their boards members with special knowledge of accountancy, agriculture and rural economy, banking cooperation, economics, and small-scale industry. The amendment also required the banks to appoint a full-time chairman who was a professional banker and not an industrialist. Furthermore, it gave RBI power to appoint and remove the chairman, any director, the chief executive officer, or any other officer or employee of the bank. It was understood that in exercising these powers, RBI would keep in view not just the interests of the banks and depositors but also the larger public interest. A key component of public interest in this context was to make banks a more effective instrument of development via faster expansion of bank branches in unbanked areas and channeling of credit to priority sectors such as agriculture and small-scale industry.

Before social control had the opportunity to prove its worth, however, political considerations led Gandhi to nationalize all fourteen banks that had deposits worth 500 million rupees or more in July 1969.[8] With SBI already nationalized, this action gave the government ownership and control of more than 90 percent of the country's banking assets and deposits. In due course, the deposits of another six private banks grew to 500 million rupees or more, and on the recommendation of the RBI governor, Gandhi nationalized them as well in 1980. Therefore, from 1969 until 1991, when the license permit raj finally gave way to more liberal policies, the government remained in firm control of the banking sector.

This control in turn allowed the government to freely employ the country's banking resources to promote the twin goals of expanding the banking network to rural and semi-rural areas and diverting credit flow to priority sectors that were considered underfinanced. In the early years following nationalization, the government used the Lead Bank Scheme (LBS) to expand the branch network. Under it, a "lead bank" was designated for each district and given responsibility to provide leadership for the expansion of banking infrastructure in that district. The program was effective in expanding branch networks by 129 percent between 1969 and 1975. Half of the new branches opened during this period were in rural areas. As a result, the share of rural branches in total branches increased from 17.6 percent in 1969 to 36.3 percent in 1975.

In 1977, the government introduced a branch license policy under which banks were allowed to open one branch each in metropolitan and urban areas for every four branches opened in rural areas. To ensure that branch expansion also resulted in the expansion of credit, rural and semi-urban branches were directed to maintain a minimum 60 percent credit-deposit ratio. Bank branch expansion as well as correction of the urban bias continued during the 1980s. By 1990, rural branches accounted for 58.2 percent of the total number of bank branches. Semi-urban branches accounted for an additional 19 percent of all branches. But this indiscriminate expansion of branches proved costly. Many branches could not be sustained on a commercial basis. In 1990, the government decided to discontinue its bank branch expansion program.

The second major initiative of the government was to reorient credit in favor of what it considered to be priority sectors. The government had been making efforts to raise the share of agriculture in credit through the instrumentality of the State Bank of India and its subsidiaries. Nationalization of another fourteen large banks gave the government the ability to intensify those efforts. In 1972, it went on to adopt a formal definition of priority sector, and in November 1974 it directed all public sector banks to raise the proportion of priority sector credit in total outstanding credit to one-third by March 1979. In November 1978, it also directed private sector banks to reach the same target by March 1980. Both sets of banks achieved the target by the assigned dates. Subsequently, the target was raised to 40 percent of outstanding credit, which too was achieved.

These efforts led to a decline in the share of formal industry in total credit from 67.5 percent at the end of 1967/68 to 38.9 percent at the end of 1979/80 and 37.5 percent at the end of 1988/89. The share of agriculture rose from 2.2 percent at the end of 1967/68 to 15.8 percent at the end of 1988/89. Exports and small-scale industry came to account for 22.6 percent of credit by the end of 1988/89.

From the mid-1960s onward, India practiced extensive credit controls. Interest rates were controlled and varied by sector as well as by the size of the borrower. Credit was rationed, so not everyone wishing to borrow could borrow, or could borrow the amount she wanted. At a broad level, priority sector lending was at subsidized rates, which resulted in an effective tax on the rates charged to non-priority-sector lending. Within both the priority and non-priority sectors, multiple rates prevailed. Under the Credit Allocation Scheme, RBI had to approve any loan exceeding a relatively low threshold. The government offered low interest rates on its debt. These low rates were sustained by the high statutory liquidity ratio that banks were required to maintain. Empirical estimates suggest that the low rates on government debt resulted in very substantial financial repression.[9]

Finally, nationalization of banks gave depositors a certain degree of confidence in the security of bank deposits. This fact helped shift household savings from physical assets to the financial sector. As incomes rose, overall household savings (including both the amounts kept in physical assets and in financial assets, mainly bank accounts) rose as well. The result was a rise in financially intermediated household savings as a proportion of GDP, from 3 percent in 1970/71 to 5.9 percent in 1980/81 and 8.7 percent in 1990/91.

Notes

1. Evidence in this regard is summarized in my book *India: The Emerging Giant* (2008), chapter 11.
2. Reserve Bank of India, *Report of the Working Group to Review the Existing Prudential Guidelines on Restructuring of Advances by Banks/Financial Institutions* (2012), 74, at https://www.rbi.org.in/Scripts/PublicationReportDetails.aspx?UrlPage=&ID=676 (accessed March 17, 2019).
3. Credit growth of foreign banks during 2016/17 was negative, but its cause was rooted in interest rate increases in the United States.
4. Unless otherwise noted, data and information in the remainder of this section are taken from RBI 2018 and from Insolvency and Bankruptcy Board of India 2018.
5. Rangan 2019.
6. Amaldi 2014.
7. Reserve Bank of India 2008, 85, table 3.10. An urban cooperative credit movement had begun in the state of Baroda in the late nineteenth century. Recognition of the need for the provision of rural credit led to spread of the movement in rural India as well. As a result, by independence, a large number of cooperative banks had come to exist in India.
8. I discuss the political circumstances leading to nationalization in greater detail in my book *India: The Emerging Giant* (2008), chapter 3.
9. Kletzer 2005.

10
Transforming Higher Education

A sound higher education system, capable not just of providing up-to-date education in all fields but also of producing scholars who compete internationally with the best in their field, is essential for any country aspiring to be a leading economic power. Good educational and health outcomes depend on the availability of good teachers and doctors. Delivery of justice likewise depends on the availability of good lawyers and judges. Industrial and technological development requires the availability of first-rate engineers, managers, and technology experts. In sum, to build a nation, one must create excellent institutions of higher education.

Apart from meeting the challenge of creating a human capital base essential to sustaining rapid growth, a country's higher education system must grapple with a variety of issues, including access, equity, efficiency, quality, financing, and public versus private provision. In this chapter I do not propose to offer an exhaustive treatment of all these issues. Instead, my main focus is on how best to replace the current archaic regulatory regime, introduced more than sixty years ago via the University Grants Commission (UGC) Act (1956), with a more modern one that is consistent with a market economy and suits contemporary India. In addition, I offer a road map for how best to speed up the quality of higher education and research.

I begin by first offering some historical background on higher education in India along the quantity and quality dimensions. In doing so, I assess India's progress against that made by China, a country that is marginally larger in terms of population and which started equally poor in the 1950s. The Chinese experience is helpful in understanding what is feasible for India in the forthcoming decades.

The Quantity Dimension: Healthy Expansion

India has made accelerated progress in expanding higher education in the post-reform era, especially during the current century. Accelerated growth has yielded larger public revenues and rising private incomes and investment resources. Increased public revenues have allowed the government to invest more resources in higher education, while higher incomes and more investment

Table 10.1 Number of Recognized Educational Institutions and Enrollment in Them

Year	Universities (number)	Colleges (number)	Students (millions)
1950/51	27	578	0.4
1980/81	110	6963	4.8
2000/2001	254	10,152	8.6
2016/17	864	40,026	35.7

Source: Ministry of Human Resource Development 2016, 2017.

resources have brought private players into the sector. Private higher education institutions (HEIs), especially colleges, have been the fastest-growing segment of higher education.

Table 10.1 shows the total number of universities and colleges, plus student enrollments, for selected years. Between 1950/51 and 2000/2001, India added 227 universities, 9,574 colleges, and 8.2 million students. In the sixteen years after the turn of the century, it added 610 more universities, 29,874 colleges, and 27.1 million students. In absolute terms, the accomplishment during the first sixteen years of the twenty-first century has been three times that during the preceding fifty years.

The progress India has made in expanding the absolute number of enrollments in higher education since 2000/2001 broadly matches that of China, which saw its enrollments rise from 5.9 million in 2000 to 37 million in 2016. Indeed, when we consider that this growth in enrollments in China took place at substantially higher income levels, India's performance looks even more impressive.

Increases in enrollments in India have taken place against a demographic transition very different from the one in China. As a result, the gross enrollment ratio (GER), which measures the gross enrollment in higher education as a percentage of the total college-age population (defined as the age group spanning eighteen to twenty-three years), has evolved very differently in the two countries. In India, the GER rose from 8.1 percent in 2000/2001 to 25.2 percent in 2016/17. For approximately similar absolute enrollments in China, it rose from 12.5 percent in 2000 to 42.7 percent in 2016. Because of the smaller and rapidly declining population in the group of eighteen- to twenty-three-year-olds, the GER in China has been higher and risen faster.[1]

The private sector has been crucial to the expansion of higher education in India. Table 10.2 shows the division between the public and private sectors in terms of universities, colleges, and enrollments. Perhaps the most dramatic

Table 10.2 Numbers of Public and Private Institutions and Enrollments in Them

Institution type	2000/2001	2016/17
Universities		
Public	245	522
Private	31	330
Colleges		
Public	4,097	8,177
Private	8,199	28,675
Enrollment: universities plus colleges		
Public	3.44 million	14.2 million
Private	4.95 million	19.3 million

Note: Private institutions include government-aided but privately managed colleges and universities.
Source: Agarwal 2006, table A3 (for 2000/2001) and Ministry of Human Resource Development 2017, 39, T-5 (tables 5 and 5a), and T-27 (table 27) (for 2016/17).

figure in this table is the large number of private (including government-aided but privately managed) colleges in 2016/17. The number of such colleges has grown more than threefold since 2000/2001 and now stands at more than three times the number of public colleges. This means that undergraduate education has progressively moved to the private sector in India. This movement has been especially pronounced in technical fields such as engineering and medicine.[2] At the university level, the public sector continues to dominate despite substantial growth in the number of private universities. More-disaggregated enrollment data (not shown in Table 10.2) reveal that in 2016/17, enrollment in public universities stood at 5.6 million, as opposed to only 1.5 million in private universities. Therefore, university education remains concentrated in the public sector.

The Quality Dimension: Some Progress but a Long Way to Go

Even as India is winning the battle to bring higher education to the doorstep of a large and increasing proportion of its youth, it is failing along the quality dimension. Colleges and universities are falling well short of providing their students with up-to-date and quality education. Relative to comparator countries, scholars from India are performing poorly on the research and innovation fronts.

It may be stated at the outset that the decline in quality is to be interpreted in a relative sense. India has not been able to move as fast as other countries in producing quality education and research. Still, in terms of absolute output of the number of graduates, research papers, and patents of a given quality, India has been making steady progress.

Rapid growth during the current century has led to a rapid rise in the demand for qualified engineers and managers. Had the economy failed to generate adequate numbers of them, the potential for high growth could not have translated into actual high growth. In a similar vein, the momentum we see in the start-up space in India and the continued growth in information technology offer evidence that the supply of skilled personnel has largely kept up with demand and that the current talent pool is substantially larger in absolute terms than it was even ten years ago.

The number of articles published in leading science and engineering journals provides objective evidence of the progress India has made in absolute terms. The US National Science Foundation has compiled country-by-country data on the number of journal articles published in the fields of physics, biology, chemistry, mathematics, clinical medicine, biomedical research, engineering and technology, and earth and space sciences beginning with the year 2003; currently these data are available through 2016. In 2003, India ranked eleventh on this list. Remarkably, by 2016, India had climbed up to outrank eight out of the ten countries it trailed in 2003. As Figure 10.1 shows, in terms of the absolute number of scientific and engineering articles published in leading journals, India now stands ahead of such countries as Japan, Germany, and the United Kingdom. Only the United States and China remain ahead of India.

Figure 10.1 shows the clear progress that India has made in catching up with some of the comparator countries. Yet its achievements remain well below what its size would suggest is possible. It is sixteen times more populous than Germany, the country right below it in 2016. Even Russia, the largest among comparator countries shown in Figure 10.1, is one-ninth the size of India. The point is brought home by Figure 10.2, which shows the United States, China, and India on a common graph. In 2003, papers published by authors in China stood at 27 percent of those by authors in the United States. By 2016, China had outdone the United States. India too has made progress relative to the United States. Papers by its authors as a proportion of those by US authors rose from 8.3 percent in 2003 to 27 percent in 2016. But this progress fades in comparison to China. Still, the proportional gap between India and China bottomed out in 2009 and has been recovering ever since, which offers hope that with more effort India can aspire to catch up with China and the United States.

With 21,950 peer-reviewed journals as of August 2017, the Scopus database provides the most comprehensive view of the world's research output in the fields

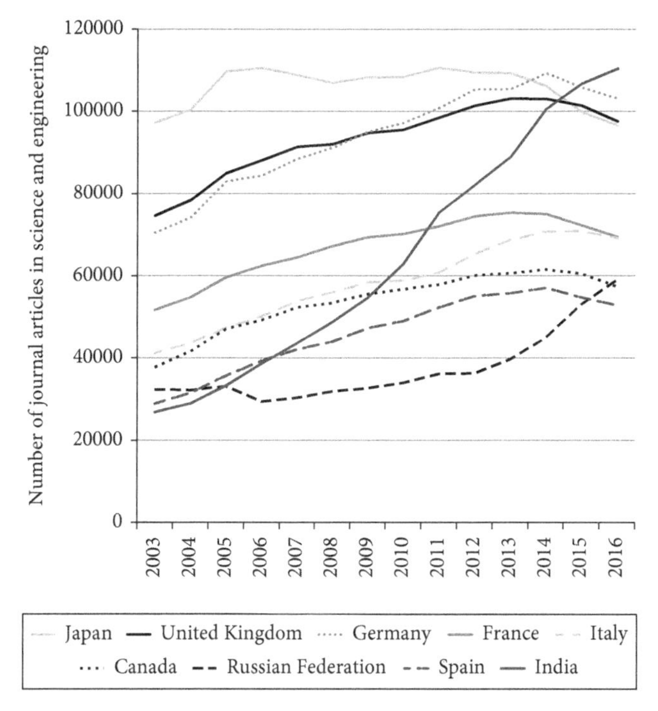

Figure 10.1 Number of Scientific and Engineering Journal Articles by Country from 2003 to 2016 for Nine Countries

Source: WDI online series "Scientific and Technical Journal Articles," attributed to the National Science Foundation (accessed on June 3, 2018).

of science, technology, medicine, social sciences, and the arts and humanities. The starting date of the database is 1996, and it is updated annually. Among other things, it allows us to rank countries not just by the number of journal articles but also by citations (both with and without self-citations). Citations (especially excluding self-citations) are an important measure of the visibility of an author's research papers.

Table 10.3 provides the rankings of India and China in 1996 and 2017 by the total number of articles in journals in the Scopus database, total citations, and citations excluding self-citations. The picture that emerges is discouraging. Although India has gone from thirteenth to fifth between 1996 and 2017 when ranked by the total number of papers, the improvement is only from sixteenth to eleventh based on total citations and from nineteenth to fourteenth based on citations excluding self-citations. In 1996, India had ranked higher than China based on total citations and citations excluding self-citations. But by 2017, China had not only surpassed India but also achieved the rank of second and third, respectively, based on those two criteria.

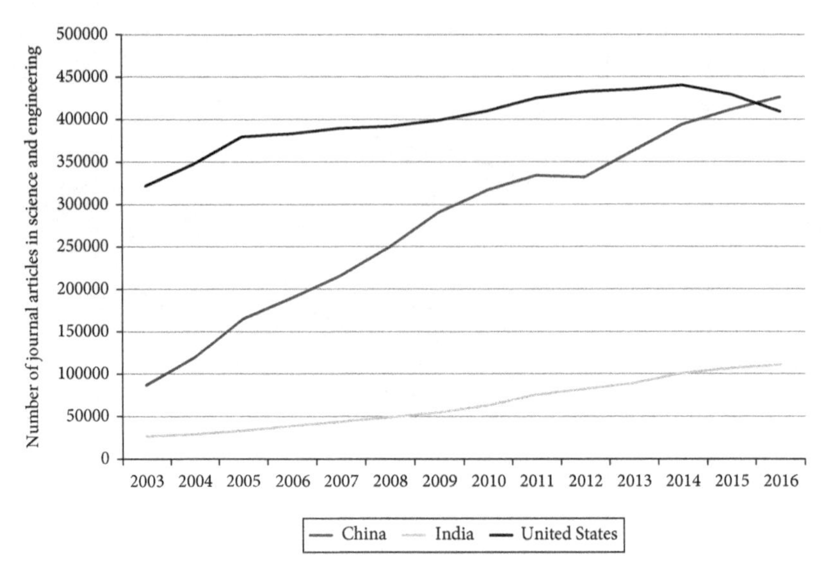

Figure 10.2 Number of Scientific and Engineering Journal Articles by Country from 2003 to 2016 for China, India, and the United States

Source: WDI online series "Scientific and Technical Journal Articles." attributed to the National Science Foundation (accessed on June 3, 2018).

Table 10.3 Rankings Based on Scopus Database According to Articles in All Subject Areas

Criterion	India		China	
	1996	**2017**	**1996**	**2017**
All subject areas				
Total papers published	13	5	9	2
Total citations	16	11	19	2
Total citations excluding self-citations	19	14	21	3

Source: Author's compilation based on Scopus database at https://www.scimagojr.com/countryrank.php?order=it&ord=desc (accessed June 7, 2018).

The Scopus database also allows us to rank countries by subject areas, which helps us identify areas of strength and weakness. Accordingly, Table 10.4 shows the rankings of India and China in the years 1996 and 2017 according to total citations in a number of key subject areas. India does reasonably well in physics, chemistry, mathematics, engineering, business, management, and

Table 10.4 Rankings Based on the Total Number of Citations in Different Subject Areas

Subject area	India		China	
	1996	**2017**	**1996**	**2017**
All subject areas	16	11	19	2
Agriculture and biological sciences	17	14	22	2
Arts and humanities	28	25	15	6
Biochemistry, genetics, and molecular biology	17	14	20	2
Business, management, and accounting	22	10	27	3
Chemistry	11	5	13	1
Engineering	14	4	10	1
Mathematics	20	7	11	1
Medicine	19	17	23	3
Physics and astronomy	17	8	13	2
Social sciences	21	14	24	5

Source: Author's compilation based on Scopus database at https://www.scimagojr.com/countryrank.php?order=it&ord=desc (accessed June 7, 2018).

accounting. But it does poorly in agricultural and biological sciences; arts and humanities; biochemistry, genetics, and molecular biology; medicine; and social sciences. In the majority of these areas, progress between 1996 and 2017 has been minimal.

In contrast to India, China has made impressive progress across all subject areas, even in the arts and humanities, where it ranked twenty-eighth in 1996 but moved up to sixth in 2017, a solid nineteen places ahead of India. In social sciences, it rose from twenty-fourth position in 1996 to fifth in 2017. In chemistry, engineering, and mathematics, it now ranks first in terms of the total number of citations.

The superior progress achieved by China is reflected in the international rankings of higher education institutions (HEIs). This is shown in Table 10.5, which reports the latest available HEI rankings from three commonly used sources: QS, Times Higher Education (THE), and Shanghai. China has seven institutions in the top two hundred according to the QS rankings, four according to the THE rankings, and ten according to the Shanghai rankings. India has only three institutions in the top two hundred according to the QS rankings and none

Table 10.5 Number of Universities from India and China in International Rankings

Country	Top 100	101-200	201-600	601 -1000	Total
QS, 2018					
China	4	3	24	9	40
India	0	3	6	11	20
THE, 2018					
China	2	2	19	31	54
India	0	0	6	24	30
Shanghai, 2017					
China	2	8	49	33	92
India	0	0	1	6	7

Source: Author's construction from rankings available online.

according to the other two rankings. None of the Indian institutions in the top two hundred in the THE rankings makes it to the top one hundred.

Taken as a whole, the data presented here offer both good news and bad news for India. The bad news is that while India has made substantial progress in expanding enrollments in higher education, it has achieved minimal progress along the quality dimension. The good news is twofold. One, even without focused effort, rising enrollments have produced progress along the quality dimension, especially in science and engineering. And two, the experience of China shows that with focused effort, India can achieve substantial improvements along the quality dimension in the next two decades.

There are two key areas where India needs to focus. First, the existing regulatory regime under the auspices of the UGC Act (1956), though suitable for the India of the 1950s, has been stifling competition among institutions at all levels today. India must learn from the experience of the successful countries and replace the current UGC regime with a more pro-competitive regulatory regime. Second, India must enhance and redirect its investments in research to improve quality while also promoting greater cooperation among HEIs, industry, and government.

International Experience

By all measures, during the last several decades, the United States and the United Kingdom have had the best universities. The United States has been home to the largest number of top-ranking universities in the world. In terms of historical ties and governance, the Indian higher education system has the greatest affinity to the system in the United Kingdom. Finally, China is a developing country with a large population that has made the greatest progress in higher education during the past two decades. If we keep these factors in view, the regulatory experiences of the three countries can offer useful lessons for India, with special reference to governance.

The United States

In the United States, degree-granting institutions are classified into three categories: public, private non-profit, and private for-profit. In the academic year 2013–14, the country had 3,039 four-year degree-granting institutions.[3] In the fall of 2015, of the 13.5 million students enrolled in four-year institutions, 62 percent were in public, 30 percent in private non-profit, and 8 percent in private for-profit institutions.[4]

The Sources of Revenue

The sources of revenue of the three types of institutions vary considerably. As Figure 10.3 shows, tuition fees are the single largest source of revenue for private institutions, both non-profit and for-profit. Tuition fees contribute as much as 90 percent of the total revenue of private for-profit institutions. Private non-profit institutions raise a large part of their revenue from gifts, private grants, and contracts, which are included in "all other revenue." Public institutions depend most heavily on federal, state, and local government grants, though even they raise one-fifth of their total revenue from tuition. Tuition fees are generally significantly lower in public institutions than in private ones. Private non-profit institutions charge the highest tuition fees on average.[5]

Governance

The US higher education system is highly decentralized. Once established, a university or college is independent of federal or state government regulation. To start an HEI, all that is required is a degree-granting license from the state in which the HEI is to be located. The difficulty of obtaining the license varies by state. The most liberal states, such as Virginia, Colorado, and Wyoming, do not require even a site visit. At the other extreme, in states such as Maine inspectors visit the campus, other university presidents must be informed, and a state legislator must introduce a bill for the grant of the license.

Public as well as private institutions are typically chartered as corporations in the United States. They are governed by boards of trustees, appointed by a state

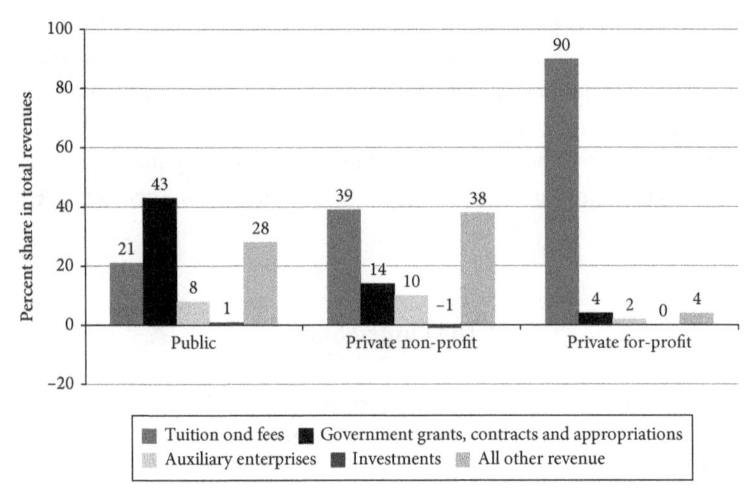

Figure 10.3 Sources of Revenues of Degree-Granting Institutions in the United States in the Academic Year 2015–16

Note: "All other revenue" includes gifts, capital or private grants and contracts, hospital revenue, sales and services of educational activities, and other revenue. Auxiliary enterprises include campus housing, dining services, on-campus bookstores and vending machines, parking and transportation services, and on-campus hotels.

Source: https://nces.ed.gov/programs/coe/indicator_cud.asp (accessed on June 8, 2018).

governor or state legislature in the case of public institutions and elected by the board itself in the case of private institutions. The institutions can have a single site or multiple campuses. In some cases they can also be systems comprising several independent institutions, as is the case with the University of California system. All institutions are autonomous with respect to administrative and academic decision-making.

Universities are also decentralized in terms of course offerings. Each department decides its course offerings and faculty teaching assignments. As long as the academic department can muster resources, it can start new courses, with the design of the course normally left to the assigned faculty member. Indeed, with individual faculty members giving their own separate examinations for the purpose of grading their students, even the contents of the same course taught in two or more sections by different faculty members during the same semester may differ.

A key instrument for promoting excellence in teaching is the evaluation of the instructor by students. At the end of each course, students at most institutions routinely fill out an evaluation form answering questions relating to the design of the course, assigned readings, classroom lectures, and the overall performance of the professor. Students may also offer additional written comments on the course.

Secret of Success

The success of HEIs in the United States is to be attributed to two key factors: availability of sufficient R&D funds and competition. Historically, the federal government has played a key role in funding university-based R&D. In the late 1960s, its share in the total R&D expenditures by HEIs had reached 73 percent.[6] That share has subsequently declined, dropping to 54 percent in 2016. At the same time, industry and university shares have risen. In 2016, industry and university shares in R&D expenditures by HEIs stood at 5.9 percent and 25 percent, respectively. Total R&D expenditures have seen steady increases, with the amount in constant 2017 dollars rising from $27.8 billion in 1990 to $73.3 billion in 2016. Figure 10.4 depicts the evolution of R&D expenditures by HEIs from 1990 to 2016.

The second important factor behind the success of HEIs in the United States has been competition for excellence across all dimensions. Universities compete for the best students, best faculty, and research funds. Faculty salaries are set competitively, with individual faculty rewarded for their higher productivity. Faculty salaries differ not just across academic departments but also within the same department depending on productivity and what market forces dictate. Universities try to build up their faculty by hiring away the best faculty at other institutions, so each institution has to respond to the bids for their best faculty by

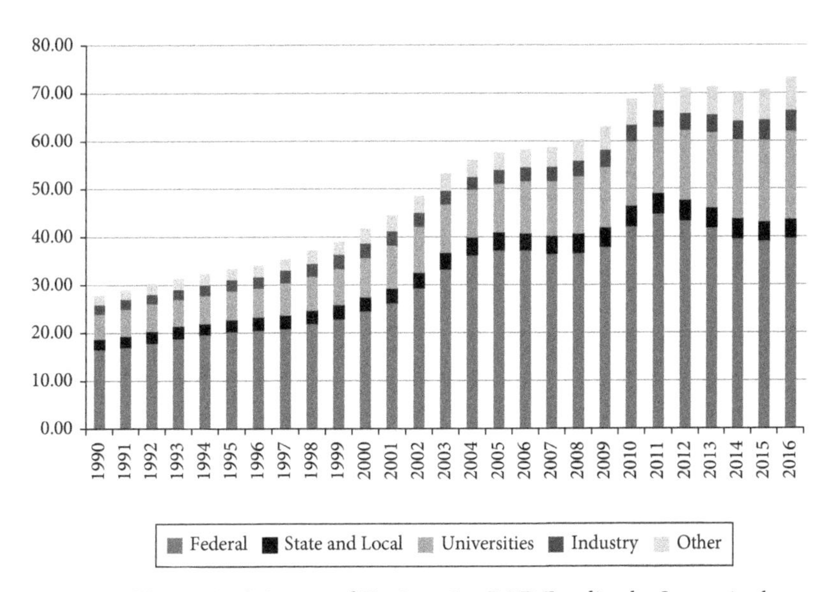

Figure 10.4 University Science and Engineering R&D Funding by Source in the United States, 1990–2016

Source: National Science Foundation, Higher Education R&D survey data series, http://www.nsf.gov/statistics/herd.

offering packages of their own. In this system, individual faculty members earn respect through publications in prestigious journals and visibility, reflected in the offers they receive from peer institutions. Even within the same academic department of the same university, salaries reflect faculty members' relative standing. In a similar fashion, universities also compete for the best students. In addition to offering scholarships and fellowships to the best students, members of the faculty may personally reach out to students to woo them to their universities.

China

Western-style HEIs in China, which began appearing in the late nineteenth century, first followed the Japanese model and then the American model. Beginning in 1949, the higher education system switched to the Soviet model. That system did well for sixteen years, but then came the Cultural Revolution, which turned HEIs into battlegrounds and administered a near fatal blow to them. It was only after Mao Zedong died and Deng Xiaoping came to the helm that higher education had a revival.

Empowering of HEIs: The Higher Education Law

The Higher Education Law (1998) governs the current Chinese higher education system. While this is a central law and vests the authority to permit the opening of new universities and provide overall guidance to HEIs in the central government, it is operationally very liberal. It decentralizes the higher education system in a manner similar to the United States.

The State Council formulates the specific standards for the establishment of new institutions of higher learning. Applications may be made to the Department of Education Administration under the State Council with a report on the proposed institution, a feasibility report, articles of association, and other prescribed materials. The Department of Education Administration then examines the application and makes a decision.

Article 32 of the 1998 law calls upon the HEIs to "work out schemes for admission and independently regulate the percentage of admission for departments and disciplines." Article 33 gives them independence to "set up and adjust disciplines and specialties." Articles 34 empowers them to "work out teaching plans, select and compile textbooks and organize activities of imparting teaching in accordance with the requirements of teaching." Article 36 authorizes the institutions to "independently carry out scientific, technological and cultural exchanges and cooperation with foreign institutions of higher learning in accordance with the relevant provisions of the state." Article 37 imparts administrative freedom to the institutions, which "independently decide on the setting up and personnel employment of such internal organizational structures as teaching, scientific research and administrative functional departments in the light of actual requirements." Finally, Article 41 fixes the responsibility for outcomes on the president of the institution while also conferring on him wide-ranging powers:

> The president of an institution of higher learning shall be fully responsible for the teaching, scientific research and other administrative work of the respective institution and exercise the following duties and powers:

(1) to draft development planning, formulate specific rules and regulations and annual work plan and organize their implementation;
(2) to organize teaching activities, scientific research and ideological and moral education;
(3) to draft schemes for the setting up of internal organizations, recommend candidates for vice presidency, appoint and relieve persons in charge of internal organizations;
(4) to employ and dismiss teachers and other internal workers, administer students' school roll and give rewards or impose penalties;
(5) to draft and implement annual fund budget proposal, protect and manage school properties and safeguard the legitimate rights and interests of the school; and
(6) other duties and powers provided for in the articles of association.

Tuition Fees as a Major Source of Revenue

Article 54 of the Higher Education Law explicitly recognizes the right of the HEI to charge tuition fees. It states, "Students of institutions of higher learning should pay a tuition fee in accordance with state provisions." Students whose families face financial hardship "may apply for subsidy or reduction and exemption of the tuition fee." Giving the institutions considerable freedom to charge tuition has been an important step toward placing them on a solid financial footing. A modest fee of RMB 100 for accommodation and RMB 20 for tuition was first introduced in 1989. Subsequently, tuition fees at public institutions rose rapidly to RMB 600 in 1992, RMB 4,000 in 1999, RMB 5,000 in 2001, and RMB 6,000 in 2005. By the mid-2000s, some private universities were charging fees as high as RMB 10,000. In 2003, higher education fees amounted to RMB 40 billion, in comparison to the national expenditure on higher education of RMB 70 billion.[7]

Promoting Excellence: Projects 211 and 985

Though the Higher Education Law in China leaves academic and administrative decisions to HEIs, the Chinese government has actively intervened with substantial financial resources to foster improvements in quality. This has been done through two major programs, Project 211 and Project 985.[8] The former was intended to help top universities improve teaching, research, and infrastructure, and the purpose of the latter was to turn some top universities into world-class institutions.

Initiated in 1995, Project 211 derived its name from the slogan "For the twenty-first century, to manage one hundred universities successfully." The project allocated RMB 36.8 billion ($4.6 billion) across 107 universities between 1995 and 2005. Of this amount, RMB 16.5 billion was spent on developing some key disciplines, RMB 7.1 billion on the establishment of a system of public service, RMB 2.4 billion on strengthening teaching staff, and RMB 10.8 billion on infrastructure.[9] Engineering and new technology, social sciences and humanities, medicine and health, environmental sciences and agriculture, and basic research were the key disciplines the project supported.[10]

Project 985 was so called because it was launched in May 1998. Its objective was to create a number of world-class universities, and all universities under this program were drawn from Project 211. The project provided for (1) reforming and improving university administrative and operational mechanisms, (2) recruiting leading scholars inside or outside China to establish strong research teams, (3) establishing the Science and Technology Innovation Platform and the Social Sciences Research Base in the selected universities, and (4) improving university infrastructure and supporting international collaborations.

Different universities entered Project 985 on different dates and received different levels of funding.[11] The top two universities, Peking and Tsinghua, were the first to enter the program and received a whopping RMB 1.8 billion ($240 million) each during the first three years of the program. Seven other universities were added to the list in 1999, though they received much reduced levels of funding. By 2003, the number of institutions covered by the project had risen to thirty-four.[12] During Phase I, spanning 1999 to 2003, special funding provided by the central government to these thirty-four universities amounted to RMB 14 billion. During Phase II, spanning 2004 to 2007, funding was RMB 18.9 billion and covered thirty-nine universities.[13] Provincial governments provided additional funds. In 2011, both Project 211 and Project 985 were closed to new entrants.

The United Kingdom

In the academic year 2016–17, the United Kingdom had 162 HEIs, which received public funding via one of the UK funding councils and returned data to the Higher Education Statistical Agency. In addition, there are nine privately owned institutions, which do not receive funding for teaching and research from the government. In 2016–17, a total of 2.32 million students were studying at UK higher education institutions. The GER in higher education in the United Kingdom stood at 57 percent in 2015. The Higher Education and Research Act (2017) has recently brought about important changes in the governance of the higher education system. In the following, I first describe the system as it functioned until 2016–17 and then describe the latest reform.

Governance of Institutions and Degree-Granting Power

HEIs in the United Kingdom are independent and autonomous legal entities with councils or governing bodies managing them. Individual institutions are fully free to appoint their own academic and administrative staff. They also determine their own entry requirements and admission procedures.

The power to award degrees in the United Kingdom is regulated by law and is granted by a royal charter (mostly before 1993) or by an act of Parliament. The Higher Education Act (1992) empowered the Privy Council to grant HEIs powers to award their own degrees.

Funding for Education

The UK government funds the institutions, but it neither owns nor governs them. Government funding has been managed at arm's length through independent funding councils.[14] Funding councils attach conditions to the grants requiring the institutions to use the funds as per the law, undertake quality assessments of education and research, and meet the specified governance standards.

During the decades immediately following the Second World War, undergraduate education for UK students was free. But the rapid expansion of education during the 1980s and 1990s resulted in declining expenditures per student, with universities finding it difficult to maintain the quality of teaching. This situation led the government to introduce tuition fees for undergraduate students beginning in 1997. The initial fee cap was set at £1,000, which was revised to £3,000 in 2006 and to £9,000 in 2010.

Students are able to finance tuition by taking loans from the government offered through the Student Loans Company. After the student begins earning and her annual earnings cross the threshold of £21,000, she must begin repaying the loan. During any period in which earnings fall below the threshold, repayments are suspended. After thirty years, any remaining debt is written off.

Funding for Research

Until recently, institutionalized research funding by the government was channeled through two sources. First, the funding councils gave an annual block grant to each institution for research infrastructure and for promoting research according to the institution's mission and priorities. These funds could also be

Table 10.6 Income of HEIs in the UK: 2014/15 to 2016/17

Source of income	£ billions			Percent of total		
	2014/15	**2015/16**	**2016/17**	**2014/15**	**2015/16**	**2016/17**
Tuition fees and education contracts	15.5	16.8	17.7	46.4	48.4	49.7
Funding body grants	5.3	5.2	5.1	15.9	14.9	14.3
Research grants and contracts	6.0	5.9	5.9	17.8	16.9	16.6
Other income	5.9	6.0	6.1	17.6	17.4	17.0
Investment income	0.2	0.3	0.3	0.7	0.8	0.7
Donations and endowments	0.5	0.6	0.6	1.6	1.7	1.6
Total Revenue	33.5	34.7	35.7	100	100	100

Source: https://www.hesa.ac.uk/data-and-analysis/providers/finances (accessed June 11, 2018).

used for research on pedagogy. Second, seven research councils, organized by fields of research, provided grants for specific research projects, contracts, and post-graduate programs. In addition to these institutionalized sources, HEIs also received funds from charities, industry, the European Union, and individual UK government departments. Recently, some changes to funding infrastructure have been made; these will be discussed later.

Overall HEI Resources

Table 10.6 provides the total incomes of the HEIs and their sources in the years 2014–15, 2015–16, and 2016–17. The total revenue of all HEIs rose from £33.5 billion to £35.7 billion over that three-year period. Tuition fees and education contracts constitute the largest source of revenue and accounted for almost half of revenue by 2016–17. This large share is truly astounding when we consider the fact that tuition fees for UK undergraduates were nonexistent until the late 1990s. Funding body grants, research grants, and contracts are the other major sources of revenue for UK HEIs.

A New Architecture for Higher Education and Research

In 2017 the UK Parliament enacted the Higher Education and Research Act. This act replaces the old system of governance through the funding councils and research councils with a new set of institutions: the Office for Students (OfS), with jurisdiction over all higher-education-related issues, and UK Research and Innovation (UKRI), with jurisdiction over research.

The OfS establishes and maintains the register of higher education providers. It formulates the regulations (including fee caps) that a proposed new institution must abide by to be entered into the register, as well as regulations that existing HEIs must satisfy in order to keep their place on the register. It also lays down conditions under which an institution may be de-registered. It has the power to impose penalties in case of violations.

Under the new law, OfS grants HEIs the power to grant degrees. It can also empower HEIs to authorize other institutions to grant degrees on their behalf. It further grants authority to HEIs to use "university" in their titles.

Assessing and rating the quality of education by HEIs is another important function of the OfS. A Quality Assessment Committee helps the OfS discharge this function. The OfS also designates other bodies to perform the assessment function on its behalf. Designated bodies are permitted to charge HEIs fees to provide assessment. The law lays down rules for the oversight of the designated bodies. The fee cap applicable to an institution can be related to its quality rating, with a higher cap permitted for an institution with a higher quality rating.

The OfS is empowered to give grants and loans to the governing body of an HEI for the provision of education and facilities or activities that the governing body considers desirable for education. Given this provision, no need remains for the Higher Education Funding Council, and the new law abolishes it.

UKRI, a separate corporate body created under the new law, has jurisdiction over research. It has the following committees:

Arts and Humanities Research Council
Biotechnology and Biological Sciences Research Council
Economic and Social Research Council
Engineering and Physical Sciences Research Council
Medical Research Council
Natural Environment Research Council
Science and Technology Facilities Council
Innovate UK
Research England

UKRI is empowered to carry out research as well as encourage and support research in science, technology, humanities, and new ideas. It is also charged with facilitating and supporting knowledge exchange in these areas. The UKRI may delegate these functions wholly or partially to the first six councils in their respective areas. Innovation UK's mandate is to carry out activities that help promote economic growth. Research England is to give financial support to the governing bodies of HEIs for research and knowledge exchange and to provide facilities required for research and knowledge exchange in science, technology, humanities, or new ideas.

UKRI also develops an overall research and innovation strategy to be approved by the government. Within this overall strategy, each council must prepare a strategic delivery plan for the period specified in the UKRI strategy paper. The delivery plan requires approval by UKRI.

A Possible Road Map for India

Evidence shows that India has done well in increasing enrollments in higher education and made some progress in increasing research output but has lagged in terms of quality of education and research during the past two decades. Research quality, as measured by citations, is of particular concern. In 1996, India ranked ahead of China along this dimension, but by 2016, it had fallen very far behind. The good news, however, is that China's experience shows that rapid progress is feasible with concerted effort.

Creating Autonomous and Independent HEIs

One feature common to the United States, United Kingdom, and China is that their HEIs are autonomous corporate entities. In the United States, many universities receive funding from federal, state and local governments, but they enjoy full autonomy in running their academic and administrative affairs. In the United Kingdom, all but a few HEIs receive government funding, and students are funded by generous government loans. But the HEIs remain independent in making their own decisions regarding academic and administrative matters. Even in China, where many institutions get much of their funding from the central or provincial governments, HEIs have a high degree of autonomy.

Recently India has begun to grant its top universities and colleges autonomy, seeing excellent results even within a short period of time.[15] The experience of other countries suggests that this process must be accelerated. The degree of autonomy must be increased, and it should be extended to many more institutions. The system should now evolve into one in which HEIs are given autonomy unless there is positive evidence to indicate that this will be harmful to the quality of education and research they deliver.

One possible option is to adopt something like the British system, under which HEIs are independent and autonomous legal entities with their own governing boards. Under such a system, government funding beyond a minimum level would be subject to quality standards. HEIs that perform well would be entitled to a larger volume of funds than those that perform poorly. And if an institution's performance falls below a given threshold, it would face the prospect of losing funding altogether.

A Higher Education Promotion Commission

The key reform India needs is to replace the UGC Act with a new law whose aim would be to promote rather than control higher education.[16] To convey that this is the intent of the new law, it may be called the Higher Education Promotion Commission Act. In the twenty-first century, India can ill afford to work with a law conceived in the 1950s. No matter how suitable it was at the time of inception, today the UGC Act is an obstacle to the growth of quality education.

The new act should be designed so that it will not be possible to resurrect the inspector raj that has become the hallmark of the UGC regime. Illustratively, we can imagine it having nine members, all eminent persons of unimpeachable integrity and having passion for the promotion of excellence in higher education. Under this conception, in the initial round, three members would be appointed for six years, three for four, and three for two. Subsequently, every two years the commission would replace three outgoing members with three new members that it would select and appoint for six-year terms. A high-level committee would choose the initial nine members, after which the commission members would select all new members.

The commission would be assisted in its work by three bodies: an Advisory Council, Office of Registration of HEIs, and a Committee for Quality Assessment.[17] The Advisory Council would consist of representatives of the states and eminent scholars from different fields. It would meet at least once a year and more frequently if the commission so desires. The council's role will be advisory but important since it will link the commission to active academics and sensitize the commission to ongoing issues that it must address.

The Office of Registration would maintain the register of HEIs. It would develop a classification of HEIs (for example, fully autonomous, partially autonomous, degree-granting, private, public, foreign-owned, college, university, and HEIs of national importance) and list each HEI in the register using this classification. The commission would formulate transparent criteria for entering an institution (including those of foreign origin) on the register under one or more categories. It would make decisions regarding the entry of an HEI applicant, whether domestic or foreign, in a timely manner. It would also formulate transparent criteria for existing HEIs to maintain their presence on the register.

Failure of an HEI to satisfy these criteria would attract punitive action, including in extreme cases removal of the institution from the register.

Access and quality of education should be the only criteria for gaining entry to the register and maintaining a spot there. Any input-based criterion should be included only if there is a clear and direct link between it and quality of education. Enforcement should be entirely based on a clear statement by each HEI on its website that it is in compliance with all the stipulated conditions; any false claims should attract severe penalties.

Degree-granting power should be vested in the commission and implemented through the Office of Registration. The commission should translate this power into action by developing transparent criteria under which an HEI can be empowered to grant degrees. Degree-granting power should be available to both universities and colleges, as is the case in the United States. This will allow first-rate colleges to develop their brand names without having to convert themselves into full-fledged universities. The commission must also specify transparent criteria under which an HEI will be granted power to authorize other HEIs to confer degrees on its behalf. This power should be available to both public and private universities as long as they satisfy the stipulated criteria.

The commission should also develop transparent criteria under which an HEI can use "university" in its title. These criteria should offer paths to directly set up an institution as a university as well as to convert an existing HEI into a university. No central or state government legislation should be required to set up a university. The commission should make decisions in a timely manner.

The Committee for Quality Assessment will help the commission to develop criteria for the entry of a new HEI applicant onto the register and for continuing to keep existing institutions there. Most importantly, it will help develop criteria for rating different categories of institutions. With its help, the commission will also identify and designate outside agencies to rate HEIs in different categories.

The commission will refrain from developing curriculums. Instead, universities and colleges with autonomy will be entirely free to develop their own curriculums. They will also be free to choose their own textbooks and other reading material for students. Universities and colleges without autonomy would follow the curriculums and textbooks of these universities and colleges, identifying on their websites clearly for each course the university or college whose curriculum they are following. In rare cases when a university or college without autonomy wishes to start a course that is not given by any institution with autonomy, the commission should appoint a committee of two or three experts who would provide a curriculum in a timely fashion.

Allocation of Government Funds for Education and Facilities

The function of allocating government funds for education and facilities (but not research) should be assigned to a separate committee that is at arm's length from the government. In drawing up criteria for such disbursements, this committee must give considerable weight to the quality of institutions as assessed by the Committee for Quality Assessment. Recently, the Rashtriya Uchchatar Shiksha Abhiyan (RUSA), a program of the central government's Department of Education under the Ministry of Human Resource Development, has made an important beginning in this direction by channeling a portion of central government funds by means of merit-based criteria. But a large chunk of this funding does not flow through RUSA. Instead, it goes directly to the states and contributes to the salaries paid at state institutions. This automatic flow needs to be replaced by a merit-based flow, with public and private institutions competing for the funds on equal footing. As long as recipient institutions accept quality-related conditions, they should be eligible to compete regardless of their public or private character. Once the commission is operational, all central government funding, including that currently disbursed through RUSA, may be unified and channeled through this committee.

Tuition Fees

Various state committees currently fix tuition fee caps. This practice may be continued, though there is a need to connect the caps to the quality of education. Institutions that provide quality education should be given more generous caps. States may be encouraged to accomplish this by connecting the caps to quality assessments by the Committee for Quality Assessment. States should be required to provide information about fees to the commission.

There also needs to be transparency in the collection of fees. Therefore, institutions should have the obligation to provide a clear statement on their websites regarding all fees that students are required to pay. Outside of the listed fees, no other fees should be permitted, and any violations must attract punitive action by the commission.

HEIs in the United States, China, and United Kingdom charge hefty tuition fees. In contrast, India has ended up with a system in which students enrolled in private colleges and universities pay high fees, while those lucky enough to get into publicly owned colleges and universities pay almost nothing. With the central and state governments both financially strapped, this has created a huge resource crunch for publicly owned colleges and universities. This needs to change.

One possible course is to adopt something like the British system, whereby generous loans are provided to cover tuition fees, but once the beneficiary begins working and her income reaches a certain threshold, repayment begins. After thirty years, any unpaid debt may be written off. Such a system will provide institutions with additional resources to improve the quality of education. It will also create greater equality between public and private institutions and encourage students to choose institutions based on quality instead of always preferring public institutions because they charge lower fees.

A National Research and Innovation Foundation

Under the existing system, research in India has been relegated to independent councils such as the Council for Scientific and Industrial Research, Indian Council of Social Sciences Research, and Indian Council of Agricultural Research, with the HEIs being teaching-only institutions. This separation of education and research has been highly detrimental to productivity in both areas, since they go hand in hand and the vast faculty resources at HEIs largely cannot contribute to research. To be sure, some research does take place at HEIs, but only at a tiny fraction of them, and it is often driven by individual faculty members' interest, with no institutional reinforcement.

This state of affairs needs to change. The role of research at HEIs needs formal recognition, as is the case in countries such as the United States, United Kingdom, and China. India must incentivize research by faculty at a significantly larger fraction of HEIs than is the case currently, with due credit given for research via both funding and reduced teaching responsibilities. To make a significant impact, much larger budgetary resources will need to be mobilized for the purpose.

The only relevant R&D expenditure data available for India are for funds allocated to the research councils mentioned earlier in this section as well as to the Defense Research and Development Organization (DRDO), the Department of Atomic Energy, the Department of Biotechnology (DBT), the Department of Science and Technology (DST), and the Department of Space. In 2014/15, the total expenditure by all these units was 350 billion rupees (approximately $5.4 billion). If DRDO is excluded, the expenditure was 218 billion rupees ($3.4 billion), and if only the research councils, DBT, and DST are included, the expenditure was just 119 billion rupees ($1.8 billion).

The upshot is that the total academic R&D expenditure in India is small and the proportion that reaches the HEIs is negligible. If India is to realize its potential, it will be necessary to beef up the funds available to HEIs for R&D. This would require both a rapid increase in R&D funds and an effort to incentivize the best researchers and their labs at the existing research councils to move to universities. If students do not get to interact directly with top researchers, they are not going to get the necessary inspiration for research. Movement of some researchers and labs to universities will also help improve research collaboration between HEIs and industry.

Institutionally, India needs to create a National Research and Innovation Foundation empowered to promote research and innovation at HEIs by offering project-based research grants to the HEIs via a peer review process. At present, only small grants are channeled to researchers at HEIs in the fields of science, technology, and biotechnology through DST and DBT (totaling just 37.22 billion rupees, or approximately $570 million, in 2014/15). Funds going to social sciences and arts and humanities research at HEIs are close to nil.

World-Class Universities

Apart from improving quality in general, India must also create a few world-class HEIs that can serve as models and inspiration for other institutions. Prime Minister Narendra Modi has already announced a project to turn ten public and ten private universities into world-class institutions. My personal view is that this project needs to be fundamentally rethought along three dimensions.

First, the total number of institutions, twenty, is excessive for two reasons. One, at present India does not have twenty universities that could rise up to rank among even the top two hundred universities at the global level in one to two decades. And two, given the tight fiscal constraints it faces, India lacks the funds to genuinely aspire to bring as many as twenty universities to global level in that length of time. Betting on as many as twenty universities at once with the existing tight fiscal constraints would spread resources too thinly. The experience of China reinforces this point. It has a larger resource base and has tried to invest in nearly three dozen universities under Project 985, but it still devoted a significantly larger volume of resources to its two best universities: Peking and Tsinghua.

Second, even if India does cut down the number of universities to be promoted, it is important not to require that number to be divided equally between public and private institutions. Good economics says that it will be best to pick the top half dozen universities regardless of ownership type. The country's reputation will gain equally whether the universities that acquire high rankings are public or private.

Finally, it is important to include two or three entirely new universities in the group. A big advantage of new universities is that the rules under which they operate can be written from scratch. One of the challenges an established university will face is the existing entrenched culture, which often emphasizes equity over excellence. A new university can stipulate from the beginning that excellence will not be sacrificed in the name of equity. If a superstar scholar can only be attracted at a salary that is twice the average of the salaries of existing faculty, a new institution can write rules such that a higher salary is acceptable. The faculty to be hired by a new institution would also be entirely new, so the institution would be in a better position to go after a block of world-class scholars with common research interests than would an established university, which can hire only a small number of additional faculty members at a time. Scholars have a strong preference to be where they can work with other scholars who have similar interests. Therefore, the ability to hire a large number of faculty members in one go has a big advantage in attracting top scholars.

Concluding Remarks

Beginning in 2000, India has made impressive progress in raising its gross enrollment ratio in higher education. It has also made progress in research output, but not at the speed necessary to place the country's HEIs among the leading institutions of the world. Going by citations, China was behind India in 1996. Today, however, not only is China ahead of India, but its research productivity in terms of papers published and citations places it at the top or in second or third place in most fields.

Indeed, the progress China has made during the last two decades is a source of great hope for India in the next two decades. India has two important advantages. First, with English as the medium of instruction as well as research, it can readily anchor itself in English-language journals and other publications. Unlike countries such as China, Japan, and Russia, its researchers are not handicapped by language in terms of accessing scholarly outlets both as readers and as contributors. Second, India also has a large number of diaspora scholars in the United States, Australia, and Canada who can be attracted back home to rapidly build up faculty in the targeted institutions.

Working against this is the fact that several countries, including Russia, Japan, and China, are ahead of India and are investing a significantly larger volume of resources to improve their rankings. As a latecomer, India will need to make a truly big push to hit what is a moving target. Nevertheless, through focused efforts, India can turn its higher education system around to rapidly advance its quality and improve its standing in the world university rankings. Reforms and mobilization of substantial financial resources will be the key to this turnaround.

As a final point, it may be noted that India also needs to reform higher education in areas covered by laws other than the UGC Act. The National Medical Commission Act (2019), which has replaced the Indian Medical Council Act (1956), has been a breakthrough piece of legislation from this viewpoint. Similar changes need to be made in areas such as Indian systems of medicine, homeopathy, dentistry, nursing, pharmacy, veterinary medicine, and rehabilitation. And while the UGC Act covers legal education, that field needs special attention.

Notes

1. Enrollments and GER data in China other than those for the year 2016 are from Li and Yang 2014, figure 1.2. The data for 2016 are from Sun Wenyu, "China's Higher Education Enrollment Rate Reaches 42.7 Per Cent in 2016," *People's Daily Online*, July 11, 2017, http://en.people.cn/n3/2017/0711/c90000-9240278.html, which in turn attributes them to a communiqué by the Ministry of Education, China.
2. See Kapur and Mehta 2008.
3. See National Center for Education Statistics, "Fast Facts," https://nces.ed.gov/fastfacts/display.asp?id=84 (accessed June 8, 2018). In addition to four-year institutions, the United States had 1,685 two-year colleges in the academic year 2013–14.
4. See National Center for Education Statistics, "Digest of Education Statistics," https://nces.ed.gov/programs/digest/d16/tables/dt16_301.10.asp (accessed June 8, 2018).
5. See National Center for Education Statistics, "Postsecondary Institution Revenues," figure 2, last updated May 2019, https://nces.ed.gov/programs/coe/indicator_cud.asp (accessed June 8, 2018).
6. See American Association for the Advancement of Science, "R&D at Colleges and Universities," https://www.aaas.org/page/rd-colleges-and-universities (accessed June 9, 2018).
7. Li and Yang 2014, 13–14.
8. Two additional less prominent interventions are the 863 Project and 973 Project.
9. Zhang, Patton, and Kenney 2013, 767 n. 8.
10. Li 2010.
11. Li 2010, 278–79.
12. See Li and Yang 2014, 17 n. 2.
13. See Zhang, Patton, and Kenney 2013.
14. There are four Funding Councils for each of the four regions of the United Kingdom: England, Scotland, Wales, and Northern Ireland.
15. Panagariya and Kumar 2019.
16. Panagariya and Kumar 2018a discuss some recent reforms, while Panagariya and Kumar 2018b and 2018c offer suggestions on reforming the current governance system of higher education.

17. This design is heavily influenced by the design of the Office for Students in the United Kingdom, with the key difference that it does not vest the power to disburse government funds in the commission. Government funds should be disbursed by another armss-length agency of the government with some consideration given to institution quality as assessed by the Committee for Quality Assessment.

11
Governance

The choice of the right policies, programs, and projects is only half of the story. The translation of broad policies into concrete laws, rules, and regulations and the effective delivery of programs and projects depends on the implementation process. This is where governance is critically important. Absent effective governance, even the best of policies, programs, and projects can fail. This is why almost all successful cases of sustained rapid growth and poverty eradication can be traced to leadership capable of making the right policy choices as well as implementing them. It is inconceivable that Singapore and South Korea could have achieved the success they did during the 1960s and 1970s without Lee Kuan Yew and Park Chung-hee, respectively, at the helm.

Implementation is integral to nearly everything that the government does. Good policies can be subverted if they are not translated into appropriate laws, rules, and regulations. Delivery of services by central and state governments, whether related to health, education, infrastructure, international trade, tax collection, defense, rule of law or dispensation of justice, depends on the process of implementation and quality of personnel along the chain of delivery. Given the all-encompassing importance of governance, it should be evident that a chapter in a book can hardly do justice to the subject. What I offer below are a few ideas to improve delivery of outcomes in a selected set of areas in which the suggested changes may offer high returns.

My recommendations in this chapter fall in three areas: consolidation of ministries, reform of bureaucracy, and economic administration. Reform of bureaucracy includes such matters as the selection and promotion of civil servants, the training of officials, file management within ministries, work culture, and the role of vigilance agencies. The aspects of economic administration I discuss include implementation of reforms in mission mode, transparency in fiscal accounting, a sunset clause on centrally sponsored schemes, tax administration, monitoring of export growth, and trade negotiation administration. With some tweaking, some of the recommendations can also be applied to governance in Indian states.

Consolidation of Ministries

The central government in India has far too many ministries. Based on data gathered by my student Vishnu Narasimhan in early 2018, India had a total of fifty-three ministries. Among nineteen major countries around the world, only Sri Lanka, with fifty-one ministries, came close to India. Canada and South Africa were tied for third place with thirty-four ministries each. As Table 11.1 shows, twelve out of the nineteen countries on which Narasimhan collected data had twenty-five or fewer ministries. Germany had the smallest number of ministries, at thirteen, followed by France, which had sixteen.

Table 11.1 Number of Ministries in Selected Countries, 2018

Country	Total number of ministries
India	53
Sri Lanka	51
Canada	34
South Africa	34
Pakistan	32
Indonesia	30
Brazil	28
China	25
Nigeria	25
Malaysia	24
Chile	23
United Kingdom	23
United States	22
Kenya	20
Mexico	19
Thailand	19
South Korea	18
France	16
Germany	13

Source: As collected by the author's student, Vishnu Narasimhan.

The large number of ministries in India is detrimental to governance for at least three reasons. First, ministries judge their importance by how much they get to spend. Therefore, they compete within the government for as large a share in total expenditures as possible, regardless of the social good they might do with those resources. This competition often leads to inefficient allocation of expenditures, with some high-return areas underfunded and certain low-return areas overfunded. When the number of ministries is large, many ministries do not have credible social or public purposes. As a result, allocating resources to these ministries can be disproportionately wasteful.

The second reason a large number of ministries is detrimental to governance is that it slows down the decision-making process in the government. This happens because too many ministries end up having jurisdiction over any given decision that the government must make. Because senior bureaucrats often pursue the narrowly defined interests of their own ministries, which may not, and often do not, coincide with the national interest—and sometimes even pursue their own personal interests, such as maximizing power and influence within the government or improving prospects for their next promotion—decisions reached through negotiation and bargaining among multiple ministries frequently fail to maximize the national interest. The divergence between what serves the national interest and what actually transpires increases with the number of ministries.

The third reason a large number of ministries is detrimental to governance is that it encourages mission creep—the government gets centrally involved in sectors that should be off-limits to it. The existence of a large number of ministries in areas that should be the exclusive preserve of the private sector illustrates this point. Unlike most countries, India has ministries for steel, textiles, electronics, information technology, food processing, heavy industries, mines, chemicals, and fertilizers. These ministries perpetuate and expand the scope of public sector enterprises in these sectors. They also become focal points for lobbying by narrowly defined special interests.

The existence of ministries that buy from or sell to other ministries sometimes gives rise to gross inefficiencies. For example, the Railways Ministry is a buyer of steel and the Steel Ministry is a seller of it. Because both activities are a part of the government, it is expected that the Railways Ministry will buy steel from the Steel Ministry even if it is a costly supplier. There have been feuds between the two ministries, with the Steel Ministry crying foul at the Railways Ministry's insistence on buying steel from private sector suppliers. When public sector steel companies perform poorly, the ministry also manages to get all kinds of duties imposed on imported steel. That makes steel costlier still for the Railways Ministry and hinders the expansion of railway lines.

Sectoral ministries have also been principal barriers to the closure of many loss-making and sick enterprises. For instance, textile firms acquired by the government during the 1980s continue to impose a cost on the taxpayer even though they have not been engaged in any manufacturing for years. At the same time, valuable land owned by these firms remains unused despite the scarcity of land for new private sector enterprises.

Many ministries should be phased out, and others should be amalgamated. For instance, the nine ministries mentioned earlier—steel, textiles, electronics, information technology, food processing, heavy industries, mines, chemicals, and fertilizers—could be replaced with just two: a ministry of industry and a ministry of services. Doing so would make it more difficult for narrow special interests to lobby successfully. Such consolidated ministries would not be able to do favors to individual sectors such as steel, textiles, or information technology. Instead, they would have to address the broader interests of industry and services as wholes.

Similar amalgamations could also be done in several other cases. A single transport ministry could replace the current ministries for roads, shipping, civil aviation, and railways. An energy ministry could be created by merging the current ministries for coal, power, petroleum and gas, and new and renewable energy. Numerous social-welfare-related ministries such as Minority Affairs, Tribal Affairs, Woman and Child Development, and Social Justice and Empowerment could also be consolidated into a single ministry. Likewise, the Skill Ministry could be merged with the Human Resource Development Ministry.

Reform of Bureaucracy

A merit-based civil service system may be either a career-based closed system or a position-based open system. In the former, civil servants are selected using a set of merit criteria that may include a competitive examination at an early age. Appointments to different positions are then made through promotion from within this pool of civil servants. In a position-based system, emphasis is placed on selecting the candidate best suited for a given position, with the choice made through open competition among internal candidates and lateral entrants from outside.

To date, India has relied nearly exclusively on the former system. Various top Indian civil services, which are classified into All India Services and Central Civil Services, recruit their employees at a young age through competitive examinations offered to candidates satisfying specific eligibility criteria. Positions are then filled from within the pool of successful candidates who choose to join the services. All India Services include the Indian Administrative Service, Indian Police Service, and Indian Forest Service. The Central Civil Services are far more numerous. They include the Indian Foreign Service, Indian Economic Service,

Income Tax Service, Indian Engineering Service, Indian Railway Service, and many others.

Bringing Competition to the Top Civil Service

Of greatest importance among the myriad government services requiring reform is the Indian Administrative Service (IAS). Sardar Vallabhbhai Patel, the first deputy prime minister and first home minister of India, had conceived of this service as the "steel frame" of the country. In his address to the first batch of IAS officials at Metcalf House in Delhi on April 21, 1947, he exhorted the new recruits to be impartial, honest, and incorruptible, to serve without expectation of reward, and to behave as servants of the public rather than rulers.

More than seventy years later, members of the IAS have all but abandoned these ideals. They predominantly see themselves as rulers rather than servants of the public. Bribe taking is far from uncommon. And a majority among them are guided by narrowly defined personal interest and the expectation of private rewards rather than a desire to advance the public interest.[1]

Some of these changes were inevitable once the fervor to serve the nation, which characterized the generation that fought against the British to win national freedom, had dissipated. Ultimately, public servants are human, and they were bound to eventually turn to pursuing the same dreams of personal progress and prosperity that other citizens do. It should have come as no surprise that the enormous power Patel conferred upon them would corrupt most of them—many in the broader sense that the high ideals Patel espoused were replaced by pursuit of power and the good life for themselves, and some in the narrower sense of receiving private favors, financial or otherwise, for services provided legally or illegally in their official capacity. The decision made in the 1950s to pursue a socialistic development model with its attendant command-and-control features contributed to the speeding up of that process.

To be sure, as one would expect from the highly selective recruitment process and the prospect of influencing the lives of more than a billion people, the IAS continues to produce some highly dedicated, honest, and brilliant officials. These officials also do their best to keep up with developments in economic thinking, technology, and other relevant areas. But there are two reasons the downside is no longer something that can be overlooked.

First, instead of being the steel frame of India, the service has become the steel armor that protects its own. Taken as a whole, it functions like a monopoly and works toward safeguarding its own power, interests, and privileges. Because the service has successfully reserved for its members nearly all top-level positions in the central and state governments, even the most poorly performing officials can count on becoming secretaries in states before retirement. And mediocre performance is generally sufficient to reach the position of secretary in the central government. In the absence of any threat of competition from outside, almost no punishment for poor performance, and nearly guaranteed promotions based on length of service, stagnation has developed among officials, while also making many of them arrogant to the point of believing that they know all there is to know as far as administration and policymaking are concerned. The result is resistance to change and unwillingness to constructively engage with experts.

Second, and more importantly, the old bias within the IAS in favor of general skills rather than specialized ones has continued. This bias made sense immediately after independence, since officials' primary duties were limited to general administration, maintenance of law and order, and provision of standard public goods such as education and healthcare. Even when it came to policymaking, common sense could go a long way because the economy was still in a primitive state at the time.[2] But today the economy is large and complex, requiring specialized knowledge.

For example, the Finance Ministry must deal with a whole host of macroeconomic policy issues ranging from inflation, fiscal deficit, and debt to banking, capital markets, tariff policy, taxation, investment treaties, and privatization. Each of these subjects is highly specialized and forms a separate area of research in economics. It is preposterous to think that an official can acquire expertise in these areas within a few months, as many of those in the IAS like to believe.

The same can be said of the tasks performed by the Ministry of Commerce. Officials of this ministry must represent India in negotiations for multilateral agreements at the World Trade Organization as well as talks regarding bilateral and plurilateral free trade agreements with trading partners. They must also negotiate on bilateral trade issues and disputes with large countries such as the United States. The economics of these negotiations and agreements is a subject of much research and debate among trade economists. Once again, it is difficult to imagine that officials who entered the service some twenty or twenty-five years ago and have not studied the subject in any depth would be in a position to adequately represent the country's interests in such negotiations.

The impact of this lack of specialized knowledge and intellectual stagnation has manifested itself in two ways: a slow pace of reforms and avoidable mistakes. With no scope for injecting fresh blood into it at top levels, the bureaucracy remains entrenched in its conventional ways and, with rare exceptions, resistant to change. With its strong bias in favor of the status quo, it has also designed rules and regulations that make any change difficult. Often multiple layers of regulations must be removed before a change can become effective. The result is that even when political leadership wants reform, change is excruciatingly slow.

A good example is the decision by the cabinet to privatize a number of public sector enterprises in 2016 and 2017. Despite this decision, the Department of Investment and Public Asset Management (DIPAM) had not privatized a single PSE until as late as August 2019. This is particularly damning because some of the units identified for privatization are listed on the stock market and the government's stake in them was 60 percent or less. Therefore, DIPAM needed to sell only a small portion of its remaining shares in those units before being able to pass their control to independent boards. The decision by the cabinet to privatize Air India also remains unimplemented.

With India in the midst of reforms aimed at replacing the old order, partially inherited from the British but mainly created during the first four decades of independence and during the second term of the United Progressive Alliance, the need for bureaucrats who understand the basic principles of economics is especially acute. This point is reinforced by the fact that within the Indian system, ministers are predominantly popularly elected members of the parliament and usually not professionals with specialized knowledge. The party in power has the option to bring professionals to the Cabinet by getting them elected as members of the Upper House of the parliament known as the Rajya Sabha since these members are elected indirectly by members of state legislative assemblies where the ruling party usually has substantial representation. Unfortunately, however, political parties exercise this option sparingly in part because they are under pressure from influential party workers to give priority to them in these elections. The net result is that the government has to rely heavily on the permanent bureaucracy for the design and implementation of new laws and the accompanying rules and regulations to bring about necessary change.

To be sure, an official can compensate for a lack of specialized knowledge by reaching out to outside experts. But this avenue has two limitations. First, to seek such knowledge, officials have to know what they do not know. Unfortunately, with intellectual stagnation and arrogance simultaneously characterizing many of them, this is not always the case. Second, the ability to identify the right expert, absorb her advice, and correctly translate it into action may require a certain minimum expertise on the part of the officials, which may be lacking.

A good recent example illustrating these problems is the slow pace at which the Department of Financial Services (DFS) in the Ministry of Finance responded to the problem of non-performing assets of public sector banks. To experts in the field, the problem had been apparent as early as 2013. By 2015, it had also been a subject of at least informal discussions within the government. Yet with the leadership in DFS unable to grasp the implications of the problem, it neither initiated corrective action in a timely fashion on its own nor made an effort to sensitize the higher levels of government to the urgency of tackling it. It was only after growth in bank credit came to a standstill in early 2017 and the top leadership recognized the need for action that the DFS bureaucracy swung into action.

Another example relates to the reform of labor laws. Economists have spilled much ink pointing to these laws as a reason for the poor performance of labor-intensive sectors in India as well as for the predominantly small size of Indian firms. Therefore, they have proposed making labor laws more employment friendly. In response, the central government recently decided to replace its existing thirty-three labor laws with four labor codes. The wage code, which the parliament has already passed into law, speaks to how poorly Labor Ministry bureaucrats understand the workings of labor markets. The code retains provisions from existing labor laws for rising minimum wages with rising levels of skill. This is a bizarre provision and one that exists in hardly any other important country. The ethical argument for a minimum wage is that an individual's wage should be enough to provide that person with a minimum living standard under prevailing social norms. But this minimum living standard cannot be higher for more-skilled individuals than for less-skilled ones.

For nearly two decades I have suggested lateral entry as a possible solution.[3] Such entry amounts to opening government positions to outsiders based on a match between the nature of duties to be performed and skills of the individual rather than appointing only those from within the existing bureaucracy to them. Appreciating full well that such a proposal strikes at the heart of the monopoly power they enjoy, IAS officials as a group remain opposed to it. With proponents of lateral entry gaining traction in recent years, officials from the service have responded by interpreting the reform as opening the system to the entry of specialized staff as consultants. This, however, is a tactical response that gives the appearance of receptivity to the reform while fully protecting the monopoly of the service over positions with real decision-making power. Genuine lateral entry requires opening positions with decision-making power—such as those of directors, joint secretaries, additional secretaries, and secretaries—to lateral entrants.

Lateral entry will bring two major advantages. First, it will subject the regular IAS bureaucracy to competition. The resulting pressure would force the members of the service to continuously improve themselves through acquiring new skills and augmenting their knowledge base rather than stagnating under the protection of guaranteed and automatic promotions. Even if new entrants end up filling only 10 to 15 percent of the positions, with current employees of IAS taking the remaining ones, the resulting competition will impact the entire service. It is the contestability of the position rather than the final outcome that is the key to change. Second, lateral entry will offer the opportunity to bring specialized skills and knowledge directly into the corridors of power. Once inside the system and bestowed with decision-making authority, the entrants would be in a position to influence the thinking of the permanent bureaucracy on a daily basis.

Recently, the government has made two radical policy shifts with regard to appointments of senior officials. First, it has opened joint secretary positions to officials of services other than IAS in a big way. As a part of this shift, in July 2019, out of a total of thirty-three new joint secretaries, it chose only seven from IAS. The remaining twenty-six came from services such as the Indian Railway Service of Mechanical Engineers, Indian Post and Telecommunication, Indian Defense Accounts Service, Indian Audit and Accounts Service, Indian Railway Accounts Service, Indian Railway Service of Signal Engineers, and Indian Statistical Service.

Second, the government has opened the door to lateral entrants for senior positions. In April 2019, it announced the appointment of nine outsiders with specialized knowledge as joint secretaries. According to media reports, the government plans to bring more outsiders with special skills and knowledge into lower-ranked government positions such as directors and deputy secretaries.

Five observations relating to these unprecedented shifts in policy toward senior appointments in central government are in order. First, the appointment of officials from non-IAS services as joint secretaries is administratively much easier and faster than bringing in outsiders through lateral entry. Therefore, these appointments are a very effective way of rapidly weakening the IAS monopoly on senior jobs and of establishing the principle of opening up senior levels of bureaucracy to individuals other than IAS staff. Some further movement in this direction is desirable. But it is equally important to recognize a key limitation of this avenue to enhanced competition for senior positions. Whereas IAS officials have the occasion to think about policymaking at various stages in their careers, the duties of officials in non-IAS services are predominantly administrative. Insofar as a key function of joint secretaries is making policy, the government should be careful not to rely too heavily on appointments of officials of non-IAS services to senior positions. Once the stranglehold of IAS is weakened and the principle of openness in the appointment of senior officials is firmly established, most positions should be thrown open to all applicants, whether insiders or outsiders. There is no reason why the IAS monopoly should be replaced by another, even if it happens to encompass all services. Talent must be tapped wherever it exists.

Second, it is extremely important that the number of non-IAS hires is rapidly expanded. Past experience suggests that IAS officials may try to discredit non-IAS entrants, whether from other services or from outside, in order to reassert their control. If the number of non-IAS appointees is small in relation to the existing stock of senior IAS officials, the latter will be in a good position to ensure the failure of the former.

Third, the dominant view among IAS staffers is that non-IAS appointees must be subject to more stringent age and experience requirements than their IAS counterparts. This is wholly inappropriate. It is time to recognize that talent is not inextricably linked to age or experience. Truly talented individuals advance rapidly in their fields, and they would not want to join the government if they would have to wait simply because their talent is not backed by additional years of age or experience. The goal should be to simply eliminate the age and experience requirements for all positions and make appointments based solely on the qualifications of the candidates. If younger current IAS and non-IAS officials within the government wish to compete for positions open to lateral hires, they should be permitted to do so as well.

Fourth, it is also important that outside candidates are brought in on fixed terms. Once that term is over, they must return to a non-government job. This will help ensure that only those confident enough of finding a good outside job after completing their stint in the government will take these jobs. Any promise of a permanent job in the government is likely to attract candidates with limited talent who are looking for a comfortable job in which they can eventually retire.

Finally, the government must demonstrate utmost transparency in and protect the integrity of the process of hiring outside candidates. Vested interests have every incentive to discredit non-IAS appointees by alleging favoritism and political interference. The present government is particularly vulnerable to allegations that it is appointing party cadres to coveted positions. Selection through the Union Public Service Commission, which is known for its independence, and making the qualifications of non-IAS hires available for public scrutiny can go a long way toward blunting such criticisms.

In concluding the discussion on lateral entry, it is useful to briefly touch on a tension of sorts between general and specialized skills in the running of the government. There is a need for greater acceptance of the view that certain tasks and positions within the government require specialized skills and knowledge. Because IAS officials tend to be generalists, they promote the fiction that they can learn to perform any specialized task within a matter of months and that they do not need any additional study or training. In its extreme form, this view translates into hostility toward those with specialized knowledge, and it can result in deliberate placement of younger IAS officials with specialized skills and knowledge in positions that are entirely unrelated to their expertise. In turn, this discourages other young officials from seeking specialized knowledge. This is counterproductive. Senior IAS officials must learn to accommodate younger colleagues with specialized knowledge.

At the same time, this pitch for a greater role for and acceptance of specialized skills should not be interpreted as a rejection of the generalized skills that characterize many IAS officials. Generalists will always remain pivotal to any well-functioning government. Indeed, to be successful in a bureaucracy, any outside entrants will have to acquire some generalized skills as well. Ultimately, what is needed is a balance between generalized and specialized skills.

Temporary Exit to Non-Government Sectors

While bringing outsiders into the government on fixed terms, the government must also encourage the temporary exit of at least a small fraction of its permanent staff for positions in non-government sectors, including the private corporate sector. Such temporary employment outside the government can serve three purposes. First, it would allow officials to see the world from the other side. They will get to see and experience firsthand how those they serve feel about their services. This may help sensitize them to the public's needs and serve them better when they return to the government. Second, outside employment will help them acquire skills that may make them more effective government employees in the future. Finally, some officials may discover that their comparative advantage lies outside the government and they may choose to permanently leave the government. This too will represent better allocation of the nation's human resources.

A common fear expressed with respect to government employees working outside the government is that it would lead to a conflict of interest during employment outside or after they return to the government. But these fears are highly exaggerated and should not deter experimenting with temporary exits, for three reasons. First, ultimately it is the individual character of the official that determines her behavior. Officials with integrity will refrain from profiting personally at the expense of the public even if they serve in the private sector for short periods, while those without scruples are likely to sacrifice public interest for personal gain even if they spend their entire working lives in the government. Second, should an official indulge in wrongdoing on account of contacts developed while working outside the government, vigilance agencies can bring that person to justice, just as they do in the case of wrongdoing by officials who never leave the government. Finally, even if there is a risk of conflict of interest in allowing officials to take temporary outside employment, we must measure this cost against the potential benefit of such movement. Movement of individuals into and out of government is a common feature in many countries including the United States.

File Management, Lower Levels of Bureaucracy, and Young Professionals

Under the current system, the lowest-level official in a ministry (in most cases, this is a member of the clerical staff) initiates a file or writes the first set of comments on a file that comes in from another ministry. Once this official has initiated the file or written comments on the file and the file travels up, the tendency is for successively higher-level officials to echo the view of the officials below. The lowest-level official sticks to the line the ministry took in the past on any given issue. This gives him a good defense in case bosses above him raise any questions. As the file travels up, higher-level officials also feel secure in endorsing what comes from below, since they can blame their subordinates in case questions are raised about the stance of the ministry. The lack of specialized knowledge reinforces this view: if you do not know the subject well, it is best to endorse what the officials below you noted on the file. Indeed, this is a perfectly safe system for senior bureaucrats who claim that they can become specialists in any area within a matter of months but actually don't.

This process leaves little room for innovative thinking within the ministry, so any major change invariably has to come from the top. To promote innovative thinking at the middle and lower levels, the government should shift to a system under which the first notation on a file comes from an official with the rank of director or higher. The official may take inputs from those below her, but the initiation of a file or the first comment on a file from another ministry must be hers. This would even encourage the official to discuss the matter up front with those senior to her, forcing greater interaction and thinking.

A related reform would be to overhaul the staff below the level of deputy secretary. Rather than rely on a large body of permanent staff at these levels, it may make more sense to bring in bright and tech-savvy young professionals in their early to late twenties on three- to five-year contracts. These youngsters can bring energy and innovative thinking to the ministry while also gaining exposure to and experience with working in the government. Once past files and records are digitized and made searchable, the young professionals can help the senior staff readily track down the history of how the ministry handled any specific subject in the past. Digital archives would eliminate the need for permanent staff as keepers of institutional memory. The government think tank NITI Aayog has made effective use of young professionals since its inception in 2015, and other ministries may learn from its experience.

Reining in Vigilance Agencies

India has far too many vigilance agencies, and there are widespread complaints that they launch investigations of officials on flimsy grounds. Such investigations demoralize officials and discourage them from taking innovative actions and making bold decisions. Fearful that any deviation from the past may open the door to questioning by the agencies, officials take the safe course of continuing with past practices, thereby perpetuating the status quo. This fear is often also why officials endorse what their juniors write on official files, since in case of an investigation the blame can be shifted to the lower-ranking official. The fact that all those whose signatures appear on a particular file take the same view of the matter further serves as a protective shield. There is a need to curb frivolous investigations that do not lead to convictions but only create an atmosphere of fear among officials. India needs to create an ecosystem in which officials can freely make decisions that are in the national interest.

Reforming Training Institutions for Officials

The government must also take a fresh look at its various training institutes and programs. Under the current system, there is a strong internal bias in training, in the sense that trainers are predominantly from within the government. Some outsiders are invited to speak, but officials' exposure to them is limited. The process should not be one in which senior officials serving as trainers effectively try to turn junior officials into their clones.

Correcting Colonial- and Princely-Era Practices in the Daily Lives of Officials

A sensitive but nevertheless important issue concerns the discontinuation of certain practices in the daily lives of officials that have been inherited from colonial and princely eras and which should have no place in a modern society. For example, multi-tasking staff (MTS) carry officials' bags, open the doors of their offices and cars for them, deliver files from one office to another for them, and serve them tea and coffee. Officials often insist on two cars and multiple drivers, with one car exclusively for family use. When it comes to very senior officials, a virtual army of MTS and contract workers can often be found hanging around their residences and offices. Few modern countries indulge in these practices. Today's officials must learn to carry their own bags, open their own doors, and get their own coffee and tea. As regards amenities, the government should consider moving to a system of cash allowances rather than the current opaque system of in-kind benefits such as cars, drivers, workers to assist at home, and large bungalows in the most expensive part of New Delhi.

Economic Administration

There are numerous areas of reform that can be loosely classified under the rubric of "economic administration." Therefore, what I discuss here is illustrative rather than exhaustive.

Reforms in Mission Mode

During his first term, Prime Minister Narendra Modi successfully deployed a governance model that relied on bureaucratic initiatives under his guidance. A key element of this governance model was the appointment of a number of groups of secretaries, with each group assigned the task of preparing presentations on projects, programs, and policies to be implemented the following year in key sectors of the economy. The prime minister, his entire cabinet, and top bureaucrats then discussed the presentations during long sessions. Once finalized, these presentations became the road maps for the following year for the major sectors.

An advantage of this approach was that bureaucrats jointly owned the proposals and therefore diligently implemented them. But when it comes to radical reforms, this approach has a downside. By nature, bureaucrats are cautious and lean heavily in favor of projects and programs rather than significant policy changes. Even when they do propose policy changes, such changes are often piecemeal and rarely go beyond tinkering.

To pave the way for radical reforms, the government must adopt a different approach. At the outset, it must identify half a dozen key areas of reform. These could potentially include labor laws, land acquisition laws, higher education, international trade, privatization of public sector enterprises, and banking reforms. In each area, a time-bound mission must be launched, with a senior bureaucrat with domain knowledge heading it. Within two months, the mission head must provide a precise road map for radical reforms with a time-bound action plan.

Each mission head must have as an adviser a professional with deep knowledge of the area of reform. A team of bright and energetic young professionals should in turn assist the mission head and adviser. The experience of NITI Aayog in recent years shows that young professionals, unencumbered by the compulsions of the regular bureaucracy, can play a critical role in helping speed up the work of ministries and missions. Designing, piloting, and implementing the reforms should be the mission's sole responsibility.

Each mission should have its own budget, with the mission head having full authority to decide how the funds are used. Rather than having to seek prior approval for each expenditure item, it should suffice for the mission to send a statement of its expenditures each quarter to the financial adviser representing the department of expenditure. It is important for India to move away from a system that relies on multi-layered bureaucratic rules to one that places trust in at least its senior officials. The mission should have similar autonomy in other areas to add to the speed of its work.

Finally, the prime minister must oversee the implementation of each of these missions and require periodic reports from the mission heads. In turn, each mission head should have direct access to the prime minister for one-on-one meetings so as to be able to freely seek his help in removing obstacles to the mission's work posed by any functionaries, departments, or ministries.

This mission-mode implementation of reforms should assume a special importance during the second term (2019–24) of Prime Minister Modi. His government has a two-thirds majority in the lower house of the parliament. Though it does not have a majority in the upper house on its own, it is able to muster enough votes from other parties and independents to pass even contentious legislations. Such a favorable situation for bringing about major changes in the economy is unlikely to be realized in the future.

Implementation of an Export Strategy

A central theme of this book has been that rapid growth of the kind that the East Asian "tiger" economies achieved in the 1960s to 1980s and that China achieved during the last three decades is not possible without major success in export markets. India must increase its share in export markets to achieve a significantly larger scale of operation in its manufacturing enterprises. For this to take place, in addition to various policy changes it also needs to signal to enterprises its commitment to the removal of barriers that hinder its cross-border trade in general and exports in particular.

Here India can learn from the experience of South Korea. In the 1960s, as South Korea embarked on its export-oriented strategy, it not only adopted policies that helped make its goods competitive in the world markets but also sent clear signals to enterprises that it wanted them to expand their engagement in the world economy. Beginning in December 1962, President Park Chung-hee initiated a process of regular, institutionalized consultations with stakeholders, including relevant ministries, industry groups, policy analysts, and exporters, to effectively communicate the policy and to identify and remove bottlenecks facing exports. He enacted the Export Committee Regulation and created an Export Promotion Committee to discuss important policies and plans for export expansion. Initially, the Ministry of Commerce and Industry was given the charge of coordinating across different departments, and the prime minister chaired the committee.

Because the process did not work satisfactorily in the early years, in February 1965, Park himself assumed chairmanship of the committee, which began meeting once a month. The committee discussed and devised policies to expand exports and address bottlenecks facing exporters. As Korea began achieving success in expanding exports, the scope of the committee expanded. Beginning in 1969, its participants came to include government ministries, the Korea Chamber of Commerce and Industry, the Korea International Trade Association, representatives of export industries, professors, and even political and legal figures.

The fact that Park himself presided over the committee sent a strong message to all relevant actors that the government was serious about its objective of expanding exports. The meetings also offered the government departments an opportunity to communicate, discuss, and modify policies while giving industry representatives a chance to bring to the notice of the government any bottlenecks they faced. Reviews of progress at the meetings in the presence of Park also placed the burden of explanation of any failures on relevant actors. This kept all involved on their toes.

Korea's approach to international trade stands in sharp contrast to that of India. India's trade concerns have been predominantly centered on imports. According to media reports, in June 2019 the government announced its intention to monitor the top fifty tariff lines, which together account for 60 percent of India's imports, to find ways to "reduce import dependence."[4] In September 2019, the commerce minister stated that the government was monitoring import trends of important goods and would take corrective steps to control sudden surges that harm Indian industry.[5]

Going by the experience of every single successful country, India would do well to build exports, which would effectively eliminate the need to cut imports to promote industry. Adopting an institutional approach involving regular review of trade policies and export performance under the chairmanship of the prime minister, as was done in Korea by President Park in the 1960s and 1970s, can ensure the success of the Make in India program through industries in which India enjoys comparative advantage. As in Korea, regular reviews by the prime minister will go a long way toward signaling to industrialists the government's commitment to building export industries. They will also put India's policymaking bodies on notice that they must work to remove the barriers exporters face. Such a process may also lead to sincere exploration of the prospects for free trade agreements that may help open markets for Indian exports in return for imports.

A New Entity for Trade Negotiations

The Ministry of Commerce has had a long-standing protectionist history in India. It has supported tariff hikes on numerous products to promote import substitution in recent years. It has also taken a rather negative approach to negotiations at the World Trade Organization as well as those for free trade agreements with the European Union and with Asian countries under the auspices of the Regional Comprehensive Economic Partnership (RCEP). At the WTO, India has refused to join negotiations on e-commerce that seventy-plus countries, including China, have initiated. At the EU and RCEP negoitations, the Commerce Ministry makes impossible demands seeking liberal entry of Indian workers to the markets of negotiating partner countries, and upon being rebuffed, it reports back that the latter are not interested in forging agreements with India. It is critical to break these logjams to maximize the opportunities trade offers India.

A possible solution to the problem is to create a new entity similar to the Office of the United States Trade Representative (USTR) and place it in charge of all negotiation. Ideally, this entity should report directly to the prime minister. If this is administratively awkward, it may be placed in the Ministry of External Affairs (MEA). In contrast to the inward-looking attitude of the Commerce Ministry, MEA better appreciates the value of external engagement and is also better able to carry out negotiations with trading partners.

Tax Administration

The central government collects taxes on personal income, corporate profits, the purchase and sales of goods and services, and international trade. Administration of each of these four components of taxes has governance problems specific to it. The subject of tax administration is vast and can hardly be covered satisfactorily in a short section of a chapter. Accordingly, I confine myself to some basic issues at a conceptual level.

Currently, at 18 percent of GDP, the combined tax revenue of the central and state governments in India is well below that in comparator countries. This creates a serious revenue problem for a government that is committed not just to undertaking significant social expenditures, building infrastructure, and raising defense expenditures but also to maintaining fiscal discipline. As a result, the pressure on tax authorities to raise more revenues is immense.

The tax authorities can raise more revenue by expanding the tax base, collecting more revenue from the existing base, or both. Unfortunately, they have found it more convenient to increase revenue from those already bearing the largest part of the burden of taxes. This approach has translated into higher tax rates on individuals in higher tax brackets, cesses (an additional tax on top of the regular tax often levied for a specific purpose), surcharges (an extra tax on the tax liability assessed at the regular rates); and challenges by tax collectors to exemptions claimed by richer taxpayers including corporations. Additionally, recognition of the fact that the government desperately needs more tax revenue has created a sense of impunity in tax collectors keen on extracting more bribes from taxpayers. The end result has been greater harassment of taxpayers, including demands for greater bribes, and damage to investor sentiment.

It is India's high tax rates and a complex web of exemptions that are at the heart of this unhappy situation. Despite the embrace of reforms for three decades, policymakers in India have been unable to rid themselves of a socialist mindset. They continue to find popular appeal in taxing the rich and corporate entities at ultra-high rates while simultaneously loading up the system with all kinds of exemptions conveniently labeled as incentives. Such a system encourages rent-seeking behavior and impedes wealth creation. What India needs instead are moderate tax rates with fewer or no exemptions. Such a system will automatically minimize the scope for tax officials to extract bribes by challenging exemptions sought by taxpayers. It will also have a favorable impact on investment and growth and undercut rent-seeking behavior.

A related problem India faces is its very large number of tax disputes. A complex tax system with ambiguously defined exemptions, scope for extracting bribes, and tax officials' fears that vigilance agencies might investigate them if they settle tax disputes rather than appeal all the way up to the final judicial authority have resulted in the accumulation of a large number of tax disputes over time at different levels of the judicial system. According to available data, there were more than 137,000 such cases related to direct taxes and 145,000 cases related to indirect taxes at the appellate tribunal, high court, and Supreme Court levels.[6] Though the government loses more than two-thirds of the cases at all levels, officials continue to pursue them either because they want to extract bribes or they want to avoid being accused by vigilance agencies of taking bribes to close the case. The slow pace of the Indian judicial system only makes matters worse.

To clear the backlog of disputes, judicial reforms aimed at speeding up resolution are needed. But there is also a need for tax simplification and administrative reforms that would help minimize the scope for bribe extraction and discourage officials from pursuing frivolous cases against taxpayers. Greater reliance on modern technology to conduct audits can help reduce human involvement in selecting the returns that are subject to scrutiny. It will shrink the space for bribe extraction while also reducing the scope for vigilance agencies to investigate officials. The decision in mid-2018 to increase the monetary thresholds for additional tax claims, below which the income tax department cannot file an appeal to the next judicial level, is an important step toward reducing the backlog of cases. The government should regularly revise these thresholds for appeals at various judicial levels.

Sunset Clause on Centrally Sponsored Schemes

The government devotes a substantial proportion of its expenditure to centrally sponsored schemes (CSSs). Expenditures on these schemes are shared by the central and state governments in pre-specified proportions. For the vast majority of these schemes, we lack any assessment of their impact. It is time for the government to carry out a serious audit of the schemes, and those failing to meaningfully serve a social purpose should be closed down. In the future, when a new scheme is begun, the ministry proposing it should be required to provide a clear statement of objectives and a timetable for their delivery. A sunset clause should accompany each CSS, and continuation of the scheme beyond the sunset date should be seriously evaluated by the prime minister's office in light of the scheme's outcomes. With rare exceptions, the government should require pilot projects prior to full launch of a scheme. Finally, states should be given full flexibility in the choice of different CSSs. Based on the choices made by the states, central allocations should be continuously rejigged across schemes. This will also help separate schemes that are aligned with states' interests from those that are not.

Transparency in Fiscal Accounting

The main documents listing public sector revenues and expenditures in India are the annual budgets of the central and state governments. These documents give a somewhat partial picture of public sector revenues and expenditures. In particular, public sector entities such as the Food Corporation of India, National Housing Bank, Rural Electrification Corporation, Power Finance Corporation, Higher Education Finance Agency, and National Agricultural and Rural Development Bank borrow funds from the market to finance expenditures on social schemes and infrastructure. These funds, called extra-budgetary resources

(EBRs), remain on the balance sheets of the entities borrowing them and are not included in the borrowing reported on the government budget. At the same time, the government covers the interest and losses of these entities when they are unable to cover them from their income streams.

There are two separate issues related to this borrowing. First, an exhaustive account of EBRs and payments made by the government to cover the interest or other expenses of borrowing entities remains unavailable. Transparency requires that all sources of funding for government expenditures, whether on- or off-budget, be listed. Likewise, public resources spent on servicing loans of off-budget entities should be transparently listed.

The second issue concerns the calculation of the fiscal deficit. Conceptually speaking, to the extent that EBRs finance expenditures on government projects, they should be incorporated into the calculation of the fiscal deficit. If the sums involved were small, this would not be a major issue. But according to some recent calculations, the central government's fiscal deficit in 2017/18 becomes 5.85 percent of the GDP if EBRs are included, whereas the officially reported fiscal deficit is only 3.5 percent of GDP.[7] Even if the exclusion of EBRs from the official fiscal deficit is standard international practice, it is important to report the figure inclusive of it. When assessing the impact of public sector borrowing on private investment, it is the larger figure that is relevant.

The final point worthy of note is that while off-budget borrowing may help the government keep the official fiscal deficit figure low, it is a costly form of borrowing. The interest rate paid by public sector entities is generally 2 to 3 percentage points higher than what the government pays on sovereign borrowing. Therefore, the eventual cost to the taxpayer would be significantly lower if the government shifted off-budget borrowing to the budget.

Concluding Remarks

The choice of policy and the identification of projects and program are critical to development and growth. But they can yield desired outcomes only if implemented effectively. This is where governance comes into play.

The subject of governance is wide-ranging, and even an entire volume exclusively devoted to it would be insufficient to do justice to the topic. As such, this chapter does no more than scratch the surface. I have briefly touched on a handful of important topics. My focus has been on subjects relating to governance at the level of the central government. Topics covered have included consolidation of ministries, reform of bureaucracy, and selected aspects of the central government's economic administration.

I have deliberately chosen not to discuss two of the most important areas of governance: the police and the judiciary. While insufficient expertise is a contributing factor, my primary reason for this choice is that justice cannot be done to these subjects without devoting at least a full chapter to each of them. Nevertheless, I note the critical importance of reforms in these areas. The police and the judiciary are central to achieving peace, security, and order and to enforcing contracts. When peace, security, and order are missing, no amount of good policy can lead to development and growth. For instance, as long as Bihar remained unsafe, it was unable to make much economic progress. When Chief Minister Nitish Kumar came to the helm in 2005, the first thing he did was to establish some order and security of life in the state. Only then he was able to reap the benefits of good policy. In a similar vein, repeated terrorist attacks and the resulting insecurity have been a major obstacle to development in the state of Jammu and Kashmir.

A poorly functioning judiciary not only undermines the objectives of peace, security, and order but additionally exerts a negative effect on growth by failing to enforce contracts in a timely fashion. Indian courts at all levels—district and subordinate courts, high courts, and the Supreme Court—have been notoriously slow in dispensing justice. More than 10 percent of the civil cases in district and subordinate courts take five years or longer to resolve.[8] In the Delhi and Bombay high courts, the average life of unresolved cases is approximately six years.[9] India thus needs major reforms in the areas of the police and the judiciary.

Notes

1. This was forcefully driven home to me when, as vice chairman of NITI Aayog, a government think tank for which the prime minister serves as chair, I offered to deliver a few lectures on the Indian economy to freshly recruited IAS officials. Much to my disappointment, my staff told me that most of the young officials would not attend the lecture unless they were served dinner with a non-vegetarian dish after the lecture. That led me to withdraw my offer after the first lecture.
2. I hasten to add that even during the early years there were occasions when expert advice could have helped avert some highly damaging decisions. One such moment was when a lone bureaucrat in the Ministry of Finance decided to introduce strict foreign exchange control in response to a balance-of-payments crisis in 1957/58 without considering the possibility of a devaluation of the rupee (see Panagariya 2008, 26–29). Had India chosen to devalue the rupee at the time, it could have maintained a far more open import regime than the one that followed the imposition of exchange control. In the early 1960s, faced with a similar situation, South Korea chose multiple devaluations, which allowed it to pursue more outward-oriented policies subsequently.
3. Panagariya 2000, 2005.

4. Chakraborty 2019.
5. The report appeared on the front page of the *Economic Times* on September 4, 2019, under the title "Will Take Steps to Control Imports That Harm Indian Industry: Goyal," https://www.pressreader.com/india/the-economic-times/20190904/281569472407866/textview.
6. Ministry of Finance 2018, 137.
7. A media story attributes the calculation to a presentation made by the comptroller and auditor general of India to the Fifteenth Finance Commission. Dinesh Narayanan, "CAG Demonstrates How Govt Relies on Off-Budget Resources to Fund Deficit," *Economic Times*, July 25, 2019, https://economictimes.indiatimes.com/news/economy/indicators/cag-demonstrates-how-govt-relies-on-off-budget-resources-to-fund-deficit/articleshow/70360281.cms (accessed August 13, 2019).
8. Ministry of Finance 2019, 100, figure 4.
9. Ministry of Finance, 2018, 134, table 1.

12
Nuggets: A Miscellany of Reforms

I have already systematically analyzed the key areas requiring deep reforms to accelerate growth to double-digit levels. The account will remain incomplete, however, without brief reference to a number of additional reform measures. Arguably, some of these measures deserve detailed consideration and separate chapters of their own. But doing so would make the volume unduly long, something I wish to avoid. Hence I choose to follow the middle path.

Macroeconomic Reforms

During the last two years of the United Progressive Alliance government, 2012/13 and 2013/14, inflation, the fiscal deficit, and the current account deficit were high. During its first term, the successor National Democratic Alliance (NDA) government managed to stabilize the economy, bringing all three indicators down. Early in its term, the NDA government adopted inflation targeting, with the Reserve Bank of India required to keep inflation at 4 percent, plus or minus 2 percentage points. RBI has been successful in achieving this target. It has also been able to hold the current account deficit below 2 percent of GDP. For the first time in history, the government has kept the fiscal deficit as a proportion of GDP from rising for seven consecutive years.

Given this macroeconomic stability, there would seem to be little reason to change course. Yet not all has been well. Though GDP growth has averaged a respectable 7.5 percent during the five years spanning 2014/15 to 2018/19, it has not accelerated in a robust manner toward a double-digit rate. Bringing prosperity to nearly all Indians within one to two decades requires growth at rates of 8 percent or higher year after year. That India remains some distance away from that goal is testified to by the fact that the growth rate declined to 5.8 percent in the last quarter of 2018/19 and to 5 percent in the quarter that followed. During the full year from July 1, 2018, to June 30, 2019, growth averaged only 6.1 percent. There is no doubt that this fragility largely reflects the restructuring that is under way due to the implementation of GST, cleanup of non-performing assets of commercial banks, and the prime minister's anti-corruption drive. But macroeconomic policies have something to do with it as well.

In particular, it is my view that the inflation rate in India has been kept excessively low in recent years. Although the assigned inflation target is 4 percent plus or minus 2 percentage points, RBI's behavior suggests that it has treated this as a mandate to hold the inflation rate at or below 4 percent. Anytime inflation appears to rise above this level, it rushes to raise its policy interest rate (the rate at which commercial banks can borrow funds from RBI overnight, also called the repo rate). But it is less inclined to cut its policy rate when inflation falls below the 4 percent threshold. The result has been a large increase in banks' real lending interest rate over the past five or six years. This trend can be seen in the data presented in Table 12.1.

According to Table 12.1, inflation has steadily fallen from 10.1 percent in 2012/13 to 3.4 percent in 2018/19. Alongside this 6.7 percentage point decline in inflation, the RBI policy rate has fallen just 1.25 percentage points. The small decline in the policy rate has in turn been reflected in small movements in the average lending rate of banks to businesses, which has fallen barely 2 percentage points. The result has been a large increase in the real interest rate paid by borrowers. Admittedly, in 2012/13, the real lending interest rate was negative, which was unsustainable. But the average real lending rate of 4.5 to 4.65 percent in 2018/19 was also on the high side by any standard. For borrowers without access to one of the major banks, interest rates are higher, and for those having to borrow from non-bank sources, they are significantly higher.

Table 12.1 Inflation Rates, RBI Policy Interest Rates, and bank Lending Rates, 2012/13 to 2018/19

Year	Consumer price index (%)	Repo rate, end of fiscal year (%)	Lending rate range (%)*
2012/13	10.1	7.5	9.7–10.25
2013/14	9.3	8	10–10.25
2014/15	5.8	7.5	10–10.25
2015/16	4.9	6.75	9.3–9.7
2016/17	4.5	6.25	7.75–8.2
2017/18	3.6	6	7.8–7.95
2018/19	3.4	6.25	7.9–8.05

*Based on rates charged by five major banks.

Source: Author's construction using data in real-time *RBI Handbook of Statistics on Indian Economy* (accessed September 6, 2019).

In addition to pushing the real interest rate facing borrowers to unduly high levels, low inflation poses another risk. A fast-growing developing country needs to restructure its economy on a continuous basis, with resources moving out of declining sectors to rising sectors. For this restructuring, adjustments in relative prices of different products and activities must serve as signals. But if inflation is held to excessively low levels, the space for relative prices to adjust shrinks. Potentially, this absence of price signals can impede the reallocation of resources from less efficient activities to more efficient ones.

The possibility that investment decisions of busiensses depend on the grwoth in nominal rather than inflation adjudted profits provides another reason why excessively low inflation may be harmful to grwoth. Symmetrically, if household decisions on financial savings depend on the nominal rather than inflation adjusted interest rate, excessively low inflation, which partially translates into low nominal interest rates, can impact financial savings adversely. These considerations add to the reasons the government should consider revisiting its current inflation target with a view to revising it upward to 5 or 6 percent. If the original intent of the 4 percent target plus or minus 2 percentage points was that a rise in the inflation rate to above 4 percent should not invite the ire of RBI, it has not been fulfilled.

One further subject relating to macroeconomy worthy of further thought is government expenditures. Prime Minister Modi has set many very ambitious targets in his quest to build a New India by 2024. Achieving many of these targets requires the rapid expansion of expenditures. Push for such a rapid expansion has in turn generated pressures at two different levels.

First, tax collection agencies are having to scramble to collect revenue as never before. In turn, this has led to increased harassment of honest and law-abiding taxpayers in high tax brackets, since they present an easier target for collecting yet more revenue. Such harassment ends up vitiating the atmosphere for economic activity in general and investment in particular. For instance, it is increasingly in the news these days that entrepreneurs prefer to register their companies abroad and then operate in India through wholly owned subsidiaries of those companies.

The second impact of ambitious targets has been that ministries responsible for delivering those targets are increasingly resorting to off-budget borrowing. According to one reliable estimate, this borrowing may be adding another 2.4 percent of GDP to overall public sector borrowing.[1] With household financial savings already low, such large public sector borrowing can starve the private sector of investment resources. To the extent that economic growth crucially depends on the growth of the private sector, it is necessary to allow some more time for the achievement of targets that are dependent on large expenditures.

Closure and Sale of Public Sector Enterprises, Monetization of Assets

Most economists adhere to the principle that government should not enter an activity unless it serves a public purpose. Activities related to defense, education, and health fulfill this condition. But in India, the government has also entered into many activities that serve no real public purpose, in the sense that moving them to the private sector would result in no sacrifice of any public purpose. Indeed, what has happened over the years in many cases is that after the activity was brought into the public sector, the ministry serving as host to it has come to attach this or that public purpose to it. If nothing else works, it labels the activity as having "strategic" importance, serving a "development" objective, or simply being a "priority" for the government.

In large part, the reason for the government to have taken over many activities with no substantive public purpose is historical. As India launched its development program, the government took the view that it was necessary for the country to build its own heavy industries such as steel, aluminum, and defense, which required large investments. It further felt that the private sector did not have the necessary financial resources to undertake these large investments. Therefore, the government had to step into these activities in the public interest. Complementing this reason was the government's objective of building a socialistic pattern of society in which the government would have a progressively larger share of new investments. Later, under Prime Minister Indira Gandhi, this objective acquired greater vigor. She went on to increase its share in production activity and ownership of resources not just through an increased share of the public sector in new investments but also through outright nationalization.

With the private sector having access to investment resources aplenty and the economy having been opened to foreign investors, the first of these rationales for the entry of the government into many activities no longer applies. Moreover, with India having chosen the market economy model over the socialistic one since 1991, the second rationale has also lost its force. Therefore, there is now a strong case for the government to exit activities it currently undertakes that do not have a public purpose. And it should make no new investments in such activities.

Privatization of Public Sector Enterprises

Unfortunately, as the saying goes, old habits die hard. Not only has the government shown no propensity to exit activities without public purpose into which it had entered in the past, but it has continued to enter into more such activities. If

India is to achieve and sustain near double-digit growth for one to two decades, it must undertake a major course correction.

Today, the scale of the government's involvement in areas in which it has legitimate reasons to be present has greatly expanded: administration, education, health, defense, and numerous anti-poverty programs. Increasingly, it finds itself seriously short of fiscal resources to fulfill its obligations in these areas. One of the unintended consequences of this resource scarcity has been the deterioration of governance in tax collection, with increased harassment of taxpayers being the result.

In such a situation, it makes no sense for the government to continue owning and managing loss-making large PSEs such as Air India and BSNL. Even if the debt of these PSEs is currently outside the government budget, taxpayers will eventually have to repay it in some form. There is no credible argument against privatization of these and other perpetually loss-making PSEs. Ministries that do not want to part with their PSEs often use the argument that the government should revive them before privatization to maximize their sales value. But the harsh reality is that this is merely a ploy to delay and possibly even thwart privatization. Past experience shows that attempts to revive sick PSEs have usually amounted to good money being thrown after bad.

The government, of course, needs to go much further than selling just the loss-making PSEs. It should extend privatization to PSEs that may be profitable as long as such action has no adverse impact on public welfare. On the one hand, the government needs additional revenues to stay on course with fiscal consolidation; on the other, ministries need to focus on their core functions, such as policymaking and implementing schemes directly related to public welfare. In cases in which looking after PSEs is virtually the only activity of a ministry, after the privatization of enterprises under its jurisdiction, that ministry needs to be closed down. Looking after PSEs that the private sector can profitably run is an unnecessary burden on the public sector's human resources.

Sometimes ownership of PSEs by ministries creates a conflict of interest. When their units perform poorly, ministries seek protective tariffs and other restrictions against imports. Such actions end up hurting rather than promoting the public interest. This has been the case with fertilizer imports, for example. There have even been instances when a ministry producing an input tries to forbid another ministry using that input from buying it from private suppliers even though the latter may sell it at a lower price. This has been an issue, for example, between the steel and railways ministries.

A final point in favor of privatization of PSEs is that private entrepreneurs are in a much better position to take risks associated with commercial activity. The government appoints chief executive officers of PSEs from among a pool of bureaucrats, often after their retirement. Not being professional entrepreneurs, they lack the skills necessary to undertake commercial activity efficiently. Their tendency is to minimize risk, including personal risk arising from any actions that might lead to investigation by vigilance agencies. The impact of this factor can be seen in the generally poor performance of PSEs relative to their private sector counterparts.

A study of privatization during the administration of Prime Minister Atal Bihari Vajpayee shows that the gains are vastly greater when the government sells majority stakes and transfers management into private hands than when it sells a minority stake and retains management control. Specifically, it finds that on average the gains from majority privatizations exceeded those from minority privatizations by 23 percent in terms of sales, 21 percent in terms of profits, and 28 percent in terms of employment.[2] Figure 12.1 offers further evidence. Net profits as well as earnings before tax as proportions of the revenue of listed private enterprises turn out to be uniformly several times those of central PSEs in manufacturing as well as services.[3]

A common bureaucratic tactic to delay privatization is to argue that it is necessary to wait so as to maximize the value of the enterprise to be privatized. Clearly, such an argument has no validity in perpetuity. Even in the short run, the argument is a red herring when the PSE is listed on the stock market and the government has no more than a 60 percent share in it. In such cases, all the government needs to do is to sell enough shares so that it no longer has a majority stake; that is sufficient for it to pass control to a private board. The government can then wait on selling its remaining shares in the PSE till such time as it feels confident that the share value has peaked. In May 2020, a number of PSEs existed in which the government had less than a 60 percent stake, and they have had cabinet approval for privatization for nearly three years. Yet the bureaucracy continued to drag its feet.

Restructuring and Closure of Loss-Making PSEs

At the end of 2017/18, there were 339 central government PSEs. Of these, 71 showed losses during the year, with their combined losses summing to 312.6 billion rupees. Many PSEs have been running at a perpetual loss with no prospects that they will turn into profit-making enterprises, thereby costing the taxpayer large sums of money every year. These enterprises perpetuate themselves by implementing repeated restructuring plans. In some cases, such as Air India and BSNL, the cost of restructuring falls directly on the taxpayer. In other cases, ministries carry out restructuring plans by using money obtained from selling a small part of the land available to the PSE. In this case, it is public resources that pay for restructuring.

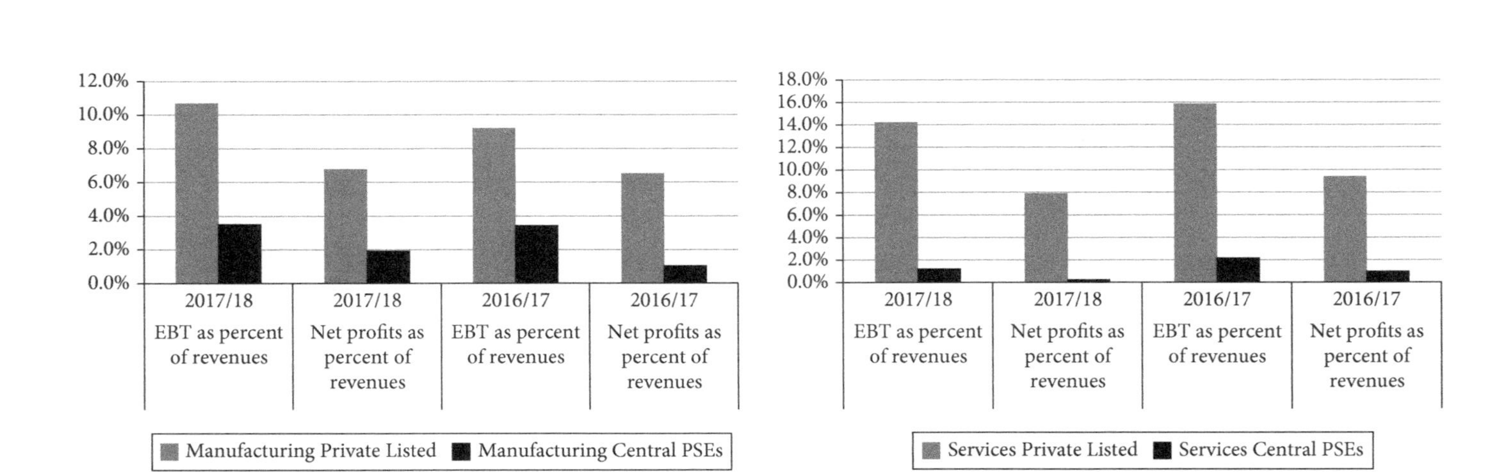

Figure 12.1 Earnings Before Tax and Net Profits as Proportions of Revenue in Central PSEs and Listed Private Enterprises

Source: Gupta and Panagariya 2019.

The government should put an end to this charade of restructuring. PSEs that serve no public interest must be allowed to restructure only if their restructuring plans meet the market test. The rule should be that any PSE that serves no public interest must seek funding from a bank for its restructuring plan at commercial terms. If the plan is commercially viable, the bank will provide financing for it. If not, restructuring should not be permitted. At that point, the enterprise should be sold to the highest bidder if a buyer can be found; if not, it should be closed down.

The government has a number of PSEs that have been dormant for many years with no production activity whatsoever. These enterprises are a net drain on public resources, since workers must be paid their salaries and factory premises maintained. In most cases, the only asset with financial value that these enterprises have is land. The government must close them down and either lay off workers with appropriate severance packages or reemploy them elsewhere in the government. Land owned by these enterprises should be deposited in a land bank or auctioned off. NITI Aayog has made such recommendations in a number of cases between 2016 and 2020, with the cabinet accepting those recommendations. But the ministries involved have not implemented the cabinet decisions.

Monetization of Public Assets

In addition to entering manufacturing activity, over the years the government has also invested heavily in many public projects such as roads, bridges, railways, airports, and ports. Each of these projects is public in the sense that, at least to a limited degree, its use by one customer does not reduce its availability to another. More importantly, investment in these projects is characterized by lumpiness: though its combined benefits across all customers exceed the cost, the benefit to any single customer or subset of customers falls short of that. As a result, without some government intervention, the project may not be undertaken.

Conventionally, these public projects have been undertaken and maintained by the government. Consequently, the government owns and maintains many of them today. At the same time, the private sector has become financially far more capable than in the past and has acquired considerable expertise in building and maintaining such projects. This has led to the two sectors coming together to form public-private partnerships, with private entrepreneurs investing in building many public projects. Unfortunately, however, many of these projects have gotten stuck on account of delays in land acquisition and environmental and other clearances, with their costs rising unduly.

As a result, private entrepreneurs have lost their appetite for such new, greenfield public projects. They are nevertheless willing and able to invest in projects that have been already completed and have established revenue streams in the form of tolls and other user charges. There are many highways, bridges, railway stations, ports, and airports that the government currently owns and manages. It can raise substantial revenues in exchange for long-term leases on them to private operators. This will be a win-win since it will bring revenues to the government, good returns on investment for private operators, and better service for customers of the projects.

One other extremely important asset that the government can monetize in win-win transactions is land. PSEs often own substantially more land than they need. Similarly, loss-making PSEs that are closed down have substantial amounts of land. Finally, many ministries, such as railways and defense, own large amounts of land. Most of these tracts of land are located in urban areas and are effectively unproductive. Auctioning them would not only bring the government revenue but, more importantly, turn valuable unproductive assets productive. It is a major national loss when so much urban land is left unused in the face of huge scarcity.

Consolidation of Subsidies, Scaling Down of Food Corporation of India

In December 2018, the government introduced a cash transfer scheme for farmers called PM-KISAN. Under the scheme, each farming household receives a cash transfer of 6,000 rupees per year. Though the sum is modest, this scheme established the principle of direct cash transfers to farmers. The government can take advantage of this new instrument to eliminate inefficiencies associated with several other transfer schemes.

The first such subsidy is that on fertilizer. The purpose of this subsidy is to keep the price of fertilizer paid by farmers below the level that would prevail absent government intervention. Because farmers are the ultimate intended beneficiaries of this subsidy, the government can transfer it directly to farmers in proportion to their land holdings along with PM-KISAN transfers. Once this is done, fertilizer prices may be allowed to find their equilibrium level in the market and restrictions on imports can be eliminated. To provide modest protection to domestic producers, the government may impose a 10 percent customs duty on fertilizer imports. On the supply side, this will allow efficient fertilizer producers to expand and force inefficient ones to contract. On the demand side, it will help eliminate wasteful use of fertilizer.

Another subsidy that can be replaced by cash transfers is that provided through minimum support prices. Because procurement at MSPs is confined principally to wheat and rice, this subsidy is concentrated in relatively rich states such as Punjab and Haryana and goes mainly to large farmers, who often have a lock on official procurement. This makes the subsidy regressive as far as income distribution is concerned. The government can make the system more efficient and less regressive by distributing the subsidy among all farmers based on the size of their holdings. This will eliminate the need for procurement of grain in order to provide a price subsidy to farmers. It will also eliminate the artificial incentive to grow wheat and rice that currently exists due to above-market MSPs for these crops. When the subsidy is calculated according to the size of a farmer's land holding, farmers on the margin will have an incentive to diversify into other crops.

One other important, closely related subsidy worth converting into a cash transfer is the food subsidy. This subsidy is not targeted specifically at farmers, though the vast majority of them do receive it because of their poverty. Since beneficiaries of this subsidy are already identified in each state and they have Aadhaar cards, the subsidy implicit in below-market grain prices under the public distribution system can be transferred in cash to each beneficiary household. Initially, the government can even begin by offering a choice between cash and in-kind transfers, letting the conversion to cash take place gradually as more and more households opt for cash. It is a reasonable conjecture that the vast majority of the beneficiaries will shift to cash within three years, since it gives them greater control over what they wish to buy and from whom. Once a majority has chosen cash, the government can extend the cash mode of transfer of subsidy to all.

If both MSPs and food subsidies are replaced by cash transfers, the government can achieve a major efficiency-enhancing reform of the Food Corporation of India. With the provision of subsidies to farmers and consumers through this institution eliminated, its operations can be dramatically scaled down. Its mandate can be limited to maintaining a small emergency stock and a public distribution system in areas where the private sector has poor reach. Procurement for both purposes should be done at market prices. If FCI wishes to maintain public distribution in areas served by the private sector, it must do so on a commercial basis, with no public funds provided to support such operations.

FCI has a huge workforce. The proposed reform would release most of these employees from their current employment. They may be shifted to other parts of the government that currently face personnel shortages. In some cases, this may require retraining the workers.

Electricity Distribution Companies

The power sector in India has faced repeated crises. The sector is too complex to be considered in detail here. Instead, I briefly discuss one component of it, distribution. In India, it is this component that is at the heart of the key problems facing the sector. Distribution companies (discoms) buy power from generation companies and supply it to users. If discoms are insolvent, generation companies are not willing to contract to sell power to them. The result is that even if users are willing to pay, they are deprived of power.

In India, discoms in most states are in poor financial condition. Among the reasons are large transmission and distribution losses, power theft, poor metering, non-payment of bills, and uncovered subsidies to users. Businesses pay ultra-high rates to cross-subsidize home users and farmers, and many state governments provide additional subsidies. But these payments remain grossly insufficient to cover the losses on low-price electricity to homes and free electricity to farmers. The result is that distribution companies accumulate losses and debt. Their poor financial condition means that they are not credible buyers of electricity from generation companies.

At the heart of the problem is the absence of genuine commercial pressure on distribution companies. With rare exceptions, they are state-level public sector companies, run by state government employees whose jobs do not depend on the health of the companies they serve. The situation is made worse by State Electricity Regulatory Commissions (SERCs), which do not function as independently as their central counterpart, the Central Electricity Regulatory Commission, does. State governments interfere with tariff setting to keep tariffs low. They also forbid distribution companies from charging tariffs to favored groups, especially farmers, without fully compensating them through budgetary resources.

The government has made repeated attempts to solve the problem, but without success. The latest such attempt was the Ujjwal Discom Assurance Yojana (UDAY), or Shining Discom Assurance Scheme, under which state governments undertook to shift 75 percent of discom debt to their budgets and improve efficiency along a set of specified parameters in return for certain subsidies from the central government. Though the scheme temporarily relieved discoms' financial burdens, it has not been successful in restoring their long-term health. Aggregate transmission and commercial losses, which represent power for which the discom did not receive any payment, calculated as a proportion of the total electricity it procured, fell from 20.8 percent in 2015/16 to 18.8 percent in 2017/18. But as of September 2019, they rose back to 21.4 percent. Likewise, as of July 2019, the gap between the average cost of supply and the average revenue realized, which UDAY had sought to eliminate, remained 0.25 rupees per unit of electricity.[4]

Ultimately, the problem cannot be solved without reform that will bring commercial pressure on distribution companies. And this requires subjecting electricity supply to competition. The government had placed the Electricity (Amendment) Bill (2014) before the lower house of the previous parliament to achieve this goal, but it failed to pass. The reform proposed in this bill is a sound one, and the government needs to implement it as soon as possible.

The key proposal in the bill was to separate distribution into network and supply businesses. This would allow multiple supply licensees in any area of supply, thereby bringing competition to the distribution of electricity. The network would still be owned by a public entity, which would be regulated to ensure that it gives equal access to potential suppliers of electricity. The bill also mandated that any subsidies to users will be provided by the central or state governments in the form of direct benefit transfers, with suppliers setting their own prices to recover their costs. In this manner, price discrimination among users will be eliminated, with DBT subsidies protecting disadvantaged users of electricity.

One further reform concerns the independence of SERCs. An independent, competent, and honest SERC has the potential to bring about significant improvement even under the current system. An effective SERC can ensure that state governments wishing to subsidize certain groups of customers pay the full cost of it, with the discom receiving the subsidy amount in full. In addition, discoms may be encouraged to contract out the collection of electricity bills to private agencies, with rewards and punishments built into contracts for extra collections and shortfalls, respectively, relative to initially specified collection amounts.

Opponents of discom reform sometimes appeal to the good performance of public sector distribution companies in certain states to bolster their case. To be sure, public sector distribution companies that are well managed and are in sound financial condition do exist. The problem, however, is that such performance can be sustained only as long as the top leadership in the state is sound and appoints competent staff to manage the state's discoms. Once the leadership changes, the companies' management and financial condition may deteriorate. For instance, discoms performed very well during the rule of Chief Minister Narendra Modi in Gujarat until 2014. But it did not take long for their performance to deteriorate after he became prime minister and a new chief minister succeeded him in Gujarat.

The Right to Education Act

The Right to Education (RTE) Act, whose principal objective was to give every child age six to fourteen access to school, was passed in 2010. By that year, only 4 percent of children in this age group were not in school. Therefore, broadly speaking, the act's mission had already been accomplished when it was passed. It was trying to solve yesterday's problem.

Data widely available even at the time the law was passed suggested that tomorrow's problem with school education was its quality. These data, painstakingly collected by the non-governmental organization Pratham and published in its Annual Status of Education Report (ASER) since 2005, were repeatedly showing low student achievements in reading, writing, and mathematics. The reports also showed at best limited improvement over time.

Unfortunately, the RTE Act was not just neglectful of the education quality problem. Under the pretense of doing good, the act even incorporated provisions that made the problem worse. Just as the Industrial Disputes Act deprived Indian workers of decent jobs, the RTE Act carried provisions that promised to deprive children of a decent education. Outcomes reported in ASER subsequent to the passage of the RTE Act showed declining levels of achievement in reading, writing, and mathematics. Only recently has this trend begun to exhibit signs of reversal.

If India is to seriously address the issue of quality of education, it must overhaul the RTE Act. Provisions that inhibit improvements in learning outcomes need to be replaced by those that would facilitate them. Here I discuss two specific provisions that are clear candidates for amendment.

First, the minimum norms and standards for schools to retain recognition by the government in the act are laid down entirely in terms of inputs, with none in terms of learning outcomes. They include a student-to-teacher ratio of 30:1 for primary schools and 35:1 for middle-level education, a well-equipped library, an all-weather building with one classroom per teacher, a kitchen for midday meals, a playground, sports equipment, and more. The act says that the government could force schools that failed to meet these standards by March 31, 2013, to close down. In recent years, several schools have met this fate under the act.

Studies show little correlation between the standards prescribed by the act and education outcomes. There are numerous low-budget schools that do not meet these standards, cater to low-income families, and yet deliver better educational outcomes than publicly run counterparts that do meet the standards. Indeed, in rural India, parents are progressively moving their children into such low-budget private schools precisely because public schools fail to provide meaningful education. It is this gap in outcomes that has been behind the large-scale hollowing out of public schools. For example, during the four years following the implementation of the RTE Act, the number of schools with fifty or fewer students rose sharply, reaching 370,000 in 2014/15. That figure represented a gigantic 36 percent of all public elementary schools in existence at the time. The per-pupil cost in teacher salary alone in these schools amounted to 40,800 rupees.[5]

Closing private schools on the grounds that they do not meet the standards laid out in the RTE Act is nothing short of criminal. By doing so, the government deprives children of a better-quality education than what public sector schools in their areas offer. The government must amend this provision by basing school recognition primarily on learning achievement outcomes and diluting greatly or even removing input standards.

In this context, the provision in the RTE Act that state governments set salary standards for all teachers, including those in private schools, must also be removed. Numerous low-budget schools run on teacher salaries that are a fraction of the salaries paid by their public school counterparts. Raising all salaries to the levels of the latter would lead to a closure of all but a tiny number of elite private schools. This too would be tragic, since studies show no correlation between teacher salaries and learning outcomes. A careful study of schools in Andhra Pradesh has shown that private schools are able to deliver learning outcomes at least as good as their public sector counterparts at less than one-third the cost.[6]

The second major provision in the RTE Act that needs amending in order to improve learning outcomes relates to the promotion of every child to the next grade each year regardless of whether or not she has achieved some minimum level of learning. This provision has two detrimental effects on learning. One, for many children, automatic promotion means that they need not bother learning the material, since they will be promoted to the next level anyway. And two, the difficulty of the material rises exponentially as the child moves to higher and higher grades. But a child who has not learned the material prescribed for earlier grades is unprepared to learn this more demanding material.

The common argument made to defend automatic promotion is that holding children back leads them to drop out of school. But it must be asked if staying in school has any value if the child is not learning anything there. Indeed, forcing such children to stay in school may even deprive them of the opportunity to pick up skills by working at home in the family trade. If there is going to be real value in attending school, school must motivate the child to learn rather than rely on automatic promotion to the next class.

Concluding Remarks

In a country such as India that has spent many decades pursuing counterproductive economic policies, there is no escaping a long list of needed reforms. During the first four decades following independence, India adopted numerous growth-retarding policies. In 1991, it began to dismantle those policies. But along the way, it also added new anti-growth policies, especially during the second term of the United Progressive Alliance between 2009 and 2014. Future reforms must address these policies as well.

In an economy with a policy regime as distorted as that in India, reforms pose an uphill battle both because the list of reforms is long and because significant beneficial impact comes with a long lag. Though the reforms of the 1990s resulted in quick macroeconomic stabilization and some early payoff in terms of growth, it was not until 2003/4 that the economy shifted to a trajectory of 8 percent growth or more. And even then, a failure to maintain the pace of reforms and a return to some dirigiste policies resulted in a loss of the momentum. Under Prime Minister Modi, the economy has returned to reforms, but there is a considerable distance to cover. Despite a setback to growth during the three quarters beginning on October 1, 2018, the current policy regime can be counted on to yield 7 percent growth in the medium run. But acceleration beyond this level will require sustained reforms.

Notes

1. Dinesh Narayanan, "CAG Demonstrates How Govt Relies on Off-Budget Resources to Fund Deficit," *Economic Times*, July 25, 2019, https://economictimes.indiatimes.com/news/economy/indicators/cag-demonstrates-how-govt-relies-on-off-budget-resources-to-fund-deficit/articleshow/70360281.cms.
2. Gupta 2013, 141–67.
3. Gupta and Panagariya 2019.
4. Mishra 2019.
5. Kingdon 2017.
6. Muralidharan and Sundararaman 2015.

13

In Conclusion: Revisiting the Past, Looking to the Future

The opportunity for India to become the third-largest economy in the world in less than a decade and to bring genuine prosperity to the bulk of its citizenry could not be brighter. In May 2019, the people of India gave Prime Minister Narendra Modi the strongest possible mandate. The National Democratic Alliance, which he leads, returned to power with a two-thirds majority in the lower house of parliament. Not since Prime Minister Jawaharlal Nehru, who contested his elections in the immediate post-independence era, when opposition parties were still emerging, have the people of India given a leader such a strong mandate twice in a row. NDA has also come to enjoy enough support from other parties and independent members in the upper house of parliament to be able to pass its bills in that house. Modi now has an unprecedented opportunity to transform the nation. Given the unflinching faith that people have placed in him, this is also his obligation.

Many commentators argue that India cannot repeat the performance of China because the global economy will not be as hospitable in the next twenty years as it was during the last twenty. But these commentators forget that the global economy was rocked by a major financial crisis triggered in 2008. Indeed, China also had to contend with the Asian financial crisis a decade earlier, in 1997. Even setting these crises aside, the global economy was much smaller and export opportunities far less generous during the years that China transformed than they are today.

For instance, in 2000, world merchandise and commercial services exports amounted to just $6.1 trillion and $1.5 trillion in current dollars, respectively. In 2017, these figures had grown to $17.2 trillion and $5 trillion, respectively. Though growth in trade has slowed down in recent years, it remains positive despite the trade war between the United States and China. No one predicts that global exports will fall in the forthcoming decades, but even if that happens, combined goods and services exports would continue to be $20 trillion.

Therefore, if economic policies within India are designed to promote efficiency, so that the country can become progressively more competitive in the global economy, it has ample scope for expanding its exports. In 2017, India's share was just 1.7 percent in global merchandise exports and 3.5 percent in global commercial services exports. If it raises these shares to even 4 and 5 percent, respectively, in a decade and maintains them at these levels in the following decade, global exports cannot be a constraint on its growth.

To put these shares in perspective, China accounted for 12.8 percent of global merchandise exports and 4.3 percent of global commercial services exports in 2017. For India, the real constraint in the next twenty years will not be the size of the global export pie; instead, it will be the size of the slice it is able to carve for itself from this pie. Rather than freeze into inaction for fear that the global economic environment will be unfavorable over the next decade, India needs to aggressively implement reforms that make its goods and services competitive in the global economy.

Productivity growth in rich countries is constrained by the rate of technological change. But this is not the case for poorer countries such as India. Low per capita income in India compared to its richer counterparts implies that its level of productivity is far below that of the latter. It follows that India has a large scope for productivity growth through catch-up with these richer economies. What is needed once again is a set of policy reforms that would enable Indian enterprises to imbibe more and more of the superior technologies that are already available. This is precisely what the East Asian "tiger" economies did during the 1960s, 1970s, and 1980s and what China did during the last two to three decades.

Therefore, it stands to reason that the problem of economic growth and transformation for India is wholly one of getting its own internal policies right. If India progressively adopts policies that improve efficiency, as measured by its ability to capture a larger and larger share of world export markets in both goods and services, it will accomplish in the next twenty years what China did in the last twenty. While I have discussed a detailed road map for these policies in the preceding pages, in this chapter I discuss the political economy challenges that Modi faces as he implements radical reforms.

Reduced but Continuing Influence of Socialism

The dominance of socialist ideas in the thinking of policymakers, whether we consider politicians or bureaucrats, has been the bane of development efforts in India. It is ironic that when it comes to the economy, communist countries such as China and Vietnam have shown a greater propensity to embrace pro-market reforms than India has. In India, even many entrepreneurs remain infected by the old socialistic ideas and readily approve of the government taking on tasks that are best performed by the private sector. The result has been an acceptance of the heavy hand of the government and a consensus around policies that undermine individual initiative and wealth creation.

In the immediate post-independence era, building a "socialistic pattern of society" was a formal objective of the government. Under Nehru, pursuit of this objective translated into a progressive expansion of the public sector, including into production activities that served no direct public purpose. This era saw the government determining even the allocation of private investment through the instrumentality of investment licensing. It subjected all private investments above a relatively low threshold to a license that only it could issue. The license specified the product to be produced, its volume, and the firm's location. On top of that, import licensing often denied the entrepreneur access to the latest technologies as well as high-quality machinery and inputs. The result was high production cost and abysmal product quality.

After Nehru, the stranglehold of socialism became tighter still. Prime Minister Indira Gandhi, who ruled from 1966 to 1984 with a small break in the middle of that period, went on to expand the scope of the government through nationalization of enterprises. She began with banks that had deposits exceeding 500 million rupees and then proceeded to take over the entire insurance sector. This was followed by nationalization of coal mines and all major oil companies. She went on to amend labor laws such that they deprived manufacturing firms with one hundred or more workers the right to terminate a worker under any circumstances. She also introduces the Urban Land Ceilings and Regulation Act, which gave the government the right to acquire empty urban lots for a fire-sale price.

After the launch of liberalizing reforms in 1991, the hold of socialism progressively weakened. Yet politicians and bureaucrats have not been able to fully free themselves of their socialist mindset. For politicians in the major national parties—Congress and BJP—the problem remains that their founding leaders, who serve as inspiration for the current leaders, have all been socialist. In the Congress Party, Prime Ministers Nehru and Gandhi were committed socialists. Both Sonia Gandhi and Rahul Gandhi, who currently lead the party, fully subscribe to the ideology of these earlier leaders. The Congress Party has also entirely disowned Prime Minister Narasimha Rao, who initiated pro-market reforms in 1991. In the BJP, while Prime Minister Modi himself is reform-minded and appreciates the role of markets, many in his party draw inspiration from Pundit Deendayal Upadhyay, who was a socialist. Therefore, reform initiatives under the present government have predominantly come from Modi himself.

The Indian bureaucracy's adherence to socialism remains deeply rooted in the education its officials received in Indian universities, where faculty members are wedded to anti-business and anti-market ideology. The young are naturally drawn to the dream of an ideal world that socialist ideology offers. This attraction is reinforced by anti-market ideas that their college teachers impart to them. The civil services in India pick up many of these youngsters at an early age. Once inside the government, they find themselves safely in the company of others like them for the remainder of their professional lives.[1]

The impact of this continuing (even if somewhat weakened) grip of socialist ideas is visible in many policy choices made even in the post-reform era. For all intents and purposes, pro-market reforms came to a standstill under the Congress-led United Progressive Alliance government between 2004 and 2014. During the second term of this government, legislation dominated by socialism proliferated, including the Land Acquisition Act, the Right to Education Act, and the Food Security Act. Though apparently intended to help the poor and the weak, each of these pieces of legislation did exactly the opposite by undermining growth. Under the Modi government, import substitution, which is also associated with socialist policies, has seen a revival. Similarly, preoccupation with micro and small enterprises, which cannot become engines of growth without flourishing medium and large enterprises, has its roots in a socialistic mindset.

The socialist undercurrent in the Indian bureaucracy means that bureaucrats have taken few initiatives toward building a pro-market economy. A small number of senior officials can be heard echoing pro-reform sentiments when they are expressed by the country's top leadership of the day, but the bureaucracy as a whole has done little to move the reform agenda forward. Prime Minister Modi even offered them an explicit opportunity to put radical reform ideas on the table by convening groups of secretaries to prepare annual road maps for action in different areas of the economy. But projects and programs rather than radical policy reforms dominated the proposals these groups put forth.

In many instances, bureaucracy has served to slow down and even block reforms that the top leadership has sought to implement. For instance, the Modi government has made the decision to privatize a large number of public sector enterprises. In 2016, the prime minister's office directed the NITI Aayog to carry out an analysis of public sector enterprises and identify enterprises that would be good candidates for privatization. After the NITI Aayog undertook the exercise and sent lists of such enterprises, the prime minister saw to it that the cabinet gave its approval for privatization of those enterprises. But once the matter went to the Department of Investment and Public Asset Management, it remained stuck there. At the time of writing (May 2020), not a single public sector enterprise has been privatized.

Labor law reform offers another example. In this case, the top leadership decided to simplify and consolidate thirty-three central government laws into four codes and asked the Ministry of Labor to perform the task. This was an excellent opportunity for bureaucrats in the Ministry of Labor to propose reforms of various anti-growth and anti-employment laws while simplifying and consolidating the existing laws. But so far the ministry has failed to rise to the occasion. The Wage Code, which has now been enacted into law by the parliament, did little to make minimum wage laws employment friendly. Even more important, according to media reports, the Code on Industrial Relations it has proposed fails to incorporate even the reforms many states have already implemented with the consent of the central government.

A final example relates to civil service reform. Prime Minister Modi has pushed for lateral entry at the top levels of bureaucracy for several years. But publicly available information suggests that the bureaucracy has slowed down the process to such a degree that only at the very end of Modi's first term were nine officials brought in from outside. According to media reports, there had been plans to bring in many more officials from outside, but this had not happened until May 2020.

It may be asked how the bureaucracy can block actions desired by the prime minister and his cabinet. Why can the prime minister not replace obstructionist bureaucrats with other officials who would carry out his mandate? There are two answers to this important question. First, a seasoned bureaucrat never says no to those above him. Instead, while stalling progress, he tells his superiors that he is in the process of taking the necessary actions. When questions get asked from above about the lack of progress, he takes just one of many steps in the process and again says that progress is under way. Given the multi-layered processes needed to bring a project to its conclusion in India, this tactic can be deployed for long enough that either the bureaucrat responsible for the delay retires or the government changes.

The second problem concerns the shortage of officials who are both competent and devoted to the agenda of the top leadership. Often these officials are already placed in departments where they are needed the most. Therefore, the prime minister does not have the luxury of moving around non-performing officials. He only risks replacing one non-performing official with another while creating additional disruption.

Remarkably, in India, even business leaders have played an insignificant role in pushing for market-friendly reforms. In most countries, businesses try to use an economic crisis as an opportunity to seek removal of regulations that impede their progress. But in India, businesses see crisis as the opportunity to seek subsidies and protection from imports. They want the government to intervene more, not less, to save their specific sector or industry.[2] With rare exceptions, even business organizations and associations, which are expected to represent the collective interest of businesses, have not bothered to push for pro-growth reforms.

What Makes Reforms Possible

This discussion points to rather bleak prospects for reforms. Indeed, it raises the question of how any reforms ever take place. My broad answer to this question is that it is principally the top political leadership that must be credited with the reforms that have been put in place to date. Prime ministers who have been determined to see India progress faster and have been perceptive enough to appreciate that the dirigiste policies of the first four post-independence decades cannot deliver prosperity to Indians have successfully implemented reforms despite India's difficult polity and bureaucratic machinery.

A complementary factor aiding progress in reforms is the positive role that specific individuals within the system have played. Though the central tendency of each set of players in the system—politicians, bureaucrats, and business leaders—has been to lean against reforms, each group has also produced some exceptional individuals who joined hands with the enlightened leadership at the top to push reforms. This has been particularly true of a handful of bureaucrats who knew how to navigate the system and became partners of the top leadership in the reform project.

From a longer-term perspective, the writings of a handful of economists have gradually helped change the minds of all Indians and have strengthened the hand of pro-reform actors in the system. Like the movement of the hour hand of a clock, gradual evolution in public opinion is not noticeable. But the change becomes visible when we compare two historical moments sufficiently far apart in time. For example, in the mid-1980s, the license-permit raj had near universal approval in India. But today it is the subject of near universal opprobrium. In 1970, when Jagdish Bhagwati and Padma Desai published the first full-scale case for a more liberal policy regime in India, they found no takers.[3] Today, those ideas have found wide acceptance, while the opposite ones, espoused most prominently by Amartya Sen, are in retreat. The result is that even though a diluted form of socialism continues to have appeal in certain powerful circles, advocates of reform have come to command a great deal of respect, especially among the young, who want change and want it sooner rather than later.

In the early phase of reforms, three events helped these ideas gain greater acceptance. First, the poor performance of the Indian economy had gradually led at least a few Indians in positions of power to conclude that the command-and-control system had failed India and that there were no prospects that it would deliver even modest growth. Second, the collapse of the Soviet Union, on which Nehru had modeled India's development strategy, brought out into the open the fact that the emperor had no clothes. Finally, for a long time Indian policymakers had disdainfully rejected the extraordinary performance of the East Asian "tiger" economies, arguing that they were too small to carry any lessons for India. But when China, a country more populous than India and a communist one at that, shed its command-and-control, even autarkic model and produced double-digit growth for a full decade, their defense of the old system fell flat.

These developments paved the way for Prime Minister Narasimha Rao—a politician from the south with no baggage—to use the occasion of a balance-of-payments crisis to give a dramatic turn to economic policy.[4] A pragmatic politician who had survived multiple splits in the Congress Party, Rao dismantled the license-permit raj in one stroke and began opening the economy to foreign trade and investment in his very first year. In the years that followed, he kept opening the door to trade and foreign investment wider while also implementing reforms in the financial sector, telecommunications, and civil aviation.

Some observers argue that Rao embraced reforms under pressure from the International Monetary Fund and the World Bank. But this is a mistaken view. At most, one can make the case that these institutions had a significant role in the first bout of reforms, though even this is arguable.[5] After the initial loans from these institutions, the Indian economy recovered quickly, with its macroeconomic stability restored; it did not need any additional loans from the IMF and World Bank and could have eschewed further reforms. But the impetus for reforms had come from within, and Rao was determined to take the process forward.

The role of the top leadership in determining the course of reforms remained crucial in subsequent years. Hounded by corruption charges, Rao lost the 1996 election, and a series of unstable coalition governments followed. They ruled the country for approximately two years. Apart from a few isolated actions, the reforms witnessed a pause during this period. But in 1998, a BJP-led coalition government, with Atal Bihari Vajpayee as prime minister, came to the helm. Like Rao, Vajpayee was reform-minded and decisive. He sought double-digit growth to eradicate abject poverty. Helped by able bureaucrats, he implemented wide-ranging reforms touching almost all areas of the economy. By the last year of his rule, 2003/4, India finally found itself on a trajectory of 8 percent growth or more.

It was this higher growth rate that strengthened the hand of reform advocates and helped shift politics in favor of liberalization. For the first time, people saw their fortunes perceptibly improve within a decade. That fact greatly sensitized them to the power of growth.

In earlier decades, improvement in living standards had occurred at a snail's pace, leaving people resigned to their fate. This sentiment is captured in the classic Hindi phrase "Aise hee chalata hai." Translated into English, the phrase means, "It goes like this only." This fatalism led people to repeatedly return the same government to power. But once they found that better policies and governance could deliver dramatically superior outcomes, their voting behavior changed. Henceforth, governments that delivered significantly better economic outcomes would be returned to office, while those failing to do so would bite the dust.[6] During the past decade, people have returned state and central governments that deliver superior economic outcomes, and kicked out those failing to do so.[7]

Prime Minister Vajpayee presided over a fragile coalition government, and in 1999 this fragility culminated in the fall of his government. Elections were held again that year and he returned to office with a slightly stronger mandate, allowing him to pursue an extensive reform agenda. In 2004, when elections were held again, however, some of his coalition partners broke away, which tipped the balance in favor of the opposition. The acceleration of growth to 8 percent during the last year of his rule had come much too late to benefit him electorally.

In May 2004, the Congress-led United Progressive Alliance came to power. In 1998, Sonia Gandhi had wrested back control of the Congress Party, and she was now at the helm. Though she opted to have Manmohan Singh, a technocrat, as prime minister, she remained the real power behind the throne. Fully wedded to Prime Minister Indira Gandhi's socialism, she steered economic policies during the following ten years with the help of the National Advisory Council, whose members were more or less committed to socialist ideology. Apart from continuing policies of trade liberalization and trimming the SSI list that reserved labor-intensive products for exclusive manufacture by very small enterprises, the reform process came to a standstill once again. Much of the progress was in expanding social spending, including the launch of the Mahatma Gandhi National Rural Employment Guarantee Scheme, under which one member of every rural household was guaranteed one hundred days of employment at a specified wage.

Robust growth on the back of the Rao-Vajpayee reforms greatly contributed to a rapid decline in abject poverty. This growth also yielded a rising volume of tax revenues, allowing the government to expand social programs aimed at combating poverty. These factors greatly helped UPA return to office in the 2009 parliamentary elections.

During its first term, UPA had not advanced a reform agenda to any significant degree, but neither did it reverse earlier reforms or introduce anti-growth policies. This allowed the Rao-Vajpayee reforms to perform their magic. But the UPA's policy stance took a turn for the worse in the second term of its government. Socialism, which had remained confined to an expansion of social spending in the first term, now began to penetrate policy. Four key pieces of legislation—the Land Acquisition Act, the Right to Education Act, the National Food Security Act, and an amendment to the Income Tax Act of 1961 giving the government power to tax retrospectively—fell into this category. The last of these measures, which gave the government the power to collect taxes on transactions going back several years and in some cases even decades, seriously damaged investor sentiment. Large fiscal deficits that resulted from the rapid expansion of social schemes, a virtual standstill on environmental clearances for infrastructure and other projects, and paralysis in decision-making in the central government culminated in poor economic outcomes. During the last two years of the

UPA government, inflation hit double-digit levels, the current account deficit ballooned, and growth fell below 6 percent. It was under these circumstances that Prime Minister Modi, who contested the 2014 election on a development platform, came to power.

Growth and Development in the Modi Era

The arrival of a new prime minister who was determined to transform India economically and socially changed the course of policy yet again, with prospects for reforms greatly improved. The Modi government moved quickly to restore macroeconomic stability. It adopted an inflation-targeting framework early in its term and successfully brought down inflation as well as the current account deficit. It committed to fiscal discipline, and adhered to it during its five years. It also successfully ended paralysis in the government and speeded up the decision-making process. During the full five-year term, GDP growth averaged 7.5 percent.

Three features distinguish Modi's approach to development from those of all of his predecessors. First, he completes his major projects and programs in a timely manner. Second, he does projects at scale. And finally, his approach is holistic in terms of coverage of economic sectors as well as geographical regions.

On the first point, perhaps the best example is the Swachchh Bharat Mission. Under the mission, Modi set a deadline of October 2, 2019, to end open defecation. At the time of the launch, this had seemed like an impossible mission. But he put the project on a war footing and successfully completed it. Some gaps may remain, and changes in behavior will have to be sustained over time, but the basic fact that toilets are now available to all Indians, especially in rural areas, is generally accepted.

Modi has also shown the ability to do projects at scale. Four projects illustrating this side of his work style are the building of toilets under SBM, the spread of Aadhaar identity cards to 1.2 billion Indians, the opening of bank accounts for all, and the delivery of cooking gas stoves to all poor households in record time. Each of these projects covered hundreds of millions of households and individuals. In his second term, Modi has now set for himself the task of bringing piped water to all rural households, an even bigger challenge than SBM.

Finally, Modi has a holistic approach to development in which he casts the net widely across sectors and regions. In infrastructure, while accelerating the building of roads and railways, he has connected numerous previously unconnected cities by air and has taken the initiative to develop transportation by waterways. He has worked not just on the expansion of the railway network but also on increasing the speed of trains, electrification of trains, and modernization of railway stations.

For ordinary citizens, Modi has digitized numerous government services to make it easier for people to access them. For businesses, he has worked with states to make it easier to do business. He has attacked corruption head-on. He has made a focused effort to develop the northeastern states, with perceptible success. For the first time, he has also taken up the task of developing islands. He has reached out and built bridges to other nations on a scale not done by any other past leader.

Finally, on the reform front, he has enacted the Insolvency and Bankruptcy Code and the National Medical Commission Act, instituted the goods and services tax, and cut the corporate profit tax to 25 percent with all exemptions ended. He has also steadily opened the Indian market wider to foreign investors in numerous areas, most notably e-commerce and defense.

Those who see the glass half full under Modi would say that, given that he inherited an extremely fragile economy and low morale among the business community and bureaucrats alike, these are impressive achievements. Those who see the glass half empty would argue that Modi failed to implement deeper reforms that would have launched the Indian economy into even more robust growth, like that clocked during 2003/4 to 2011/12. They would also point to the slowdown during the year ending on June 30, 2019, which saw the annual growth rate fall to 6.1 percent. During the last two quarters of that year, growth rates had fallen successively to 5.8 and 5 percent.

I place myself in the optimistic camp. Given where the Modi government started, restoring and maintaining macroeconomic stability along all major dimensions during the entire five-year term and accelerating growth to 7.5 percent per year is no mean achievement. Pessimists have more of a case when they point to the slowdown in growth in the first year of his second term. But this must be seen in the light of two major factors impacting growth: the ongoing cleanup of non-performing assets in public sector banks and the assault on corruption.

Among many problems inherited by the Modi government was the vast stock of restructured loans at public sector banks, many of which were on the way to turning into NPAs. Unfortunately, both the Department of Financial Services in the Ministry of Finance and the Reserve Bank of India neglected this problem until, in early 2017, data convincingly showed that growth of credit by public sector banks had collapsed. At that point the government did move swiftly, but the problem had become much larger by then. The process of cleanup is now well under way, but it will take a year or more for the financial sector to return to normal operation.

The cleanup of NPAs and the follow-up tightening of rules governing defaults have impacted economic activity in at least four ways. One, many leading entrepreneurs and corporations must absorb the lost value of their assets, which is testing their will to undertake new investments. Two, on the supply side, with the rules of the game having changed, banks are being a lot more cautious in lending. Three, the banks' balance sheets are still in the process of recovery, so banks' capacity to expand credit is limited. Finally, entrepreneurs no longer have the option to restructure loans and continue business as usual, as they did under regulatory forbearance by the Reserve Bank of India.

Turning to the second factor, in the early years of Modi's government, entrepreneurs underestimated the resolve of the prime minister to combat corruption. Many among them thought that demonetization, a key step in this fight, resulted from bad advice to the prime minister and that once the economy had been remonetized, they would return to business as usual.[8] But that is not how the reality unfolded.

The government continued to close loopholes in laws and tighten enforcement, including by collecting data from bank accounts into which discontinued high-denomination rupee notes had been deposited after demonetization. Space for money laundering, both internally and externally, was also steadily reduced. Tax evasion has been made difficult. As a result, the manner in which transactions take place has been undergoing a fundamental change. For instance, in real estate, it is no longer the case that buyers can make half or more of the payment for a house purchase in cash and escape the tax due on that part of the price.

Both of these factors—the NPA cleanup and the fight against corruption—are forcing economic restructuring. Developments in the banking sector are almost certain to help raise productivity in the medium to long run, though they do set back growth in the short run. Under the new rules, banks can no longer lend or restructure loans irresponsibly. Symmetrically, entrepreneurs cannot borrow and invest recklessly in the hope of evergreening loans with no consequences. It is the more productive projects, rather than well-connected entrepreneurs, that will have priority in banks' lending operations.

The impact on productivity of the fight against corruption is more uncertain, especially in the short and medium run. A key role of bribes is to speed up the decision-making process. They motivate bureaucrats who do not make decisions at all or make them slowly to move speedily. Therefore, as bribe giving and bribe taking become more difficult, the impact on productivity would be negative unless officials are held accountable for delays in decision-making. Increased fear of being charged with wrongdoing in cases when rules are not clearly spelled out would also make investors hesitant to undertake certain transactions.

Despite these adverse effects on growth, the case for Prime Minister Modi's anti-corruption drive remains strong, for three reasons. First, ending corruption helps improve the nation's moral fabric. An honest nation is a prouder nation. Second, corruption rewards the dishonest, those willing to break the law knowing that they can bribe their way out of punishment even if caught. By most metrics of ethics, this is an unfair system. Law should reward the honest and punish the dishonest. Finally, in the long run, eradication of corruption is almost certain to improve productivity. Once the principle that those caught breaking the law will be punished is firmly and credibly established, decision-makers in the government will come to accept the reality that there is no money to be made by delaying or blocking decisions. Indeed, they themselves would come under scrutiny for delaying decisions. That would pave the way for clean and swift decision-making in administration.

Looking Ahead

Based on the experiences of countries that have sustained high growth rates for two or more decades, India has the potential to grow at near double-digit rates in the next two decades. India's own growth at a rate of more than 8 percent during the period from 2003/4 to 2011/12, on the back of the Rao-Vajpayee reforms, reinforces this proposition. The slowdown to a 6.1 percent growth rate during the year ending on June 30, 2019, has shaken the confidence of many observers of the Indian economy, but their judgment has been colored by immediate weakness in the economy.

Fundamentally, the Indian economy remains sound and will return to a growth rate of over 7 percent in another year. One important indicator pointing in this direction is that gross fixed capital formation, which in 2018/19 was 29.3 percent of GDP at current prices and 32.3 percent at constant 2011/12 prices, remains robust. With investment staying at this high level, financial markets improving, and the government taking corrective actions, growth is unlikely to stay tepid for long.

That having been said, India cannot take rapid growth and transformation for granted. Instead, continuing that pattern of growth will require concerted reforms and steady progress in building infrastructure. Setting aside the details, which I have already spelled out in the preceding pages, eight broad points are worth underlining as I conclude this volume.

First, it is necessary to recognize the importance of policy reform for faster growth. The projects and programs on which the Modi government has laid heavy emphasis in its first term are necessary but not sufficient. The government represents only one of the two legs on which an economy walks. People—farmers, workers, professionals, business people—represent the other leg. Mobilization of their energies and talents requires a liberal policy framework.

Over the past seven decades, India has put in place far too many laws, rules, and regulations that unduly constrain private actors. There has been a tendency to enact another law or write another regulation whenever the government is faced with an issue, without thinking through the effects that the law or regulation may have in other areas. Laws and regulations should be written to deal with situations that arise frequently. One-time or anomalous situations that existing laws and regulations happen not to cover need not trigger the addition of another law or regulation. Instead, such situations should be flexibly dealt with within the existing legal framework, with the precedent recorded for future reference.

Reforms since 1991 have gone some distance toward unshackling private actors, but much remains to be done. Progress slowed considerably during the ten years of UPA rule, and while it has seen a revival under Modi, much greater acceleration in policy reform is required in the coming years to fully unleash the energies and talents of the people.

Second, policymakers must not lose sight of the fact that if they want to steadily expand government spending, they also need to continuously undertake policy reforms to accelerate and sustain high growth. When the economy is growing at a healthy pace, it is easy for the government to take that growth for granted and become complacent. But the economy is not like the mythological goddess Kamdhenu—it cannot keep giving the desired volume of revenues in perpetuity without due nurturing.[9]

The United Progressive Alliance government made precisely this mistake in its second term by returning to dirigiste policies while continuing to increase social spending to win elections. The strategy backfired, with growth receiving a setback and inflation touching double-digit levels.[10] When an economy with a long history of command-and-control policies grows in response to reforms, new bottlenecks emerge, requiring further reforms. During the past several decades, India has built so many layers of regulation in so many areas that removal of a few layers in a few areas is insufficient to allow the energies of entrepreneurs full play.

Third, the government must recognize the importance of policy stability. When a government changes policy and retroactively subjects investors to costs that did not exist at the time they made investment decisions, it has a chilling effect on future investments. For instance, the decision by the government in 2012 to amend the Income Tax Act of 1961 with retrospective effect sent shivers down the spines of investors. The decision by the Supreme Court in 2014 to cancel all allocations of coal blocks made during the period 1993–2012 had a similar effect.

Though the Modi government put a lid on retrospective taxation under the amended law and passed a law under which coal blocks are now auctioned rather than administratively allocated, it too has had its share of actions contributing to policy uncertainty. A recent example is the policy on electric vehicles. The government announced without due analysis target dates for conversion of cars and motorbikes from internal combustion engines to electric ones. These dates were far more ambitious than even those the United States is predicted to achieve.

Those announcements created much uncertainty among auto manufacturers regarding future investments. Though the targets have since been withdrawn, the announcements have not been without cost. Along the same lines, frequent changes in GST rates and personal income tax rates, delayed implementation of reductions in the corporate profit tax rate, and frequent renegotiations of electricity purchase agreements have contributed to uncertainty in the minds of entrepreneurs.

Fourth, policymakers need to come to terms with the fact that without creating conditions for the migration of half or more of the agricultural workforce out of agriculture into industry and services, India cannot make those workers prosperous. Output per worker in agriculture remains low, so redistributing this output in favor of farmers and away from intermediaries in the supply chain through marketing reforms cannot go very far. Nor is the increase in productivity in agriculture a viable solution to the problem of farmers' low incomes, for any increase in output will bring a decline in price that would wipe out the gains from increased output. Redistribution from non-agricultural workers to agricultural workers also has its limits, since the overall income in India is low. Indeed, excessive reliance on this redistribution can undermine incentives to work and to invest in industry and services, compromising growth.

Fifth, policymakers must further recognize that the bulk of current employment in industry and services is concentrated in micro and small enterprises. These enterprises are characterized by low productivity, high underemployment, and barely subsistence-level wages. The prospect of employment in them is not enough of an attraction for most agricultural workers to migrate out of their current employment. Therefore, the key to pulling the economy out of the current equilibrium is a set of reforms that would help firms grow larger, especially in sectors with high employment per unit of investment, such as apparel, footwear, furniture, and other light manufactures.

Sixth, export markets remain the key to bringing about the transformation India seeks and needs. Survival in the export market requires high productivity and steady increases in it. It also requires continuous product innovation to retain existing customers and win new ones. Enterprises that rely on export markets are typically large and therefore better able to exploit scale economies. The existence of these firms plays a critical role in creating a competitive ecosystem in which smaller firms also become more productive.

Seventh, contemporary developments in the Chinese economy offer a rare opportunity to bring many multinationals currently operating in that country to Indian shores. Real wages in China are now two to three times those in India on average. This has made many large enterprises in China, especially in employment-intensive activities, uncompetitive. They are seeking alternative production locations.

The trade war between the United States and China has given yet another reason to many enterprises currently in China to migrate elsewhere. India can greatly benefit from this situation by making India an attractive destination for these enterprises, which bring capital, technology, management techniques, and valuable links to the world markets in a single package. By making India an attractive production center for these enterprises, India can create a vast volume of job opportunities for its workforce while also capturing the global export markets for many products.

The eighth and final point is something for Indian entrepreneurs to ponder. It is a paradox that in an economy in which capital is scarce and entrepreneurs continuously complain about high interest rates, they also overwhelmingly opt for highly capital-intensive sectors and technologies. For instance, as of 2018, India's largest corporation, Reliance Industries Limited (RIL), has $110 billion in assets but employs just 250,000 workers in total. This translates to just 5 jobs for each $2.2 million in assets. In comparison, India's largest exporter of apparel, Shahi Exports, employs 1,260 workers for each $2.2 million in assets. But most formal sector entrepreneurs in India choose to invest in RIL-like capital-intensive industries. Those following the lead of Shahi Exports are few and far between.[11]

Indian entrepreneurs need to consider why they do not invest more in employment-intensive sectors in which India has a clear comparative advantage. If there are specific regulations that deter them from entering these sectors, they must seek to have those regulations withdrawn. Spreading India's scarce capital over a larger workforce is a win-win. It would not only go a long way toward accelerating growth on a sustained basis but also bring genuine prosperity to millions of currently underemployed workers. After all, in today's world, true glory for a nation can come only when everyone gets to share in it.

Notes

1. As an example, on a visit to St. Stephens College during my years at the NITI Aayog, I was surprised by the deep skepticism toward pro-market reforms among students there. The college has been a steady contributor of IAS officials for decades.
2. The case of the auto industry during the slowdown in 2019 is a case in point. See Panagariya 2019c.
3. Bhagwati and Desai 1970.
4. In the 1991 parliamentary elections, former prime minister Rajiv Gandhi led the Congress Party. But he was assassinated during election campaign, and his widow, Sonia Gandhi, asked Rao to take the helm. Consequently, Rao, who had had his bags packed and been set to retire to Hyderabad, became the prime minister.
5. Panagariya 2008, chapter 5, esp. n. 1.

6. Bhagwati and Panagariya 2004 first enunciated this hypothesis. Gupta and Panagariya 2014 tested the hypothesis empirically.
7. At the center, UPA was voted out in 2014, while Modi was voted back in 2019. States in which competent governments have been repeatedly returned to power include Bihar, Orissa, Madhya Pradesh, and Gujarat. States in which poorly performing governments got thrown out include Uttar Pradesh, Maharashtra, and Chhattisgarh.
8. In November 2016, the government ended the legal tender status of the two highest-denomination currency notes, valued at 500 and 1,000 rupees. The idea was that those holding vast quantities of these notes would have to account for how they got them. If these sources of income had gone unreported in the past, those depositing the notes would then be subject to prosecution.
9. In Indian mythology, Kamdhenu is a goddess in the form of a cow who provides her owner whatever she desires.
10. Panagariya 2019c.
11. Panagariya 2018.

References

Agarwal, Pawan. 2006. "Higher Education in India: The Need for Change." Working Paper No. 180. Indian Council for Research on International Economic Relations, New Delhi.

Ali, Mohammad. 2015. "23 Lakh Apply for 368 Peon Posts in Uttar Pradesh." *The Hindu*, September 17. https://www.thehindu.com/news/national/other-states/23-lakh-apply-for-368-peon-posts-in-uttar-pradesh/article7660341.ece (accessed January 5, 2019).

Amaldi, Durgadas Ramkrishna. 2014. "Mumbai's first bank, 1720: The beginning of banking on the Bombay island," *Prajnan* 43 no. 1, 9-49.

Bain, Marc. 2017. "One Very Basic Job in Sneaker Manufacturing Is Testing the Limits of Automation." *Quartz*, April 24. https://qz.com/966882/robots-cant-lace-shoes-so-sneaker-production-cant-be-fully-automated-just-yet (accessed November 22, 2018).

Bertraud, A. 2011. "Mumbai FAR/FSI Conundrum: The Perfect Storm: The Four Factors Restricting the Construction of New Floor Space in Mumbai." http://alainbertaud.com/wp-content/uploads/2013/06/AB-Mumbai-FSI-Conundrun-Revised_June-2013_kk-ab1.pdf (accessed August 27, 2019).

Bhagwati, Jagdish, and Padma Desai. 1970. *India: Planning for Industrialization: Industria lization and Trade Policies Since 1951*. London: Oxford University Press.

Bhagwati, Jagdish, and Arvind Panagariya. 2004. "Great Expectations." *Wall Street Journal*, May 24.

Bhagwati, Jagdish, and Arvind Panagariya. 2013. *Why Growth Matters*, New York: Public Affairs. (Published in India under the title *India's Tryst with Destiny* by Harper Collins.)

Chakraborty, Subhayan. 2019. "Piyush Goyal Takes 12 Major Decisions to Boost Exports, Industrial Growth." Business Standard, July 1. https://www.business-standard.com/article/economy-policy/piyush-goyal-takes-12-major-decisions-to-boost-exports-industrial-growth-119060800034_1.html (accessed September 4, 2019).

Chandramouli, C. 2011. "Housing Stock Amenities and Assets in Slums—Census 2011." http://censusindia.gov.in/2011-Documents/On_Slums-2011Final.ppt.

Cohen, Stephen. 2001. *India: Emerging Power*. Washington, DC: Brookings Institution.

Dehejia, Rajeev, and Arvind Panagariya. 2016. "The Link Between Manufacturing Growth and Accelerated Services Growth in India." *Economic Development and Cultural Change* 64, no. 2: 221–64.

Economic Advisory Council to the Prime Minister. 2018. *Report of the Logistics Development Committee on Key Challenges in Logistics and Development and the Associated Commerce-Policy Reforms for Ease of Doing Business/Trade in India*. New Delhi: Government of India.

Fields, Gary. 1980. *Poverty, Inequality and Development*. Cambridge: Cambridge University Press.

Foster, Andrew, and Mark Rosenzweig. 2009. "Are Indian Farms Too Small? Mechanization, Costs, and Farm Efficiency." http://www.bu.edu/econ/files/2009/09/Rosenzweig_Seminar-Paper.pdf (accessed December 18, 2018).

Gupta, Nandini. 2013. "Selling the Family Silver to Pay the Grocer's Bill? The Case of Privatization in India." In *Reforms and Economic Transformation in India*, edited by Jagdish Bhagwati and Arvind Panagariya, 141–67. New York: Oxford University Press.

Gupta, Nandini, and Arvind Panagariya. 2019. "Selling PSEs Improves Efficiency, Frees Government to Do the Business It Is Meant to Do." *Economic Times*, October 18. https://economictimes.indiatimes.com/news/economy/policy/view-selling-pses-improves-efficiency-frees-government-to-do-the-business-its-meant-to-do/articleshow/71655897.cms.

Gupta, Poonam, and Arvind Panagariya. 2014. "Growth and Election Outcomes in a Developing Country." *Economics and Politics* 26, no. 2: 332–54.

Hasan, Rana and Karl Robert L. Janoc. 2013. "Labor Regulations and Firm Size Distribution in Indian Manufacturing." In *Reforms and Economic Transformation in India*, edited by Jagdish Bhagwati and Arvind Panagariya, 15-48.

Hull, Dana. 2018. "Musk Says Excessive Automation Was 'My Mistake.'" Bloomberg, April 13. https://www.bloomberg.com/news/articles/2018-04-13/musk-tips-his-tesla-cap-to-humans-after-robots-undercut-model-3 (accessed November 22, 2018).

Insolvency and Bankruptcy Board of India. 2018. *Quarterly Newsletter October-December 2018*, Volume 9. https://www.ibbi.gov.in/publication (accessed September 1, 2019).

Ito, Takatoshi, and David E. Weinstein. 1996. "Japan and the Asian Economies: A 'Miracle' in Transition." *Brookings Papers on Economic Activity* 1996, no. 2: 205–72.

Kapur, Devesh, and Pratap Mehta. 2007. "Mortgaging the Future? Indian Higher Education." *India Policy Forum* 2007: 101–57.

Khatkhate, Deena. 2006. "Indian Economic Reform: A Philosopher's Stone." *Economic and Political Weekly* 41, no. 22: 2203–5.

Kingdon, Geeta Gandhi. 2017. "Put the Onus on Teachers." *Indian Express*, January 14. https://indianexpress.com/article/opinion/columns/education-schools-children-board-exams-mass-cheating-put-the-onus-on-teachers-4473156.

Kishore, Adarsh. 2008. "India—The Emerging Giant or Has It Emerged?" *Business Standard*, May 8. https://www.business-standard.com/article/opinion/adarsh-kishore-india-the-emerging-giant-or-has-it-emerged-108050801066_1.html.

Kletzer, Kenneth. 2005. "Liberalizing Capital Flows in India: Financial Repression, Macroeconomic Policy and Gradual Reforms" *India Policy Forum* 2005: 227–75.

Kux, Dennis. 1992. *India and the United States: Estranged Democracies 1941–1991*. Washington, DC: National Defense University Press.

Kwon, Huck-ju, and Ilcheong Yi. 2008. "Economic Development and Poverty Reduction in Korea: Governing Multifunctional Institutions." *Development and Change* 40, no. 4: 769–92.

Maddison, Angus. 2006. *The World Economy, 1-2001 A.D.*, volume 2. Paris: OECD. Available at https://www.oecd-ilibrary.org/development/the-world-economy/the-world-economy-1-2001-ad_9789264022621-21-en.

Mishra, Prachee. 2019. "Overview of the Power Sector." PRS working paper, September. https://tinyurl.com/y3p869hy.

Li, Haizheng. 2010. "Higher Education in China: Complement or Competition to US Universities?" In *American Universities in a Global Market*, edited by Charles T. Clotfelter, 269–304. Chicago: University of Chicago Press.

Li, Mei, and Rui Yang. 2014. "Governance Reforms in Higher Education: A Study of China." IIEP Research Papers. International Institute for Educational Planning, UNESCO, Paris.

Mahalanobis, P. C. 1969. "The Asian Drama: An Indian View." *Economic and Political Weekly* 4, special number, 1119–32.

Ministry of Finance. 2018. *Economic Survey 2017–18*. New Delhi: Government of India.

Ministry of Finance. 2019. *Economic Survey 2018–19*. New Delhi: Government of India.

Ministry of Housing and Urban Poverty Alleviation. 2015. *National Urban Rental Housing Policy (Draft)*. New Delhi: Government of India. http://mohua.gov.in/upload/uploadfiles/files/National_Urban_Rental_Housing_Policy_Draft_2015.pdf (accessed June 9, 2019).

Ministry of Human Resource Development. 2016. *Education Statistics at a Glance 2016*. New Delhi: Government of India. https://mhrd.gov.in/educational-statistics-glance-2016 (accessed September 2, 2019).

Ministry of Human Resource Development. 2017. *All-India Survey on Higher Education 2016–17*. New Delhi: Government of India. http://aishe.nic.in/aishe/reports (accessed September 2, 2019).

Muralidharan, Karthik, and Venkatesh Sundararaman. 2015. "The Aggregate Effect of School Choice: Evidence from a Two-Stage Experiment in India." *Quarterly Journal of Economics* 130, no. 3: 1011–66.

National Sample Survey Office. 2014a. *Level and Pattern of Consumer Expenditure 2011–12*. NSS Report No. 555. New Delhi: Ministry of Statistics and Program Implementation, Government of India.

National Statistical Office. 2014. *Drinking Water, Sanitation, Hygiene and Housing Conditions in India: July 2012–December 2012*. New Delhi: Ministry of Statistics and Program Implementation, Government of India.

National Statistical Office. 2017. *Key Indicators of Unincorporated Non-Agricultural Enterprises (Excluding Construction) of India: July 2015–June 2016*. New Delhi: Ministry of Statistics and Program Implementation, Government of India.

National Statistical Office. 2019. *Periodic Labor Force Survey: July 2017–June 2018*. New Delhi: Ministry of Statistics and Program Implementation, Government of India.

Panagariya, Arvind. 2000. "Bringing Competition to Bureaucracy." *Economic Times*, September 27.

Panagariya, Arvind. 2005. "Bringing Competition to the Top Civil Service." *Yojana* (Planning Commission, New Delhi), August, 9–13.

Panagariya, Arvind. 2008. *India: The Emerging Giant*. New York: Oxford University Press.

Panagariya, Arvind. 2012. "A Forgotten Revolutionary." *Times of India*, June 28. https://timesofindia.indiatimes.com/edit-page/A-forgotten-revolutionary/articleshow/14434370.cms.

Panagariya, Arvind. 2018. "Apparel Industry Holds the Key for India's Job Creation Requirements." *Economic Times*, January 18. https://economictimes.indiatimes.com/news/economy/policy/apparel-industry-model-holds-the-key-for-indias-job-creation-requirements/articleshow/62514682.cms.

Panagariya, Arvind. 2019a. *Free Trade and Prosperity: How Openness Helps Developing Countries Grow Richer and Combat Poverty*. New York: Oxford University Press.

Panagariya, Arvind. 2019b. "Reforms, Please, Not Stimulus: Sagging Sectors of the Economy Should Not Expect Bailouts from the Government." *Times of India*, August 21. https://timesofindia.indiatimes.com/blogs/toi-edit-page/reforms-please-not-stimulus-sagging-sectors-of-the-economy-should-not-expect-bailouts-from-the-government.

Panagariya, Arvind. 2019c. "India's Choices in 2019: Modi Has Reforms to His Credit, UPA Free Rode on Vajpayee's Reforms." *Times of India*, February 6. https://timesofindia.indiatimes.com/blogs/toi-edit-page/indias-choices-in-2019-modi-has-reforms-to-his-credit-upa-free-rode-on-vajpayees-reforms.

Panagariya, Arvind, Pinaki Chakraborty, and M. Govinda Rao. 2014. *State Level Reforms, Growth, and Development in Indian States*. New York: Oxford University Press.

Panagariya, Arvind, and B. Venkatesh Kumar. 2018a. "Liberating India's Best Colleges: HRD Minister Javadekar Has Just Announced the Most Far Reaching Reforms in Higher Education." *Times of India*, February 15. https://timesofindia.indiatimes.com/blogs/toi-edit-page/liberating-indias-best-colleges-hrd-minister-javadekar-has-just-announced-the-most-far-reaching-reforms-in-higher-education (accessed September 2, 2019).

Panagariya, Arvind, and B. Venkatesh Kumar. 2018b. "It's Time to Replace the UGC Act." *Hindu* April 17. https://www.thehindu.com/opinion/op-ed/its-time-to-replace-the-ugc-act/article23565106.ece (accessed September 2, 2019).

Panagariya, Arvind and B. Venkatesh Kumar. 2018c. "A Path Breaking Legislation: HECI Bill Can Uplift Indian Higher Education, but Requires Some Correctives Before Enactment." *Times of India*, July 5. https://timesofindia.indiatimes.com/blogs/toi-edit-page/a-path-breaking-legislation-heci-bill-can-uplift-indian-higher-education-but-requires-some-correctives-before-enactment.

Panagariya, Arvind, and B. Venkatesh Kumar. 2019. "How Autonomous Colleges Are Breaking India's Rigid Degree System." *Economic Times*, May 17: https://economictimes.indiatimes.com/industry/services/education/how-autonomous-colleges-are-breaking-indias-rigid-degree-system/articleshow/69380082.cms?from=mdr (accessed September 2, 2019).

Panagariya, Arvind, and Vishal More. 2014. "Poverty by Social, Religious and Economic Groups in India and Its Largest States: 1993–94 to 2011–12." *Indian Growth and Development Review* 7, no. 2: 202–30.

Panagariya, Arvind, and Dani Rodrik. 1993. "Political Economy Arguments for a Uniform Tariff." *International Economic Review* 34, no. 3: 685–703.

Planning Commission. 2011. *Report on Indian Urban Infrastructure and Services*. New Delhi: Government of India

Prasad, Ravi V. 2015. "30th Year of Assassination: Memoirs of Indira Gandhi." https://www.news18.com/news/india/30th-year-of-assassination-memories-of-indira-gandhi-723277.html (accessed August 17, 2019).

Rangan, M. C. Govardhana. 2019. "Thank RBI's February 12 Order for Jet Airways' Rescue." *Economic Times*, March 26. https://economictimes.indiatimes.com/markets/stocks/news/thank-rbis-february-12-order-for-jet-airways-rescue/articleshow/68571804.cms?from=mdr (accessed September 1, 2019).

Reserve Bank of India. 2008. *Report on Currency and Finance 2006–08*. Bombay: RBI. https://www.rbi.org.in/Scripts/AnnualPublications.aspx?head=Report+on+Currency+and+Finance (accessed August 30, 2019).

Reserve Bank of India. 2018. *Report on Trends and Progress in Banking 2017–18*. Bombay: RBI. https://www.rbi.org.in/scripts/AnnualPublications.aspx?head=Trend%20and%20Progress%20of%20Banking%20in%20India.

Varshney, Ashutosh. 1995. *Democracy, Development, and the Countryside: Urban Rural Struggle in India*. New York: Cambridge University Press.

Yoo, Jungho. 1997. "Neoclassical Versus Revisionist View of Korean Economic Growth." Development Discussion Paper No. 588. Harvard Institute for International Development, Harvard University.

Zhang, Han, Donald Patton, and Martin Kenney. 2013. "Building Global-Class Universities: Assessing the Impact of the 985 Project." *Research Policy* 42: 765–75.

Index

For the benefit of digital users, indexed terms that span two pages (e.g., 52–53) may, on occasion, appear on only one of those pages.

The letter *f* following a page locator denotes a figure, the letter *t* denotes a table.

Aadhaar biometric identity system, 27–28, 29, 52, 236, 250
Adidas, 75
agricultural development
  APMC Model Law, 23–24, 52
  cotton industry, 23–24, 52–53
  crop diversification in, 47–49
  productivity enhancing, 51–54
agricultural development reforms
  bringing prosperity to farmers, 51
  GM seeds, 52–53
  growth rates, 51
  land-leasing laws, 53
  MGNREGA, 53
  procurement, 51–52
agricultural policies, overview, 34–36
Agricultural Price Commission, 20
agricultural produce marketing committees (APMCs), 49–50
agricultural sector
  area cultivated under major crops, 48*t*
  cooperative movement, 34
  crop insurance, 35
  diversification, 47–49
  GDP share, 38–39, 39*f*, 41–42, 42*t*, 51
  government assistance, 35–36
  growth, 38*t*, 46–47, 51, 98*t*
  minimum support prices (MSPs), 38, 51–52, 54
  non-farm rural economy vs., 33–34
  public distribution system (PDS), 27, 51–52
  tariff reductions, 27–28
  tiny land holdings, 43–46, 45*t*, 53, 65–66
agricultural sector, reforms
  land reform, 28, 34
  marketing, 47, 49–50, 52
agricultural sector workforce. *See also* farmers
  diversification, 49
  economic growth and, 7–9, 8*f*
  GDP per worker, 54
  GVA added per worker, 44*f*
  migration to industry and services, 50, 51, 54–55, 56–57, 255
  per-worker output, 40, 42–44, 42*t*, 44*f*, 50
  statistics, 41*f*, 43–44
agricultural sector workforce employment
  Japan, 40–42
  outside India, 40–42
  share, 33, 40–42
  South Korea, 40–42, 43–44
  statistics, 41*f*
  United Kingdom, 40–42
Air India, 23, 211
air pollution, 114, 118
airline industry, 23, 27–28, 162, 211
Airports Authority of India (AAI) Act, 23
All India Services, 208–9
Antyodaya Anna Yojana program, 24
apparel industries
  automation in, 75
  custom duties, 94
  distribution and employment in, 67*f*
  exports of clothing and accessories, 68*f*
  factory architecture, 102
  firm size and distribution of employment, 67–68
  global competitiveness, 93, 94
  tariffs on, 93
Asian financial crisis (1997), 242
asset reconstruction companies (ARCs), 148
auto industry, 71n6, 93
automation, 74–76

Bangladesh, 87, 94
Bank Investment Company (BIC), 169–70
Banking Regulation Act, 158
banking sector. *See also* financial systems
  consolidation option, 170
  corruption in the, 252
  credit collapse, 158–59

banking sector (*cont.*)
credit expansion, 149–50, 150*f*
functions, 145
government rescues, 146
growth, contribution to, 145–46
IBC process outcomes, 159–61
insolvency resolutions, 159–61, 159*t*, 160*t*
investment, 134
key position, 145
loan classification and restructuring, 146–47, 152–53, 153*f*, 156–57
nationalization of the, 244
post-digital technologies, 145
priority-sector lending, 171
private investment policies, 170–71
recapitalizing, 147–48
reforms (1991–2002), 146–49
resolution vs. recognition, 156–58
rural banking, 166
underperformance, 171–72
banking sector, foreign banks
credit expansion, 150*f*, 150, 153*f*
credit-deposit ratio, 163*f*, 164
norms of entry for, 148
NPAs and restructured standard loans, 155*f*
return on assets, 164*f*, 164
wage bill as percent of income, 165*f*
banking sector, history
early post-independence, 174–76
post-nationalization, 146
pre-independence (1720–1947), 172–74
social control and nationalization (1967–1991), 146, 162, 176–78
banking sector, NPAs
accumulation episodes, 146
action taken on, 158–59
avoiding creating new, 161–62
branch expansion polity, 146
credit growth and, 158
percent of loans, 146
reducing the number of, 147–49
reduction of, 148–49, 251–52
as restructured loans, 150–56, 153*f*, 155*f*
banking sector, private banks
credit expansion, 150*f*, 150, 153*f*
credit growth, 158
credit-deposit ratio, 163*f*, 164
governance, 165–68
norms of entry for, 148
NPAs and restructured standard loans, 155*f*
return on assets, 164*f*, 164
social goals, promoting, 165–66
wage bill as percent of income, 164–65, 165*f*
banking sector, public banks
credit expansion, 150*f*, 150, 153*f*, 158, 164
credit growth, collapse of, 251
credit-deposit ratio, 163*f*, 164
efficiency, 163
governance, 165–68
government dilution in, 147–48
NPAs and restructured standard loans, 154*f*, 154, 157
privatization alternatives, 169–70
privatization of, 162–69
restructured loans, 250
return on assets, 164*f*, 164
social goals, promoting, 165–66
wage bill as percent of income, 165*f*
banking sector, scheduled commercial banks
credit expansion, 150*f*, 153*f*, 158
insolvency resolution, 159–61, 159*t*
NPAs and restructured standard loans, 153*f*
percent of shares of bank groups, 165, 166*f*
Bankruptcy Code, 251
banks, available to all, 250
basic amenities, public access to
drinking water, 115–17, 123*t*
lighting, 123*t*
public hygiene, 115–18, 123*t*
sanitation, 24, 117–18, 123*t*, 250
Benami Transactions (Prohibition) Act, 111–12
Bengal famine of 1943, 34
Bhagwati, Jagdish, 247
Bharat Sanchar Nigam Limited (BSNL), 23
black money, 111–12, 113
bond market, 141–42
bonds, 132–33
Brazil, 105
Bright Discom Assurance Scheme, 237
British Crown rule (1858–1950)
economic effect, 3, 4*f*, 10, 14, 29
global GDP share, 4*f*
labor laws, 98
brokers, 134
Bureau of Industrial and Financial Restructuring, 160
bureaucracy reforms improving governance
blocking, examples of, 245–46
colonial-era practices, discontinuing, 217–18
competition, instituting, 209–15
file management process, 216
Indian Administrative Service (IAS), 208–10, 212, 213–14
innovative thinking, encouraging, 216
lateral entry, 212–14
merit-based civil service, 208–9

princely-era practices, discontinuing, 217–18
specialized knowledge, 210–12, 246
temporary employment in non-government sectors, 215
training institutions for officials, 217
vigilance agencies, 217
young professionals, contracted, 216
Bus Rapid Transit System (BRTS), 114

capital markets, 140–43
cash transfer system, 235–36
Central Bureau of Investigation (CBI), 165–68
Central Vigilance Commission (CVC), 165–68
Chile, 141
China
corporate debt, 141
economic growth, post-WW II, 6–7, 6*t*, 10–11, 14–15
economy, 242, 243, 247
enterprise migration away from, 88, 255–56
export-oriented strategy, 219
GDP share vs. per capital income, 38
global competitivess, 255
global economic position, historically, x, 3, 4*f*, 10
industrialization, 75–76
ISI model, rejection of, 15
labor force declines, 87–88
path to transformation, 77–78
pro-market reforms, 243
rural-to-urban migration, 105, 106
space shortages, 107–8
trade war with US, 74, 77, 87–88, 242–43, 256
China-India compared
apparel industries, 67*f*, 87
economy, 243
exchange rate, 91
export performance, 74
higher education, 180, 182, 184–86, 185*t*, 186*t*, 190–92, 196, 200, 202
multinational investments, 77, 255–56
production structure, 87
wages, 65–66, 66*f*, 77, 255
China-India compared, exports
clothing and accessories, 68*f*, 75
electrical/electronic, 69*f*
footwear, 69*f*
global, 74, 242, 243
civil service reform, 208–9, 246
Clean India Mission, 117
Coastal Regulation Zones (CRZs), 110
Cohen, Stephen, ix–x
commodity exchanges, 134
Companies Act, 169–70
Complete Sanitation Campaign, 24
Congress Party, 27
Congress-led United Progressive Alliance, 245
corporate debt, 152, 161, 162
corporate debt market, 140–43
Corporate Debt Restructuring (CDR) framework, 152, 161, 162
Corporate Insolvency Resolution Process (CIRP), 159–61
Corrective Action Plan (CAP), 157
corruption
banking sector, 252
governance, improving by ending, 209
government, 28, 29
real estate sector, 110, 252
cottage industries, 16
cotton industry, 23–24, 52
custom duties, 94

debt market, 140–43
debt recovery appellate tribunals (DRATs), 148–49
debt recovery tribunals (DRTs), 148–49, 160
Dehejia, Rajeev, 72
Deng Xiaoping, 190
Department of Investment and Public Asset Management (DIPAM), 211
Desai, Morarji, 162
Desai, Padma, 247
direct benefit transfers (DBTs), 29, 53
drainage, urban vs. slum, 123*t*
drinking water, availability, 115–17, 123*t*

East Asia, tiger economies, 6–11, 6*t*, 243
East India Company, 3
economic administration, improving
export strategy, 219–21
methods of, 205
mission-mode, 218–19
sunset clause on centrally sponsored schemes, 223
tax administration, 221–23
trade negotiations, a new entity for, 221
transparency in fiscal accounting, 223–24
economic growth
opportunities for India, 242
post-WW II, East Asia, 6–11, 6*t*
sources of, 5
economic reforms, implementing
bureaucratic, 245–46
civil service, 246
future of, 253–56

economic reforms, implementing (*cont.*)
labor laws, 244, 245–46
land acquisition, 244
Modi era growth and development, 250–53
possibility of, 246–50
pro-market reforms, 244, 245, 246
socialism, movement away from, 243–46
economy
British Crown rule (1858–1950), 3, 4*f*, 10, 14, 29
future (2021–2031), predicting the, 4–5
global position (1990–2005), 29
global position historically (1 CE 1000 CE), x, 3–4, 4*f*, 10, 29
nationalization, 244
present-day, 4–5
productivity growth in the, 243
economy (1950/51–1980/81)
balances owed in payment for WWII participation, 18, 19
cottage industries, 16
development model, 15–20
economic policy, 19–20, 21
employment objective, 16
export performance, 17–18, 18*f*
foreign investment regime, 19–20
GDP growth, 12, 13*t*, 14, 18–19, 20
government interventions, 19–20
import constraints, 18*f*
import-export proportion of GDP, 24
industrial productivity and specialization, 16–17
industrial sector growth, 21
per capita income, 13*f*, 14, 25
price controls, 20
public sector nationalization, 19–20
self-sufficiency, movement toward, 15, 16
economy (1950/51–2001)
dirigiste policy regime, 3
global GDP share, 3, 4*f*
economy (1950/51–2018)
GDP growth, 12–14, 13*t*
imports-exports as a proportion of GDP (1950–51–2011/12), 18*f*, 18, 19*f*
per capita income (1950/51–2011/12), 13*f*, 13–14
economy (1981/82–1988/89)
economic policy, 21
GDP growth, 12, 13*t*, 14
growth rates, 21
per capita income, 13*f*, 14
economy (1988/89–2002/03)
balance-of-payments crisis, 21
education in the, 24
food self-sufficiency, 24
GDP growth, 12, 13*t*, 14
imports-exports proportion of GDP, 24
infrastructure development, 23
macroeconomic policy reforms, 22–23
mobile revolution, 23
per capita income, 13*f*, 14, 25
poverty reduction, 25, 26*f*
privatization, 21–22, 23
reforms, 21–22
social spending, 24
SSI reservation list, 22
stabilization, 21–22
tariff reductions, 21–22
tax system, 22
economy (2003/4–2017/18)
bankruptcy law, 29
education in the, 25, 27, 28
employment guarantees, 25, 27, 35, 53, 105–6, 249
fiscal deficit and inflation, 28
food security, 25, 28
foreign direct investment, 27–28
GDP, 12, 13*t*, 14, 27–28, 29
government corruption, 28, 29
growth, 24–25, 27–28
growth rates, 28, 29
imports as a proportion of GDP (2012/13), 24
liberalization of, 27–28
per capita income, 13*f*, 14
policy setback to growth (2004–14), 27–28
poverty reduction, 24–25, 26*f*
privatization, 27–28
reforms (1991/92–2007/08), 22–23
reforms (2014–18), 28–29
retrospective taxation, 28–29
social spending, 25, 27
SSI reservation reductions, 27–28
tariff reductions, 27–28
tax system, 29
economy (2017/18–2020)
GDP, ix–x
global position, ix–x
growth rates, 5
prosperity, pursuit of, ix
education
the economy and, 24, 25, 27, 28
right to, 25, 27, 28, 249–50
electric vehicles policy, 254–55
Electricity (Amendment) Bill, 238
employee rights, 97–99, 100
Employee State Insurance Act, 98

Employees Provident Funds and Miscellaneous Provisions Act, 98
employment. *See also* jobs; workforce; *specific industries*
- apparel industries, 67*f*
- fixed-term contracts, 85–86
- informal unincorporated enterprises, employment in, 57–58, 61*t*
- micro-small, and medium enterprises (MSMEs), 76
- opportunities for, 73
- service sector, 41*f*
- start-ups, 76
- temporary in non-government sectors, 215
- underemployment, 57–59
- unincorporated enterprises, 57–58, 61*t*, 83
- well paid, creating, 73

Employment-Unemployment Survey [EUS], 58
entrepreneurs and entrepreneurship, 76, 85, 86, 182, 252, 256
Environmental Protection Act, 110
establishment enterprises, 83
export expansion, for manufacturing-led growth, 87–88
export pessimism, 15
export-centered strategy, 74–76
exporters, indirect taxes on, 93–94
export-import restrictions, 86
export-led growth, 74, 91–93
export-led growth, policy reforms indicated
- AEZs, 95–96
- export expansion, 87–88
- free trade agreements, 94
- import substitution, 88–90
- labor market reforms, 97–102
- reimburse indirect taxes to exporters, 93–94
- the rupee, 90–91
- tariffs, 91–93
- tax simplification and predictability, 96–97
- trade facilitation, 94–95

export-oriented strategy, 219–21
exports
- average clearance time for, 94–95
- China-India compared, 68–69*f*, 74, 75, 242, 243
- in the global economy, 242–43
- growth, future of, 255
- growth statistics, 242–43
- improving governance through, 219–21
- just-in-time delivery requirement, 94–95
- large firms, 66–70
- Lerner symmetry theorem on, 89–90
- manufacturing-led growth, 93–94
- of merchandise, globally, 74
- proportion of GDP, post-independence, 18*f*

exports, China-India Compared
- apparel, 75
- clothing and accessories, 68*f*
- elictrical/electronic, 69*f*
- footwear, 69*f*
- globally, 74, 242, 243

Factories Act, 60, 98
farmers. *See also* agricultural workforce
- DBTs to, 53
- electricity provided to, 35
- fertilizer subsidy scheme, 35, 235
- improving lives of, 33, 35–36
- incomes, decline in, 37–46
- perpetual distress, reality of, 36–37
- small, disadvantages to, 45–46, 47, 49–50

farmers, bringing prosperity to
- accelerating growth, 46–47
- cash transfer scheme, 235–36
- challenge of, 46–50
- diversification, 47–49
- income redistribution for, 43–44
- marketing reform, 49–50
- paths to, 54–55
- reforms, 51–54
- share of final prices paid, 47, 49–50

Fields, Garry, 2
financial crisis (2008/10), 24, 150, 242
financial institutions, 133–34
financial markets, 135, 143
financial services, 77–78
financial systems. *See also* banking sector
- commercial flows, sources of, 137–38, 137*t*, 138*t*
- corporate debt market, 140–43
- debt and equity instruments, 132–33
- debt and equity markets, 138–40, 140*f*
- overview, 131*f*, 145–46
- primary and secondary markets, 133
- regulation, 135–36
- savers channels of transmission to borrowers, 132

First Gulf War, 21
Flexible Structuring of Long Term Loans to Infrastructure and Core Sector Industries (5:25), 157
floor space index (FSI), 102, 110–11, 114, 127
Food Corporation of India (FCI), 20, 52, 236
food self-sufficiency/security
- 1943–1980s, 34–35
- economy (1950/51–1980/81), 20

food self-sufficiency/security (*cont.*)
economy (1988/89–2002/03), 24
economy (2003/4–2017/18), 25, 28
National Food Security Act (NFSA), 35, 45–46
reforms recommended, 45–46
footwear automation, 75
footwear exports, 69*f*, 94
Foster, Andrew, 46
France, 38, 40–42

Gandhi, Indira, 16, 19–20, 34–35, 84, 162, 244, 249
Gandhi, Rahul, 244
Gandhi, Sonia, 244, 249
genetically modified (GM) seeds in cotton, 23–24
global competitiveness
apparel industries, 93, 94
China, 255
large firms, 67
multinationals, recruiting, 77, 255–56
global economy
apparel market, 75
China-India compared, exports, 74
exports in the, 74, 242–43
financial crisis (2008/10), 242
India's share, 242–43
trade wars, 74, 77, 87–88, 242–43, 256
global marketplace, 67, 71n6
Golden Quadrilateral project, 23
goods and services tax (GST), 96, 251
governance, bureaucracy reforms in improving
colonial-era practices, discontinuing, 217–18
competition, instituting, 209–15
file management process, 216
Indian Administrative Service (IAS), 208–10, 212, 213–14
innovative thinking, encouraging, 216
lateral entry, 212–14
merit-based civil service, 208–9
methods of, 205
princely-era practices, discontinuing, 217–18
specialized knowledge, 210–12, 246
temporary employment in non-government sectors, 215
training institutions for officials, 217
vigilance agencies, 217
young professionals, contracted, 216
governance, economic administration in improving
export strategy, 219–21
methods of, 205
mission-mode implementation of reforms, 218–19
sunset clause on centrally sponsored schemes, 223
tax administration, 221–23
trade negotiations, a new entity for, 221
transparency in fiscal accounting, 223–24
governance, improving through
corruption, ending, 209
ministries consolidation, 206–8
Green Revolution, 20, 35, 39, 52–53
growth, future of
employment-intensive sectors, investment in, 256
export markets, 255
firms, growth of, 255
government spending, requirements for, 254
manufacturing as the engine of, 72–74
migration, creating conditions for, 255
multinationals, recruiting, 77, 255–56
policy reforms importance, 253
policy stability and, 254–55
private actors, removing constraints on, 253–54

H. R. Khan Committee, 141
Hasan, Rana, 65
higher education
China compared, 180, 182, 184–86, 185*t*, 186*t*, 190–92, 200, 202
growth in, 179–81, 180*t*
importance of, 179
quality dimension, 181–86
United Kingdom compared, 192–96, 200
United States compared, 187–90, 200
higher education institutions (HEIs)
China, 190–92, 196, 199
compared globally, 196
growth in, 179–80
international rankings, 185–86, 186*t*
private sector growth, 180–81, 181*t*
United Kingdom, 192–97, 199
United States, 187–90, 196, 199
higher education, path to progress
autonomous and independent HEIs, 196–97
government funding, 199
Higher Education Promotion Commission, 197–98
national research and innovation foundation, 200–1
tuition fees, 199–200
world-class HEIs, creating, 201–2

Higher Education Promotion Commission Act, 197–98
Hong Kong, 6–7, 6*t*, 10–11
hygiene, public, 115–18, 123*t*

import substitution, 88–90
imports
  average clearance time for, 94–95
  constraints, 18*f*
  Lerner symmetry theorem on, 89–90
  proportion of GDP, 18, 19*f*, 24, 88–89
Income Tax Act, 249–50
India, future of
  economic transformation, components of, 77–78
  population, 5
  poverty in, 5
India, post-independence
  leaders of, ix, 10
  poverty, x
  socialism and command-and-control policies, ix, 10
India, recommendations for reforms for
  electricity distribution companies, 237–38
  food subsidies, 236
  macroeconomic policy, 227–29
  public sector enterprises
    loss-making, restructuring and closure of, 232–34
    monetization of assets, 234–35
    privatization of, 230–32, 233*f*
  Right to Education (RTE) Act, 238–41
  subsidies, consolidation of, 235–36
Indian Administrative Service (IAS), bureaucracy reforms, 208–10, 212, 213–14
Industrial Disputes Act (IDA), 84–86, 98, 99
industrial sector
  GDP share, 39*f*, 39, 41–42, 42*t*
  growth rates, 21, 38–40, 38*t*, 51, 98*t*
  GVA added per worker, 44*f*
  migration into the, 50, 51, 54–55, 56–57, 255
  nationalization, 244
  per-worker output, 42–43, 44*f*
  per-worker productivity, 59
  tariff protections, 91
  wages, 56
  workforce employment, 41*f*
industrialization, urbanization and, 103
infrastructure development, 95, 96, 114–15, 157, 234, 250–51
Insolvency and Bankruptcy Code (IBC), 29, 157, 158–61, 251
Insurance Regulatory and Development Authority of India (IRDAI), 136
Integrated Child Development Services (ICDS), 24
investment services, 134
IT-enabled services (ITES), 77–78

Jandoc, Karl, 65
Japan
  agricultural workforce, 40–42, 50
  corporate debt, 141
  economic growth, post-WW II, 6–7, 6*t*, 10–11
  GDP share vs. per capital income, 38
  minimum-wage laws, 99
Jet Airways, 162
jobs. *See also* employment
  high-productivity, creating, 78, 86–87
  low-productivity, 56–57, 59
  in technology, 182
Johnson, Lyndon B., 34–35
Joint Lenders Forum (JLF), 157

Kapoor, Radhicka, 63
Kisan credit cards, 23–24
knowledge, specialized, 246

labor laws
  British Crown rule, 98
  medium firms, 98
  reforms, implementing, 244, 245–46
  small firms, 97–98
  workforce, 97–102
labor-intensive manufacturing, policy reforms
  autonomous employment zones (AEZs), 95–96
  export expansion, 87–88
  free trade agreements, 94
  import substitution, 88–90
  indirect taxes to exporters, 93–94
  labor market reforms, 97–102
  land ownership, 102–3
  the rupee, 90–91
  tariffs, 88, 91–93
  tax simplification and predictability, 96–97
  trade facilitation, 94–95
labor-intensive sectors, 83–86
land acquisition, 108, 109, 125, 127, 244
Land Acquisition Act, 28, 86, 102, 109, 249–50
land conversion rules, 109–10
land ownership, 108–9
land reform, 28, 34
land shortages, 125, 127

land-leasing laws, 53
large firms
apparel industries, 67*f*, 67–68
criticality of, 64–70
employment in, 67*f*
export markets for growth, 87
export performance and efficiency, 66–70, 67*f*
export-import restrictions, 86
global competition, 67
in labor-intensive sectors, lack of, 67*f*, 83–86
land procurement and ownership, 86, 102
manufacturing productivity, 66–70
restrictions on, 83–85
wages, 66*f*
Lerner, Abba, 89–90
Lerner symmetry theorem, 89–90
license-permit raj, 247, 248
light manufacturing, 84, 85
lighting, in urban vs. slum households, 123*t*
logistics sector, 94–95, 102–3
Lok Adalat, 160

macroeconomic stability, 250, 251
Maddison, Angus, 3–4
Mahalanobis, P. C., 99
Mahatma Gandhi National Rural Employment Guarantee Act (MGNREGA), 25, 27, 35, 53, 105–6, 249
Make in India, 86–87, 88–89
Malaysia, 141
manufacturing
automation in, 75
factors favoring, 77
FSI limitations, 102, 110–11, 114, 127
human labor in, 75
labor-intensive. *see* labor-intensive manufacturing
large firms, criticality of, 64–66
large firms productivity and exports, 66–70
manufacturing employment
China compared, 65–66
compensation, 63, 63*t*
economic growth and, 7, 8*f*
in firms of differing sizes, 63–65, 64*t*, 65*f*
GVA added per worker, 61, 62, 62*t*
hired workers, statistics, 63*t*
South Korea, post-WWII, 7, 8*f*
wages, China compared, 65–66, 66*f*
manufacturing-led growth
automation and, 78
rapid, importance of, 77–78
services growth and, 72–76, 73*t*
manufacturing-led growth, policy reforms
AEZs, 95–96
export expansion, 87–88
free trade agreements, 94
import substitution, 88–90
indirect taxes to exporters, 93–94
labor market reforms, 97–102
land ownership, 102–3
the rupee, 90–91
tariffs, 88, 91–93
tax simplification and predictability, 96–97
trade facilitation, 94–95
Mao Zedong, 190
market economy, creators of the, ix
marketing reforms, agriculture, 47, 49–50, 52
medium firms
apparel industries, 67–68
employment in apparel, 67*f*
labor laws, 98
in labor-intensive sectors, 83–86
manufacturing wages, 66*f*
as sources of jobs, 76
micro enterprises, 76, 86–87
micro-small, and medium enterprises (MSMEs), 76
migrant workforce
housing availability, 112, 113
slums and, 119–20
migration, rural-to-urban
China, 105, 106
creating conditions for, 255
to industry and services, 50, 51, 54–55, 56–57, 255
slum dwellers, 124–25
minimum support prices (MSPs), 54
minimum-wage laws, 86, 99–101, 245–46
mobile revolution, 23
modern India, term usage, ix
Modi, Narenda, ix, 28–29, 201, 218, 238, 242, 243, 244, 245, 246, 250–55
Mumbai, 106, 107–8, 112, 117, 120
Musk, Elon, 75

National Dairy Development Board (NDDB), 20
National Democratic Alliance, 242
National Food Security Act (NFSA), 25, 28, 35, 249–50
National Highway Development Project (NHDP), 23
National Medical Commission Act, 251
Nehru, Jawaharlal, 19, 20, 34, 84, 242, 244, 247
New India, ix–38

New Telecom Policy (NTP), 23
NITI Aaygog, 245
non-agricultural workforce, 63*t*
non-farm rural economy
  agriculture vs., 33

own-account enterprises (OAEs), 83

Park Chung-hee, 219–21
Patel, Sardar Vallabhbhai, 209
Pension Fund Regulatory and Development Authority (PFRDA), 136
Period Labor Force Survey [PLFS], 58
population redistribution. *See* migration, rural-to-urban
poverty, x, 9–10
poverty reduction, 24–25, 26*f*
Pradhan Mantri Jan Dhan Yojana financial inclusion program, 167–68
Prasad, Ravi V., 34
Prime Minister's Gram Sadak Yojana (PMGSY), 23
protectionism, growth and, 74, 88, 91
public distribution system (PDS), 27
public sector enterprises, 245
public services
  drainage, 123*t*
  drinking water, 115–17, 123*t*
  lighting, 123*t*
  in slum households, 122–24, 126
  solid waste management, 117–18
public spaces, clean, 117–18

rail-based transportation, 114
railroads, 103
Rao, Narasimha, 149
Rao, P. V. Narasimha, ix–6, 21–22, 24, 244, 248, 249
Rao-Vajpayee reforms, 253
rapid transit systems, 114
Rashtriya Uchchatar Shiksha Abhiyan (RUSA) program, 199
real estate, demand for, 111–12, 113
Real Estate Regulation and Development Act, 137–38
real estate sector, corruption in, 110, 252
Recovery of Debts Due to Banks and Financial Institutions Act), 148
Regional Comprehensive Economic Partnership (RCEP), 94
Reliance Industries Limited (RIL), 256
rent controls, 112–13
Reserve Bank of India (RBI)
  authority, 167–68
  classification requirement, 146–47
  early detection of NPAs, 161–62
  government expansion of duties, 158
  insolvency responsibility, 158–59
  policy interest rate, 171
  privatization role, 169–70
  regulatory authority, 135–36, 171–72, 251–52
  treatment of restructured loans by, 150–51, 152, 153–54, 156–57, 158
Right to Education Act, 25, 27, 28, 249–50
robophobia, 77–78
Rorsted, Kasper, 75
Rosezweig, Mark, 46
rural economy, non-farm, 33–34
rural policies, overview, 34–36
rural population, 37, 105–6
Rural Roads Program, 27
rural workforce. *See also* migration, rural-to-urban
  in agriculture, 48
  annual compensation by sector, 63, 63*t*
  employment guarantees, 27, 35, 53, 105–6, 249
  employment statistics, 59*t*
  migration, rural-to-urban, 105–6
  non-farm, 33
  statistics, 48
  unemployment, 63*t*

sanitation, availabity of, 24, 117–18, 123*t*, 250
SARFAESI Act, 160
Sarva Shiksha Abhiyan (SSA), 24
scarcity factor, 130
Scheduled Castes and Scheduled Tribes, 25
Scheme for Sustainable Structuring of Stressed Assets (S4A), 156–57, 161
Securities and Exchange Board of India (SEBI), 136, 168
securities markets, 133, 139, 143
Securitization and Reconstruction of Financial Assets and Enforcement Security Interest (SARFAESI) Act, 22–23, 148
service sector growth
  accelerated, effects of, 77–78
  employment, 41*f*
  GDP share, 39*f*, 39, 41–42, 42*t*
  GVA added per worker, 44*f*
  manufacturing growth driving, 72–76, 73*t*
  migration into, 255
  per-worker output, 42–43, 44*f*
  per-worker productivity, 59
  workforce share, 45*t*
service sector growth rates, 38–40, 38*t*, 51, 98*t*

74th Constitutional Amendment Act, 107
Shahi Exports, 256
Shanghai, 107–8
Shastri, Lal Bahadur, 20, 34
Singapore
 economic growth, 14–15
 industrialization capitalization in, 75–76
 ISI model, rejection of, 15
 path to transformation, 77–78
 post-WWII economic growth, 6–7, 6*t*, 10–11
 production structure, 87
Singh, Manmohan, 24, 27–28, 249
slums, urban
 deficiencies, 128
 population, 128
 rehabilitation and redevelopment of, 119–27, 121*t*, 122*t*, 123*t*
small firms
 apparel industries, 67–68
 employment in apparel, 67*f*
 labor laws, 97–98
 limitations of, 66–67
 as sources of jobs, 76
 wages, 66*f*
small-scale industries (SSI) reservation list, 22, 27–28, 84
socialism, ix, 10, 88, 175–76, 243–46, 249–50
South Korea
 agricultural workforce, 40–42, 43–44, 50
 agriculture, GDP percentage, 43–44
 economic growth, post-WW II, 6–11, 6*t*, 7–9*f*, 14–15
 export-oriented strategy, 219–21
 farmers, living standard for, 43–44
 GDP share vs. per capital income, 38
 import substitution, 88–89
 industrialization capitalization in, 75–76
 ISI model, rejection of, 15
 manufacturing-services growth link, 72
 path to transformation, 77–78
 production structure, 87
Special Economic Zones (SEZs), 95
start-ups, 76, 182
State APMC (Development and Regulation) Model Law, 23–24, 52
State Bank of India (SBI), 146
State Electricity Regulatory Commissions (SERC), 237, 238
stocks and stock exchanges, 133, 134
Strategic Debt Restructuring (SDR) scheme, 156, 161
Swachchh Bharat Mission (BSM), 117, 250
Taiwan
 economic growth, post-WW II, 6–7, 6*t*, 10–11, 14–15
 industrialization capitalization in, 75–76
 ISI model, rejection of, 15
 manufacturing-services growth link, 72
 path to transformation, 77–78
 production structure, 87
tariff reductions
 agricultural sector, 27–28
 economic effect, 21–22, 27–28
 industrial sector, 91
tariffs
 apparel industries, 93
 competitiveness and, 91
 export-led growth and, 91–93
 industrial sector protections, 91
 manufacturing-led growth and, 88, 91–93
 rationalizing for growth, 91–93
tax evasion, 110, 111, 252
tax system, 29
taxation
 corporate, 97, 251
 exporters indirect taxes, 93–94
 goods and services, 96, 251
 Income Tax Act, 249–50
 retrospective, 254–55
 retrospective taxation, 28–29
Telecom Dispute Settlement and Appellate Tribunal (TDSAT), 23
Telecom Regulatory Authority of India (TRAI), 23
telecommunications, 77–78
tenancy laws, 113
Tesla, 75
textile industry, 84–85, 93
trade
 exports-to-GDP ratio, 7*f*
 post-WW II East Asia growth and, 10–11
 transportation and, 94–95, 102–3
trade liberalization, 88–89, 249
trade sector, 62*t*, 63*t*
Trade Union Act, 97–98
trade war, China-US, 74, 77, 87–88, 242–43, 256
transportation networks
 expansion limitations, 128
 need for, 128
 railroads, 103
 slum households, 120–22
 trade and, 94–95, 102–3
 trucking model, 103
 urbanization and, 114–15
transportation systems, 125–26

trucking model, 103
Trump, Donald, 77
Tyagi, Ajay, 141

Ujjwal Discom Assurance Yojana (UDAY), 237
Unified Payments Interface (UPI) system, 29
uniform goods and services tax (GST), 29
unincorporated enterprises, employment in, 57–58, 61*t*, 83
unions, 97–98
United Kingdom, 38, 40–42, 50, 141
United Progressive Alliance [UPA] administration, 22, 23, 25, 27–28, 96, 211, 249–50, 254
United States
  agricultural workforce, 40–42, 50
  corporate debt, 141
  food assistance, 34–35
  GDP share vs. per capital income, 38
  higher education in the, 187–90, 188*f*
  industrialization capitalization in, 75–76
  trade war with China, 74, 77, 87–88, 242–43, 256
University Grants Commission (UGC) Act, 179, 186, 197
Upadhyay, Pundit Deendayal, 244
urban development, problems and reforms
  affordable housing, 107–12
  air pollution, 118
  cleanliness-related challenges, 115–18
  rental housing, 106, 112–13
  transportation networks, 106, 113–15
Urban Land Ceilings and Regulation Act (ULCRA), 108, 125, 127, 244
urban population
  basic amenities, access to, 123*t*
  housing type and ownership, 122*t*
  per capita expenditure, 37
  percentage in slums, 121*t*
  slum-dwelling, 119–27, 121*t*, 122*t*, 123*t*
urban population growth, 105, 106
urban workforce
  annual compensation by sector, 63, 63*t*
  employment, 59*t*, 63*t*
  GVA added per worker by sector, 62*t*
urbanization
  contributors to, 105–6
  economic growth and, 9*f*, 9
  industrialization and, 103
  land shortages, 108
urbanization rates, 105–6
Uruguay Round agreements, 74

Vajpayee, Atal Bihari, ix–6, 22–23, 24, 149, 232, 248, 249
Vietnam, 38, 87, 94

Wage Code, 99–100, 245–46
wages
  China-India compared, 65–66, 66*f*, 77, 255
  industrial workforce, 56
  large firms, 66*f*
  manufacturing, 65–66, 66*f*
  minimum-wage laws, 86, 99–101, 245–46
  rural workforce, 63, 63*t*
waste management, 117–18, 123*t*
water, availability of, 250
workforce. *See also under specific industries or sectors*
  GVA added per worker, 62
  labor laws, 97–102
  non-agricultural, 59–60, 62*t*
  well-paid job creation, 77–78, 83
  women in the, 40, 41–42, 98
workforce compensation, 57, 62–63, 63*t*
workforce protections, 84–86, 97–99